AMERICA ON FILM

MODERNISM, DOCUMENTARY, AND A CHANGING AMERICA

In *America on Film*, Sam B. Girgus traces how the representation of being "American" in films of recent decades differs dramatically from portrayals in classic mid-century Hollywood film. In works such as *Mississippi Masala, Lone Star, Malcolm X, Raging Bull, When We Were Kings*, and *Bugsy* he finds new and ethnically varied characters that reembody American values, ideals, and conflicts. Such films dramatize a transformation in the relationship of American identity and culture to race and ethnicity, as well as to sexuality, gender, and the body. *America on Film* charts these changes through analysis of cinematic tensions involving fiction, documentary, and modernism. As an art form that combines fragments of reality with imagination, film connects the documentary realism of the photographic image to the abstraction and nonrepresentation of modernism.

Sam B. Girgus is professor of English at Vanderbilt University. He is the author of *Hollywood Renaissance: The Cinema of Democracy in the Era of Ford, Capra, and Kazan; The Films of Woody Allen; The New Covenant: Jewish Writers and the American Idea;* and *The Law of the Heart: Individualism and the Modern Self in American Literature,* among other titles. A recipient of a Rockefeller Fellowship and other scholarly and teaching awards, he has lectured and taught extensively in universities throughout America and the world.

AMERICA ON FILM

MODERNISM, DOCUMENTARY, AND A CHANGING AMERICA

SAM B. GIRGUS
Vanderbilt University

CAMBRIDGE
UNIVERSITY PRESS

PUBLISHED BY THE PRESS SYNDICATE OF THE UNIVERSITY OF CAMBRIDGE
The Pitt Building, Trumpington Street, Cambridge, United Kingdom

CAMBRIDGE UNIVERSITY PRESS
The Edinburgh Building, Cambridge CB2 2RU, UK
40 West 20th Street, New York, NY 10011-4211, USA
477 Williamstown Road, Port Melbourne, VIC 3207, Australia
Ruiz de Alarcón 13, 28014 Madrid, Spain
Dock House, The Waterfront, Cape Town 8001, South Africa

http://www.cambridge.org

First published 2002

Printed in the United Kingdom at the University Press, Cambridge

Typefaces Sabon 10/13 pt. and Gill Sans   *System* LATEX 2_ε [TB]

A catalog record for this book is available from the British Library.

Library of Congress Cataloging in Publication Data

Girgus, Sam B., 1941–
    America on film : modernism, documentary, and a changing America / Sam B. Girgus.
        p.   cm.
    Includes bibliographical references.
    ISBN 0-521-81092-2 – ISBN 0-521-00931-6 (pb.)
    1. United States – In motion pictures.   2. Documentary style films – United States –
    History and criticism.   3. Motion pictures – United States.   I. Title.
    PN1995.9.U64 G57   2002
    791.43'6273–dc21   2001052853

ISBN 0 521 81092 2 hardback
ISBN 0 521 00931 6 paperback

To

Arielle Gianni,
Zachary Isaac, and
Mia Victoria

CONTENTS

ACKNOWLEDGMENTS

After more than eleven years at Vanderbilt University, I again feel compelled to express my special appreciation to those students whose consistent work and contributions in so many different film and culture studies classes have helped me to develop my teaching, thinking, and writing. Over the years, these Vanderbilt students have made it possible for me to fulfill the hope of my first years in graduate school for a career in which, to paraphrase Thoreau again, loving, living, and learning cohere. These film and culture studies students include: Gayle Rogers, Marc Popkin, Adam and Brook Rabinowitz, Ross Dinnerstein, Ashley Hedgecock, Jamie Mauldin, Courtney Carlisle, Brook Beaumont, Jen Conger, Jennifer Kate Whatley, Leigh Tyson, Lowery Parker, Jennifer Slovitt, Ryan Osborn, Melissa Spencer, Frank Laughlin, Ben Scott, Isaac Rogers, John Craft, Matt O'Brien, Lindsay Denardo, Natalie Rose, Raffaella Braun, Erin Mulligan, Natalie Neptune, Nathan Tharal, Meredith Nethercutt, Jessica Wasserman, Noah Abrams, Jessica McHugh, Jennifer Morse, Alexander Mack, Emily Abbott, Anthony Wilson, Dean Masullo, Tikenya Foster, Frances Henderson, Lisa Barnes, Sean Heuston, and Tommy Anderson.

In addition, former students who continue years of learning and growing together include: Chad Gervich, Amanda Restifo O'Brien, Eothen Alapatt, Scott Evans, April Foscue, Dru Warner, Brit Farwick, Ann McDonald, Lisa Siefker, Eddie O'Neill, Jackie Leitzes, Hilton Keith, Dana Oldani, Cakki Hogan, Oliver Luckett, Lauren Petty Banta, Amity Wang, Kristi Boernhoeft Sands, Katie McCall, Alyson Goldman, Dr. Jen Giordano, Beach von Oesen, Tamsen Love, Alison Barnes, and Aimee DeSantis. To those who have grown silent over the years, they know who they are; I am sure that they will be called upon someday to answer to a higher academic authority for failing to keep in touch.

Former mentors remain great teachers and friends, most especially Joel Jones. However, it would be hard to exaggerate the personal and professional significance to me of new colleagues and friends. Jerry Christensen's personal, intellectual, and academic friendship and support have proven profoundly important to me and others. His work at Vanderbilt has not only given energy, imagination, and depth to film studies, but to all areas related to the humanities. Similarly, the efforts of Chancellor E. Gordon Gee to promote institutional change and progress at Vanderbilt have matched the energy and time that he has expended on working individually and personally with students, faculty, staff, alumni, and friends of the university. Also, Gilberto Perez and Thadious Davis were gracious enough to look at some chapters of my work and offer suggestions. James Naremore has been a source of help and encouragement as well.

Old friends and colleagues remain the bedrock of personal and academic fulfillment: John Halperin, Robert Mack, Cecelia and Bill Tichi, Leah and David Marcus, Carol Burke, Lynn Enterline, Sacvan Bercovitch, John Cawelti, Cristina Giorcelli and Giovanni Baptista, Emory Elliott, Carol and Keith Hagan, Brian and Judy Jones, Gerry and Ann Calhoun, Leonard Nathanson, Kathy Conkwright, John Bomhoff, Gregg Horowitz and Ellen Levy, Betty Herbert, Gene and Susan Wright, Ed Hotaling, "Maddie" Marion, Jim and Martha Bomboy, TimoTeo Tuazon, Derah Myers, Jane Ritter, Bill Nagel, Lisa Stewart, Magda Zaborowska, Zsuzsa Manness, Cindy Lyle, Camille Holt, Ginia McPhearson, Melissa Perkins, J. Delayney Barber, Mary Bess Whidden and Angela Boone, and Ham and Arlette Hill. I would like to note with great sorrow the loss of a special friend. Julie Jones made everyone she knew feel significant, not in a casually conversational or superficially political way but by sharing a person's hopes, fears, aspirations, and ambitions. I always appreciated this quality in Julie in regard to my own friendship with her, but only recently did I realize how many others also felt the same way. Besides her husband, who has been the closest of friends for more than thirty years, and her family, a whole college and community in Colorado benefited from her sensitivity and grace. We think of her and miss her everyday.

New members of our department revivify enthusiasm for literary studies, including Deak Nabers, Tina Chen, Sean Goudie, Dennis Kezar, Tony Earley, and Kathryn Schwarz. The support of senior faculty for film and cultural studies has proven invaluable, including Jay Clayton, Vereen Bell, Mark Wollaeger, Michael Kreyling, Chris Hassel, Sheila Smith-McKoy, Paul Elledge, Mark Jarman, Teresa Goddu, Kate Daniels, Roy Gottfried, Mark Schoenfield, John Plummer, and Hal Weatherby. I also would like to thank Dean Richard McCarty, Michael Schoenfeld, Lucius Outlaw, William Luis, Nicholas Zeppos, and Michael Rose for their support.

Once again, I have the great pleasure to thank Beatrice Rehl of Cambridge University Press for giving me the kind of support and help that most of us only pray for and dream about. Additionally, I would like to thank Sarah Wood of Cambridge University Press and John Needham, formerly of the press as well as Lia Pelosi for her editing assistance. Also, I thank the staff at the Film Still Archives of the Museum of Modern Art in New York, and I express special appreciation for all of the help I have received from the staff of the Department of English and the Learning Resource Center at Vanderbilt: Janis May, Penny Peirce, Natalie Baggett, Erika Smart, Sarah Corbitt, Carolyn Levinson, Dori Mikus, Jamie Adams, and Carol Beverley.

The burden on my grown children has probably diminished somewhat since I now seem to go for advice, help, and counsel to my grandchildren, Arielle Gianni, Zachary Isaac (Ziggy), and Mia Victoria. Still, I again express my ever-increasing love, respect, and admiration to my daughters, Katya, Meighan, and Jennifer, who continue to amaze me everyday with their extraordinary success and accomplishments in life and their truly magnificent achievements as loving and caring people. As in the past, I remain proud and thankful for Ali, Jeff, and Erik for bringing so much to our family. Similarly, to our own mothers, Rebe and Aida, and our families, I wish to express my love and appreciation: Audrey and Harris Shapiro, Danny and Emily Vafa, Negi and Jean Darsess, Ellen and Gene Winter, and Joan Girgus. Yet again, to Scottie, our heart and center, Abuella, thanks for everything, including taking me along as driver and partner on her European "fantasy grant" of a lifetime.

FILM AND MODERNISM IN AMERICA

Documentary and a Democratic Aesthetic

Gertrude Stein once claimed that "America was the oldest country in the world" because America was "the first country to enter into the twentieth century." She went on to explain that while America entered the new century in the 1880s, "other countries were still all either in the nineteenth century or still further back in other centuries."[1] Stein's idea vividly dramatizes the influence of America upon modernistic consciousness and life during the twentieth century. By the 1920s, American leadership of film as both an art form and a popular art for the masses became especially significant in energizing and defining this modernist impulse. For some, as Gilberto Perez notes, the conventional association of modernism with film as the newest art form of the last century can be considered problematic.[2] However, for himself, Perez clearly adheres to a school of thought that finds film and modernism to be inexorably interlinked in complex and important ways throughout the last century. On the debate over the modernism of film as an art form, Perez maintains, "Film, which sets in motion the photographic look into the actual appearance of things, has been the preeminent art form of the twentieth century as the novel was of the nineteenth."[3] Dudley Andrew in a recent article on the history of film studies would seem to agree.[4]

This special relationship between film and modernism provides insight into the complexity of film as an aesthetic form and cultural force and into the diversity of modernism as a way of thinking and living. Film as an expression, engine, and source of modernism, brings together in the same discussion two basic ways of viewing modernism that have often diverged from each other in critical and historical discussion. Film relates literary and intellectual modernism to the social, economic, and political forces of modernization that have revolutionized life for millions throughout the world since the late-nineteenth century.

Miriam Bratu Hansen makes a convincing case for the importance to both modernism and film of their inherent interconnections. She argues,

> [t]he cinema was not just one among a number of perceptual technologies, nor even the culmination of a particular logic of the gaze; it was above all (at least until the rise of television) the single most expansive discursive horizon in which the effects of modernity were reflected, rejected or denied, transmuted or negotiated. It was both part and prominent symptom of the crisis as which modernity was perceived, and at the same time it evolved into a social discourse in which a wide variety of groups sought to come to terms with the traumatic impact of modernization. This reflexive dimension of cinema, its dimension of *publicness*, was recognized by intellectuals early on, whether they celebrated the cinema's emancipatory potential or, in alliance with the forces of censorship and reform, sought to contain and control it, adapting the cinema to the standards of high culture and the restoration of the bourgeois public sphere.[5]

Hansen's articulation of film as a bridge between modernism as thought and expression, and modernization as public and social life, suggests a multiplicity of modernisms that involves a concomitant danger. Asserting "there is more than one modernity – and that modernism can, and should, be used in the plural," Hansen presciently warns that efforts to overcome previous monolithic notions of modernism can create new forms of the old problem of narrow definitions. She says the "attack on hegemonic modernism runs the risk of unwittingly reproducing the same epistemic totalitarianism that it seeks to displace."[6] She continues,

> the critical fixation on hegemonic modernism to some extent undercuts the effort to open up the discussion of modernism from the traditional preoccupation with artistic and intellectual movements and to understand the latter as inseparable from the political, economic, and social processes of modernity and modernization, including the development of mass and media culture. In other words, the attack on hegemonic modernism tends to occlude the material conditions of everyday modernity which distinguish living in the twentieth century from living in the nineteenth, at least for large populations in western Europe and the United States.[7]

Hansen stands among many students of modernism, including Christine Stansell, who try to mitigate the putative "opposition" of "hegemonic modernism" to the "modern life-world." Hansen writes,

"We should not underrate the extent to which modernism was also a popular or, more precisely, a mass movement."[8]

Among these other contemporary thinkers Hansen provides a substantive addition to earlier studies of modernism by an influential generation of scholars who tended to concentrate on defining modernism as intellectual and artistic movements and sensibilities, and psychological states of mind and being. Literary and cultural critics, such as Irving Howe, Richard Ellmann, and Charles Feidelson, Jr., were disposed to describe the origins and meaning of modernism and "the modern tradition" in such terms of thought and imagination, as opposed to emphasizing historic associations and social conditions. These thinkers, as I once noted, consider "the modern as referring to more than contemporaneity." As Ellmann and Feidelson say, "The term designates a distinctive kind of imagination – themes and forms, conditions and modes of creation, that are interrelated and comprise an imaginative whole."[9]

Similarly, an essay and collection on modernism by Howe, which coincidentally mimic the ontological complexity of their subject by appearing and reappearing in a variety of published forms, identify and delineate the various elements and forces that comprise modernism. Howe's essay summarizes succinctly "modernist culture" by associating it with widely-recognized themes:

> the collapse of the certainty of the "Voltairean I," the symbolism of Virginia Woolf's claim that "On or about December 1910 human nature changed," the idea of culture and the self at war with themselves, the artistic quest to reinvent reality, the emergence of a pervasive ironic consciousness, skepticism regarding the value of history and tradition, the notion of the problematic nature of being human, the fascination with perpetual change and movement as well as the obsession with inner being and psychology, the uncertainty of objective reality, and the dominance of subjectivity.[10]

Howe then proceeds to itemize nine other specific categories or "topics concerning the formal or literary attributes of modernism." These topics include: the rise of the avant-garde as a movement, the loss of belief, artistic autonomy or self-sufficiency, the decline of aesthetic order or coherence, the minimal concern for nature, the dependence upon the shock value of perversity, an identification with primitivism, a new novelistic arrangement of the character and personality of the hero, nihilism as a crucial literary force.[11]

Now, after years of theorizing about postmodernism, a new generation of scholars and thinkers, such as Hansen and Perez, has recently returned to the modernistic imagination to discuss the development since the late-nineteenth century of an original relationship of art to society and of the individual to culture and history. Thus, James Naremore and Patrick Brantlinger aver the interrelation of modernistic consciousness and social forms of modernity. They proffer a "cultural typology" that relates "social formations and artistic production" in the form of "six artistic cultures."[12] These cultures include: high art, modernist art, the avant-garde, folk art, popular art, and mass art.

Other recent critics and thinkers of modernism readdress Stein's insight about America and modernism by associating the creative imagination of modernism specifically with the transforming power of America. For example, Peter Nicholls writes, "Modernity was now imagined as a kind of disease whose ravages, felt equally in aesthetic, moral, and psychological realms, were attributable to a general malady often called "'Americanisation.'"[13] Proffering a more generous view of America's influence on modernism, Christine Stansell writes: "By 1915, even Europeans had overcome their snootiness to pronounce New York as that place to which all roads led."[14] Thomas Crow relates the liberations and turmoil of the avant-garde to the New York School's history of promoting various interactions of modernism involving high art, popular and mass culture, and the commodification of artistic fashion and taste from the late 1930s to the early 1950s.[15]

The advent of film, as previously noted, occurred concomitantly with the breakthrough of modern consciousness and sensibility in multiple forms and modes throughout all domains of public and private life. At the same time, America, which entered the twentieth century early, as Stein asserted, also became a fertile ground for nurturing this special new art form of modernism – film. Although America shared with Europe in the origins of film, with the rise and success of Hollywood, American technology, innovation, and wealth came to dominate the development of the medium as an art form and an industry. The cultivation of film as both art and entertainment for the masses soon became a major aspect of America's contribution to what Nicholls considers the transformation by modernism of the relationship of language to experience.[16]

The constructive and meaningful "juncture of cinema and modernity" that Hansen desires occurs at the intersection where documentary and fiction film meet.[17] Documentary does more than merely complement the connection between film and modernism. Documentary helps to define that relationship, strengthening the links that sustain film's adherence to modernism.

What many critics claim to be the intrinsic documentary nature of all film probably requires greater appreciation. Arguably, even in a fiction film the photographic image constitutes a form of documentary representation, the classic Bazinian notion of the visual image of reality. A fiction film invariably becomes its own documentary. As Perez says,

> Every film has an aspect of documentary and an aspect of fiction.... All films may be documentary and all films may be fictional, but some are more documentary, and some are more fictional, than others. The term *nonfiction film*, though often used, is not to be preferred. Documentary film doesn't mean avoiding fiction, for no film can avoid fiction: it means establishing a certain relationship, a certain interplay, between the documentary and the fictional aspects of film so that the documentary aspect may come forward in some significant way.[18]

By virtue of its innate documentary nature, all film, including fiction film, comprises some documentary record. Such documentary self-consciousness contributes to the modernism of film as an art form. Following these proclivities, the earliest films often were, in fact, primitive documentaries of modern experience and existence. Ever since the Lumière brothers' *Workers Leaving the Lumière Factory* (1895), documentary has informed and entertained audiences about their lives in the modern age. Often credited for making the first documentary with their footage of the female factory workers, the Lumieres' work led to an initial predominance of documentary in the form of "actualities," or brief films, about random subjects from everyday life. However, as experience and developing techniques of editing and filmmaking made fiction easier to film, such fictional works replaced documentaries in popularity.[19]

Often defined in terms of nonrepresentation and abstraction, modernism also incorporated documentary realism. In the 1920s, the connection of modernism with documentary achieved fulfillment in the work of several major directors and editors. The documentary films of Dziga Vertov and Walter Ruttmann justify the claim of the importance of both film and documentary in the development of modern consciousness. The seminal cinema of Vertov and Ruttmann records the emergence of documentary as crucial in film's complex work of generating, structuring, and mediating modern self-awareness. In their documentary films, the movie screen forms a topography of moving visual images that integrates various modernisms, popular culture and thought, and felt experiences of common, everyday reality.

Vertov's documentary, *Man With a Movie Camera* (1929), synthesizes artistic creativity and technical innovation with social and cultural consciousness. Founded on an ideology and style of filmmaking that epitomize modernism, Vertov's work exudes energy and vitality, incessant movement, compression, and the interrelation of time and space, creative montage, and systematic self-reflexivity. These qualities make *Man With a Movie Camera* a milestone of modernism and film, what Seth Feldman describes as "a high point in early modernism's desire to wed art and the machine."[20] Vertov's film captures in the excitement and volatility of its very artistic form the exuberance and chaos of its subject – everyday modern urban life. Like Ruttmann's *Berlin – Symphony of a Great City* (1928), Vertov's *Man With a Movie Camera* dramatizes a major function of documentary of surveying and structuring aspects of modern life. It creates a visual ambience for the formation of social and personal identification in the midst of urban alienation and chaos. Even in its brilliantly mobile and dynamic style of modernism, the film frames and structures the chaos of modern urban existence.

A sunrise to sunset composite urban portrait, Vertov's film compares with other urban documentaries of the time, but also contrasts with them in its self-reflexive fascination with an ideology and aesthetic of the camera itself as a means for presenting and portraying reality even more efficiently and creatively than the human eye. What Vertov dubbed kino-pravda or "cinema truth" later became widely known through the French translation as cinema-verite. Given the complexity, diversity, mutability, and mobility of modern life – especially in the growing cities – documentary mediated such turmoil by helping people accommodate and assimilate themselves to the modern experience. Vertov's film enacts and exhibits his revolutionary thesis of the potential of documentary to convey and transform reality through its capacity to supersede "the limits of time and space." In his provocative manifesto, *The Council of Three* (1923), he asserted:

> I am kino-eye, I am a mechanical eye. I, a machine, show you the world as I see it. . . . Free of the limits of time and space, I put together any given points in the universe, no matter where I've recorded them.[21]

Unfortunately, the brilliant and original impulses of both Vertov and Ruttmann for creating and pursuing a form of pure documentary were eventually deflated and ultimately undermined. This was due, in part, to the engagement of both men with totalitarian forces from opposite ends of the political spectrum.

Denis Arkadievitch Kaufman was born in Bialystok, Poland while that region was annexed by Czarist Russia. Vertov's two brothers,

Mikhail and Boris, were also pioneers of cinema. Mikhail became an important Soviet filmmaker in his own right, as well as the cameraman for his brother's films, including *Man With a Movie Camera*. Boris escaped during the revolution, gained recognition for his film work in Paris, and went on to the United States to become an exceptional cinematographer for such directors as Sidney Lumet and Elia Kazan, receiving an Academy Award for his work on Kazan's *On the Waterfront* (1954).[22] Early in his career, Denis Kaufman adopted the name Dziga Vertov, meaning spinning top in Ukrainian, as a sign of his commitment to the innovation and dynamism of modern film and documentary. Under the bureaucratization of Soviet film and art, he faded into the shadows as an editor and compiler of newsreels and documentaries. Vertov's steady withdrawal from prominence and leadership contrasts sharply with the career of another politically radical and artistically modernistic innovator of film and documentary, Luis Buñuel. Buñuel was born in Spain but worked famously throughout the world on his films, although his only documentary, *Las Hurdes* (*Land Without Bread* [1932]), a brief film about peasants living in abominable conditions was shot in the poorest region of Spain. The unconventional surrealism of the documentary continues a style he achieved through his collaboration with Salvador Dalí on *Un Chien Andalou* (1928) and *L'Age d'Or* (1930).

In contrast to both Vertov and Buñuel, Ruttmann's documentary innovations became aligned with reactionary, fascist politics through his association with Nazi film, especially with his involvement as an advisor to Leni Riefenstahl on the notorious documentary, *Triumph of the Will* (1936), her classic propaganda film about the Nuremberg Nazi Party Convention of 1934. Ruttmann died while making a war newsreel for the Germans on the Eastern front.

The work and experience of Vertov, Ruttmann, and Buñuel seem relevant to many of the issues raised by Perez about the innate relationship and tension between documentary and fiction in film. Fiction as aesthetic and social mediation, even in the kino-pravda of Vertov and Ruttmann and the surrealism of Buñuel, suggest the difficulty of achieving the ambitious hopes of Vertov and others to create a form of pure documentary that captures reality with minimal intrusion from fiction. Also, extreme political and social forces from the left and right seem to have helped subvert the fulfillment for both Vertov and Ruttmann of their initial impulses and ideals concerning documentary.

Bill Nichols, a leading authority and scholar of documentary theory, seems somewhat less sanguine than Perez over the implications of the intrinsic relationship between fiction and documentary. Nichols delineates the practical and theoretical difficulties facing the documentary filmmaker who wishes to attenuate fictional elements. He writes,

> Stopping the action to realign the camera transforms history into mise-en-scene; it becomes a cue that we have crossed into the realm of narrative fiction. Subjectivity, rather than enhancing the impact of a documentary, may actually jeopardize its credibility and shift the focus of attention to the fictional representation of an actual person or event. Our identification with specific social actors therefore has less of the intensity common to fiction.[23]

While this crossing "into the realm of narrative fiction" may pose no oppressive danger for some students of documentary, to Nichols it typifies a new trend that should be taken into account when theorizing about or making documentary film. He says, "A tendency in recent writing on documentary is to stress its link to narrative. Documentaries are fictions with plots, characters, situations, and events like any other." To Nichols, such contamination of documentary by narrative and fiction vitiates the hopes of classic documentary directors – he cites Vertov, John Grierson, Paul Rotha, and Pare Lorentz – to establish in documentary "a morally superior form of filmmaking" that can contribute to understanding society with a sobriety that remains unavailable to fiction. He says, "This insistence on a narrative, constructed basis to documentary undercuts claims for the moral superiority of documentary to fiction."[24]

Nichols recognizes that the power of the argument for "documentary as a fiction" to degrade documentary's alleged moral superiority will not be answered adequately by making another case for the superiority of documentary as verifiable empirical evidence and argument. He persuasively writes, "This critique of documentary as a fiction like any other needs to be questioned without resorting to the assumed superiority of an analytical, essayist, and fact-based discourse."[25]

Instead of proclaiming a new faith in the importance of documentary by virtue of its capacity for critical analysis, Nichols delineates differences between fiction and documentary that need to be appreciated for documentary to retain its uniqueness and potency as an art form and social force. He says,

> Documentary shares many characteristics with fiction film but it is still unlike fiction in many ways. The issues of the filmmaker's control over what she

or he films and of the ethics of filming social actors whose lives, though represented in the film, extend well beyond it; the issues of the text's structure,
and the question of the viewer's activity and expectations – these three angles from which definitions of documentary begin (filmmaker, text, viewer)
also suggest important ways in which documentary is a fiction unlike any
other.[26]

As Noel Carroll says, "Nichols eschews those facile deconstructions of
the boundary between fiction and nonfiction that conclude that nonfiction film is just like any other kind of fiction." While oppugning
Nichols's argument against a "viable notion of objectivity" in nonfiction film, Carroll notes that to Nichols "nonfiction film is fiction, but
it is not exactly like other forms of fiction film."[27] Thus, Nichols's theoretical argument helps install valuable aesthetic and social criteria for
employing and analyzing documentary without requiring documentary's abandonment of relevant and applicable forms of fiction that
can help documentary tell its story or deliver its message. Nichols's
introduction into the discussion of the "three angles" from which to
examine documentary institutes a process for analyzing and evaluating documentary. This emplaces a workable method and strategy for
"testing" the validity, legitimacy, and authenticity of documentary.
Nichols notes, "This testing depends on the work of realism and its
ability to render the impression of reality, a sense of the historical
world as we, in fact, experience it, usually on a quotidian basis."[28]
Such pragmatic testing of documentary, in William James's sense of
investigating the consequences of beliefs and actions, could inhibit the
propensity to turn documentary into propaganda for various totalitar-
ianisms, ideologies, groups, and enterprises. Examining and testing the
relationship of fiction and documentary in all of its implications and
manifestations in a particular work or body of work obviously should
render insight into the aesthetic and social significance of such work.

As a dynamically mobile frame in continuous action that opens to
endlessly expansive interior and outer spaces, film and documentary
continue more than a century of cultivating modernisms. Modernisms
as states of being, mind, social life, and interaction achieve expression
and regeneration in film. The admixtures of fiction and documentary
that dramatize and represent modernisms in film occur with challenging rapidity. A phrase by Jean-Luc Godard graphically suggests how
cinema aesthetics and structure intrinsically relate to the volatility of
modernism. A character in Godard's *Le Petit Soldat* (1960), says, "To
photograph a face is to photograph the soul behind it. Photography

is truth. And the cinema is the truth, twenty-four times a second."[29] Of course, this statement, as Gilberto Perez reminds us, concerns the number of frames of film per second that usually are both shot and projected. Godard's insight about film suggests that the inherent nature of film as a medium of movement – as a representation of experience and reality that in itself entails ephemerality and transition – makes film seem to many to be especially appropriate as a source and means for rendering, dramatizing, and documenting a society and culture of modernisms built on change. Itself constructed out of movement and change, film as an art form can be identified fairly with modernism as the culture and consciousness of change.

The movement and change that define film art accentuate its nature as an art of fragments and pieces of imagination and reality. For twenty-four frames a second, only slashes and pieces of reality occur, confirming Buñuel's visual metaphor for film and modernism of the sliced eyeball in *An Andalusian Dog*. Here again Perez's insights into the modernism of film proves helpful. Citing earlier observations by Raymond Williams, Perez emphasizes how modernism inheres in the temporal, spatial, and narratival fragmentations of film. Indeed, the very techniques of filmmaking and the elements of film construction emphasize such fragmentation. The actual language of filmmaking and construction with such terms as shots, cuts, angles, and fades dramatizes a composition process of slices, pieces, and parts consistent with multiple modernisms. Referring to this essential fragmentary nature of film and modernism, Perez says:

> The fragmentary view characteristic of our modernity has been ... especially characteristic of film. Film is indeed an art of fragments: a painting is a whole, a theater stage is a whole, but on the movie screen we see merely a part, a piece of a larger field extending indefinitely beyond our view.[30]

However, in making this continuing case for the inherent modernism of film, Perez also pushes beyond the importance of the modernistic fragmentation of film to maintain the originality of the way such fragmentation ultimately coheres in film art. The genius of film concerns the operation of fragmentation within broader aesthetic and cultural contexts. Film gives form and significance to the tension between on screen and off screen spaces, between presence and absence. Film represents reality through suggestion and assumption regarding unknown offscreen frontiers. Perez urges that in contrast to the completeness of framed paintings, "film images make sense ... only as fragments of an implied larger field, only if we keep in mind at each moment what lies unseen out of frame." He continues:

> Yet what lies unseen is not something we should miss seeing; rather we should accept it as an offscreen background to the image on screen, the detail that by virtue of being brought into view is being designated, by the convention of the shot . . . as just the part we should be seeing at the moment, the detail that matters.[31]

This discussion of film as an art form of fragments and pieces of reality running at twenty-four frames a second on a ribbon of perpetual change relates to the theory of the inherent connection between film and documentary. Perez's "implied larger field" includes an assumed relation to documentary images. If all film incorporates some element of documentary, then putting the fragments of film together includes the organization of film's documentary sense of reality.

Thus, the construction of the implied field constitutes how all film manifests the exchange between fiction and documentary. The structuring of the implied field through the dialogue between fiction and documentary demonstrates the uniqueness of film as an art form and social document to represent and transform reality. It also can be argued that as a modernistic and documentary medium of fragments, film uniquely documents its way of reconstructing reality. While media or languages other than film also self-reflexively articulate their processes and systems of meaning, film in its special way documents them.

The relationship between the construction of the implied field and the dialogue between fiction and documentary accentuates the importance of documentary testing. Documentary testing places the implied field in historical, social, and cultural contexts that question the consequences and meanings of such fields. The intervention of documentary testing can challenge the formation through documentary and fiction of yet another unitary, dominant, and oppressive modernism. Even as it insinuates questions of authenticity and consequences into film, documentary, as an inherent element of all film, can at the same time continue its creative and imaginative function of contributing to film as an art form.

This merging of creative potential with pragmatic truth-seeking acquires special importance when film and documentary engage the broader cultural dimension in which modernism converges with ideology, social practice, and moral meaning. For much of the last century, antidemocratic, totalitarian impulses found sustenance in the fragmentation, energy, dynamism, diversity, and multiplicity of modernism. Film and documentary in those circumstances often stimulated and served antidemocratic mass movements. This history of support that various modernisms in film rendered antidemocratic totalitarianism dramatizes the urgency involved in cultivating the practice of a democratic aesthetic in film and documentary. A democratic aesthetic of film and documentary would meld the creativity of film art and the diversity and depth of documentary under conditions of pragmatic testing for realism, intellectual pluralism, empirical validation, and ethical consistency. A democratic aesthetic of film and documentary also would regard the volatile fragmentation of film in the light of the social and aesthetic history of modernism.

Without minimizing what James Naremore describes as the antimodernism as well as the conservatism of much of Hollywood during the last century, it also can be claimed that a democratic aesthetic often has made American film a modernistic medium of change.[32] Especially during the last decades of the last century, American film has often participated in the instigation of social change and become a living record of it, thereby helping to overcome prejudices and stereotypes that it has also perpetuated.

Consistent with the discussion so far of modernism and film, the essays in this collection explore the tension and interaction of fiction and documentary form to analyze film's relationship to change in America, generally a culture, society, and ideology of change. Concentrating primarily on the latter decades of the past century, the discussions in the book propose American film as representating and dramatizing transformations of ideology or systems of belief, institutions, and patterns of behavior. These are transformations in the meaning of being an American, including the most basic questions concerning what it means to look like, think like, and act like an American. One of the most significant contributions of "America on Film" during the past several decades has been the promulgation through film of conceptions and representations of American identity that complicate and diversify American identity and culture.

Accordingly, in the opening chapters and section, the book suggests the literal reembodiment of the meaning of America in African Americans as developed in some contemporary films, such as Mira Nair's *Missisippi Masala* (1992) and John Sayles's *Lone Star* (1996). The films portray this reembodiment as a challenge to the vitality at the end of the century of the American idea and creed. The next section of the book develops this theme of reembodiment by examining boxing films as a kind of sub-genre that dramatizes extraordinary changes, conflicts, and continuities occurring in the American experience. For example, *Raging Bull* (1980) subverts conventional assumptions about the male body and masculine strength by proposing through complex cinematic strategies, including documentary-style filming, the acceptance of vulnerability and softness as an external sign of inner change and renewal.

The boxing chapters especially proffer a tradition of continuing change regarding race and ethnicity. While *Body and Soul* (1947) establishes a model for what could be called a "Spartacus" metaphor for the black fighter–gladiator as a sacrificial figure for white redemption, that view changes radically with *When We Were Kings* (1996), Leon Gast's documentary film about the 1974 heavyweight championship match, "Rumble in the Jungle," in Zaire between Muhammad Ali and George Foreman. Norman Mailer's notion in the 1970s of boxing as "another key to revelations of Black, one more key to black emotion, black psychology, black love" achieves graphic emotional, ideological, and visual fulfillment in *When We Were Kings*.[33]

In these opening sections, the tension in film between fiction and documentary stylistics helps structure a continuing discussion about the nature of film as an aesthetic form and as a social document. As an elaboration of this discussion about film as art and document, the next section of the book concentrates on the problem of translating narrative literature into a movie image. The difficulties and opportunities involved in operating between literature and film introduce new complexities into the discussion of the nature of film. Literature can be treated as a written document to be adhered to and recorded faithfully on the screen. However, literature also can be considered a source and impetus for creating a quite different and unique artistic work in the form of film. Such issues provide some of the background in the chapter that develops a comparison of F. Scott Fitzgerald's *The Great Gatsby* (1925) with Barry Levinson's *Bugsy* (1991), a film about the Jewish gangster "Bugsy" Siegel. These issues also obtain in the following chapter on the making of Saul Bellow's *Seize the Day* (1956) into a 1986 film of the same name, directed by Fielder Cook and starring Robin Williams as Tommy Wilhelm, the novel's main character. However, these films suggest very different views about the reembodiment of the American idea. In the *Bugsy* chapter, the theme of the reembodiment of the American idea of renewal, personified so famously in the mysterious figure of Gatsby, switches to a Jewish gangster and his volatile girl-friend, a change that emphasizes how new representations of American culture and character broaden the spectrum and consensus that comprise American identity. However, a different sense of American character in the modern age emerges in the novel and film version of *Seize the Day*. For both Bellow and director Cook, the search for renewal turns into masochistic self-destruction. Rather than being the focus of renewal, the body becomes the center of destructive forces.

The concluding chapters of the book continue to exploit the tension between documentary and fiction in film as a means for studying the relationship of film and modernism to pervasive changes in America. From a humorous perspective of profound psychoanalytical prescience and pessimism, Charlie Chaplin's *Modern Times* (1936) develops the dichotomy between documentary and fiction in film acting to reveal changes in representations of the body as signs of changing sexual and gender relations. In the film, the documentary images of the actors, Chaplin and Paulette Goddard, encounter their fictional representations on the screen, thereby enacting portentous transformations of the body, sexuality, and love for American film and culture. As a result of this interaction between documentary and fiction, the bodies of Goddard and Chaplin become signifying systems of complexity and power. The film prophesizes the predominance of deathly impulses in the commodification of the body and the commercialization of modern life. These developments suggest a radical diminution of the historic exaggeration in American rhetoric, language, and humor of the powers of the lone individual to shape the future.

The final chapter brings the book back to where it began, with the issue of transforming the representative face and body of America through the figure of Denzel Washington, this time in Spike Lee's recreation of the charismatic and controversial African American leader Malcolm X. In *Malcolm X* (1992), documentary and fiction engage each other on several levels – acting, history, rhetoric, and social drama – that transfer the battle for equality and freedom to the screen and make the film an historic aesthetic force and social document.

In sum, this work attempts to develop the double entendre of "America on Film," meaning representations and renderings of America in various films but also how America has helped to transform film itself, including the documentary form. The films of the past two or three decades that are discussed here also provide a powerful link to classic films of earlier generations of directors and actors such as

John Ford and John Wayne, Frank Capra and Jimmy S
Rossen and John Garfield, among many others. As disc
various chapters, direct and immediate continuities o
classic and contemporary films regarding central issue
culture and character, especially pertaining to race and
der, and individual identity. For example, startling cont
found between John Ford's classic *The Searchers* (1956) and *Lone Star*,
and between Frank Capra's celebrated *It's a Wonderful Life* (1946)
and *Mississippi Masala*.[34] At the same time, the contrasts and differences between films of the classic era and contemporary films speak
to, as noted throughout this essay, extraordinary changes in the culture. Many of these films discussed in this book provoke the concerns
voiced by critics and historians about the accelerating massification of
American culture that suggests equally profound and pervasive changes
in American character. While many of the films dramatize the democraticization of relations of race, ethnicity, and gender, they also indicate the emergence of issues related to the steady expansion of the
ineluctable dominance of technology, media, and consumption. As depicted in these films, such forces and institutions suffuse culture and
society today, broadening the range of opportunities and challenges for
individuals and groups. However, the forces also involve potentially serious changes in the qualities of character that have long been deemed
part of American identity and continuity: independence, responsibility, discipline, commitment, and personal and social action. Of course,
such questions and issues have persisted since the earliest discussions
in our history about American identity and character.

America on Film dramatizes the history of America as an ideology
and narrative of, to use a phrase from Levinson's and Warren Beatty's
Bugsy, "fresh starts" in which individuals and the culture face the
challenge of potential new beginnings, as in *Mississippi Masala*, *Lone
Star*, and *Raging Bull*. The threads of continuity and contrast between
classic and contemporary cinema suggest the meaning of America as an
on-going dialogue between conviction and uncertainty. The details of
this dialogue entail a form of gambling that sustains the endless contest
between faith and corruption.

America on Film includes the sadness of Chaplin's dispossessed
Tramp on the road and the emasculation of Tommy Wilhelm as well
as the faith of "Bugsy" Siegel repeating Gatsby's sacrifice for his vision
of success and America. *America on Film* marks the amazing transformation of the black boxer from a sacrificial Black Spartacus figure to

the triumph of Muhammad Ali and the complex symbolism of struggle and redemption of Washington's and Lee's Malcolm X. American film also demonstrates continuing ambiguities and conflicts in making Washington a star of national significance and authority in an era of changing but stubborn racial uncertainty, as indicated perhaps by the rejection of him for an Academy Award for best actor for his portrayal of "Hurricane" Carter in *The Hurricane* (1999) after similarly denying him for *Malcolm X*. Of course, Hollywood in its own blockbuster fashion at last seemed to correct its repeated denials to Washington and its historic neglect and mistreatment of blacks by giving Academy Awards in leading actor categories on March 24, 2002 to Washington for *Training Day* (2001) and Halle Berry for *Monster's Ball* (2001), while also nominating Will Smith for *Ali* (2001) and giving Sidney Poitier the Academy's Lifetime Achievement Award.

Thus, *America on Film* suggests that film continues to both reflect and create America at the end of one century and the beginning of another. Amidst powerful historic and cultural continuities, the films discussed in this book indicate the persistent interconnection of film as a modernistic art form of change and America as a culture of transition and transformation. Film as our modernistic art form generates and promotes new ways of thought and action, belief and behavior while undermining and sustaining others. Like America, film battles itself, ever changing and remaining the same.

PART ONE

EMBODYING A NEW RACE FOR AMERICA

The Question of American Hope in *Mississippi Masala* and *Lone Star*

CHAPTER ONE

EMBODYING A NEW RACE FOR AMERICA

Mississippi Masala

Throughout the 1990s, the media reflected and cultivated a national obsession with the putative transformation of America by waves of Third World immigration. Changes in immigration policy that went back to the 1960s opened the floodgates to people of color. Previously untapped reservoirs of peoples from Asia and South America replaced Europeans as the primary source for a new peopling of America. Both exploiting and influencing the national concern with immigration, the media's focus on the subject achieved heightened intensity with a special Fall 1993 immigration issue of *Time*. Featuring, as Susan Gubar notes, a computer-created woman's face that was meant to suggest "a mix of several races," the magazine's cover carried the somewhat sensationalistic title, THE NEW FACE OF AMERICA, with a subtitle that seemed intended to arouse concern and perhaps alarm, "How Immigrants Are Shaping the World's First Multicultural Society." In its opening paragraphs, the magazine's editors explained:

> A nation of immigrants from the beginning, the U.S. has welcomed most newcomers, grateful for any new pair of hands to tame its vast interior or help stoke its huge industrial engine. For more than a century, most of the new arrivals were from Europe. But in the 1960s the U.S. undertook a basic shift in national policy, from one stacked in favor of European immigrants toward one that favored the rest of the world, particularly Third World nations. The full effects of that policy have exploded only in recent years. The past decade has seen the greatest rise in immigration since the great wave of 1901–10. Immigrants are arriving at the rate of more than 1 million a year, mostly from Asia and the vast Hispanic world.[1]

After proffering this brief historical and cultural background, "The Editors" in their introductory explanation continued to suggest the potential effects of this yearly influx of more than a million people of color:

> The impact of these new immigrants is literally remaking America. Today more than 20 million Americans were born in another country. Given that there are higher birthrates among the mostly young Third World arrivals, demographers are predicting that the U.S. before long will have to redefine just who its minorities are. In 1950, for example, 75% of all the minorities in the U.S. were African Americans. Hispanics now number about 24 million, and by 2010 – little more more than a dozen years from now – they will have surpassed blacks in number.[2]

The 2000 census proved *Time* to be conservative in predicting the speed of population change. As the *New York Times* reported on March 8, 2001, "The Hispanic population in the United States has grown by more than 60 percent in the last decade, pulling to rough parity with blacks as the largest minority." Attributing the shift to "immigration" and better "counting," Eric Schmitt wrote that Hispanics "soared to 35.3 million from the 22.4 million" in 1990 in contrast to a rise of about 16 percent for blacks to 34.7 million. The tone of subsequent *Times* articles echoed the 1993 *Time* piece, one with a graph of "The Changing Color of America" and another by Susan Sachs about how "the rise of a specific Latino identity" was "redefining minority."[3]

In the 1990s, filmmakers also came to appreciate the importance of the reemergence of immigration as a crucial national issue. Of course, going back to its origins as a form of urban and working class entertainment, American film often demonstrated an interest in portraying the lives of immigrants, as well as in attracting ethnic minorities to theaters. Moreover, the ethnic roots of the film industry in America have been studied for years. Consistent with this history of personal, artistic, and economic interest in immigrants, American film has renewed its concern by focusing on the issue of new immigration.

Accordingly, three years after *Time*'s special immigration issue, a Sunday edition of the *New York Times* of June 23, 1996 described how the waves of Third World immigration to America influenced changes in American film. In the piece, Sanford J. Ungar, communications scholar and author of work on immigration, maintains the emergence of an important group of new films that provides "reliable information about and meaningful insight into the immigration experience." Reflecting growing public and political discussion of immigration, Ungar notes, "While politicians bash immigrants, film makers – and novelists along with them – tell us gripping immigrant stories, recording them before they disappear." Ungar then concisely summarizes an extensive historical background of such films.

> Immigration has long provided grist for movie makers, of course. During the silent era, humor was found in the antics of the awkward, newly arrived outsider. The 30s brought films like "Angels With Dirty Faces," about gangs of toughs, most of them Irish (who were themselves only emerging from pariah status). By 1961, a gang of Puerto Rican immigrants could be found duking it out with the home-grown variety in the movie "West Side Story."

As part of this background, Ungar also dutifully emphasizes the significance of popular films about Jewish and Italian immigration by Barry Levinson, Paul Mazursky, and Francis Ford Coppola. In the light of this history of films about immigrants, Ungar asserts how things have changed. "But in recent years the theme of immigration has been used in more explicit fashion and handled in a far more complex and subtle way."[4] Ungar's list of new immigration films includes, James Gray's *Little Odessa* (1995), Mira Nair's *The Perez Family* (1994), Wayne Wang's *Joy Luck Club* (1993), Ron Howard's *Far and Away* (1992), Gregory Nava's *Mi Familia* (1995), Angel Muniz's *Nueba Yol* (1996), and Goran Paskaljevic's *Someone Else's America* (1995), as well as an impressive number of films about immigration in other countries such as Hanif Kureishi's and Stephen Frears's *My Beautiful Laundrette* (1985), about Pakistanis in England.

The new films in Ungar's delineation dramatize the hardship and turmoil of contemporary immigration. They present a story of struggle, challenge, and often, ultimate triumph by modern immigrants that in many ways revisits the experiences of previous generations of immigrants. However, Ungar's article especially considers two films that indicate a deeper transformation, a change closer to the restructuring and reformation of the American people that *Time*'s discussion of immigration suggests. One of these films, John Sayles's *Lone Star* (1996), focuses on the historic clash of cultures – Hispanic, Anglo, and African American – on the Texas–Mexico border. The other film, Mira Nair's *Mississippi Masala* (1992), extends its reach far beyond our borders to consider issues of ethnicity, race, colonialism, and ideology that connect America with Africa and Asia. Nair's film drives home the impact that specific communities have on American culture. Also by injecting the Third World's postcolonial presence into Mississippi, by juxtaposing and even intermixing different peoples, *Mississippi Masala* exceeds traditional and current immigration films in visually enacting and dramatizing the image on *Time*'s cover of a new composite American face and body.

Like *Lone Star*, *Mississippi Masala* acts out and displays the reembodiment of the American idea in people of color. The film dramatizes the engagement of the classic American ideology of individual and group renewal with the racial realities of contemporary immigration. Nair's film reexamines American cultural and national history to articulate, problematize and complicate the myth and ideology of America as a New World Garden inhabited by all the peoples of the world who cohere together to form a distinctly new race. *Mississippi Masala* demonstrates awareness of the historic basis of the idea of Americans as a new people united by an ideology of a transforming democracy of individuals and peoples. Echoing Tom Paine and Hector St. John de Crèvecoeur, the words of Herman Melville inform the cultural tensions, conflicts, and contradictions that comprise the core of the idea of America in the film. Melville famously wrote:

> There is something in the contemplation of the mode in which America has been settled, that in a noble breast, should forever extinguish the prejudices of national dislikes. Settled by the people of all nations, all nations may claim her for their own. You can not spill a drop of American blood without spilling the blood of the whole world.[5]

Significantly, *Mississippi Masala* juxtaposes such idealism as expressed in Melville's creed of common national identity with parallel documentation of the difficulty of fulfilling this ideology when it comes to color and race. The film, therefore, engages the classic American ideology with questions regarding the relevance and significance of the American idea in our times.

Thus, while *Mississippi Masala* and *Lone Star* dramatize the reembodiment of the American idea for people of color, they also suggest a need for examining the condition of the ideology that these new Americans embody. The films pointedly reexamine America in terms of people and immigrants of color who challenge the capacity of the American Creed and American Idea to maintain the historic processes of self-renewal. The possibility arises in *Mississippi Masala* and *Lone Star* of the emergence in our time of a ghostly representation of the American spirit that can not invest in new Americans of color the power of renewal and rebirth that inspired and influenced white immigrants

Figures 1 and 2. Denzel Washington and Sarita Choudhury transform and advance the American Dream as lovers with different roots in *Mississippi Masala.* (Museum of Modern Art/Film Stills Archives)

from Europe. Do the potential and promise of America still obtain in a world of color engulfed in the transformations of globalism?

In addition, the films present interesting contexts for this question of the application of the American idea to people of color. *Mississippi Masala* and *Lone Star* consider whether the American experience has been so radically altered by forces of change at the end of the twentieth century as to impugn the relevance of the American idea today. The films question whether an ideology and culture that triumphed for generations still pertain for a new century of technological, demographic, and environmental transformation.

Both *Mississippi Masala* and *Lone Star* raise such questions through the use of a form of informed docudrama. The films provide documentary-style contexts of historical and cultural authenticity that lend credibility to their fictional events and characters. *Mississippi Masala* opens with a kind of educational docudrama that carefully constructs a world stage of events, ideologies, and attitudes with enough energy, intensity, and authenticity to sustain the complexities of the film's development. In the opening scene, Mira Nair creates a vivid international mise-en-scene that establishes the tone for the entire film of complex and diverse interaction and exchange. The film opens in Kampala, Uganda during November 1972 and focuses on the plight of the upper-class and elitist Lohas family, which faces Idi Amin's expulsion of all Indians. The husband, Jaymini ("Jay"), a prominent and successful attorney, is, ironically, an advocate of the rights of blacks in Uganda. He is played by Roshan Seth, an established Shakespearean actor. The wife, Kinnu (Sharmila Tagore), undergoes her own terror and humiliation during the expulsion. The injustice and brutality they endure dramatizes the vulnerability of any minority group in a society that defines individual and cultural identity primarily in terms of ethnicity and race. After a sympathetic black man, Okelo, who has been a close friend to the family, enables Jay to leave prison in order to undergo ultimate expulsion, Jay protests his loyalty and devotion to Africa and Uganda. His passionate plea repeats his courageous public stand against Amin's racist and biased politics and practices. He exclaims:

> I was born here! I have always been Ugandan first, Indian second. All my life I have devoted to justice – I have been called a traitor and a bootlicker by my fellow Indians. Uganda is my home.

In response, Okelo, who has been his friend since childhood and his savior after rescuing Jay from arrest and prison, repeats in his restrained manner the ideological sloganeering of Amin. About Jay's claim that Uganda remains his home, Okelo responds: "Not anymore. Africa is for Africans. *Black Africans.*" Okelo has internalized racial thinking at least to the point of accepting its inevitablity and refusing to resist it.

Moreover, an additional irony in Okelo's attitude occurs in the film's suggestion of a special bond between Okelo and Jay's wife, Kinnu, one that at least implies his possible fatherhood of the daughter, Mina. Throughout the film, statements refer to Mina's black coloring, especially as an impediment to attracting a wealthy and prominent Indian husband. Also, Kinnu somewhat surreptitiously brings a framed photo of Okelo and Mina as a momento with her to America where the photo reappears in a highly-visible place. Stunned by his rejection by country and friend, Jay repeatedly looks upon Okelo, and even the photograph that snugly frames Okelo and Jay's daughter, with silent resentment and ambiguity. Such resentment appears especially strong when Jay observes Okelo's final departing embrace of Kinnu at the airport in Kampala. This uncertainty over paternity obviously subverts the case for rigid racial divisions.

The drama and emotion of the break with Okelo further personalize the experience of expulsion for the Lohas family that includes a horrible encounter with bullying police who terrorize Kinnu. The personal soon becomes general and historic when the film cuts from the Kampala airport to a tracing of the journey on a map that begins with East Africa and then moves North from Uganda up to the Mediterranean, goes due West over Europe, moves slowly over the Atlantic Ocean to America, and ends at last in Greenwood, Mississippi, where the Lohas family finally settles. As the camera traces the journey, the soundtrack dramatically changes from a soft and sensuous Asian melody to a strident Southern blues and rock beat. This combination of sound and visualization signifies the global dimension of the expulsion and suggests ensuing emotional and cultural changes. The visual tracking by the camera and the sound shift also emphasize the film's theme of globalism and internationalism. All parts and peoples of the world now connect and relate to each other, and each part and people require recognition and achieve significance. This mapping documents the significance of the Indian diaspora and suggests the importance of relating this particular dispersal of people to other diasporas, including the millions of African slaves and immigrants who came to America, as well as the Jews, who literally began traveling centuries ago throughout different parts of the world from Europe to South America and elsewhere before settling in America.

Of course, globalism, internationalism, and colonialism influence the nature and meaning of the American part of the Indian journey, by far the predominant part of the film's time and story. Although expulsion and diaspora dramatize African cruelty and repression under Amin and his program, a powerful residue of white oppression and colonialism also leaves a serious mark on the film. After the family's departure and the mobile illustration of their journey, the film starkly jumps eighteen years ahead to August 1990 and Greenwood, Mississippi. The family has gone there to be with other displaced relatives and Indians. Jay helps manage an unfashionable motel belonging to a relative, while Kinnu operates her own business, a liquor store, in the black part of the city. Again, they are strangers, but as in Africa, they maintain a position over blacks. In a sense, in their situation in Mississippi, the

Indians continue as the agents of the exploitation and domination of a white governing class over people of color.

The story behind Mira Nair's decision to place the family and the major portion of the film in Mississippi reenforces the film's rendering of both perdurable colonialism and unremitting globalism. Herself born in relative comfort in Bhubaneswar, the capital of the Indian state of Orissa, what she describes as "the original hick town," Nair received a full scholarship to Harvard to study theater and went on to her career in experimental and documentary film.[6] Thus, as Samuel G. Freedman notes, Nair was "only fifteen years old in 1972" and "does not remember hearing news of Amin's edict." He says:

> Rather, she learned of it elliptically through Mr. [V. S.] Naipaul's novel, *A Bend in the River*, which is set in an unnamed African country, and more directly through an article by Jane Kramer in *The New Yorker* about an Indian family that had moved from Kampala to London under the dictator's expulsion order.[7]

Without the personal experience of the expulsion from Uganda, Nair felt compelled to research the situation for her film.

She discerned a comparison between the colonial situation of Indians in Africa and the experience of Indians in the South in the Indians' control over the motel industry. Freedman reports:

> In the precarious existence of Uganda's Indians, Ms. Nair found a parallel to those countrymen increasingly operating motels in the American South. With her documentarian's talent for research, she drove from South Carolina to Mississippi in March 1989. So numerous were Indian-owned motels that one or two billboards for competitors bluntly stated, "100 percent American."[8]

Freedman compares the situation of these Indian motel entrepreneurs to new Korean immigrants in black urban ghettoes whose success and prosperity as store owners often result in the enmity of local black residents. He writes:

> The reasons for the boom became readily clear to Ms. Nair. Sponsored for immigration, trained in the trades and sometimes even lent money by relatives, Indians could buy motels for as little as $100,000. Much like Koreans with greengroceries, the Indians could rely on family members for labor and could conduct business with only a cursory knowledge of English.[9]

The continuity Nair perceived between Africa and America for Indians and African Americans undermines the reputed uniqueness of the American experience and counters the inherent self-centered narcissism of the ideology and myth of American exceptionalism and renewal. It is significant that throughout *Mississippi Masala*, Jay yearns for Uganda and repeatedly petitions the government to restore his wealth and position. The film ends with his return to Uganda where he learns of the death years earlier of Okelo. He also witnesses the dilapidated and miserable condition of his once-beautiful home, a lovely estate that, in fact, became Nair's own home which she shares with her Indian-born husband, Mahmood Mamdani. Mamdani was raised in Uganda, and returned there to teach political science after receiving a doctorate from Harvard. The couple met while Nair worked on the film, and they have a son named Zohran.[10]

Accordingly, Nair's own commitment to Africa and her family life there and the use of Africa as a frame for *Mississippi Masala* establish more than a narrational and geographic frame for the film. The opening and end provide an ideological frame for understanding the American experience in the film. America remains part of the world and part of a history of European and Western domination of Africa and the East. To a degree, in *Mississippi Masala*, white America assumes the role of "the British, who," as Nair told Freedman, "had wedged them [the Indians of Uganda] in, were the experts in divide and conquer."[11]

As part of this Third World and postcolonial view of America in the film, it also should be emphasized that Nair not only identifies in part with Africa and her life there, she primarily sees herself as Indian and adamantly eschews any identity for herself as a marginalized American, although she recognizes the "marginalized" as the people who occupy her central concerns. Admitting that "I'm interested in marginal people – people who are *considered* marginal." She also says, "I can't imagine growing old in America. Some of us must grow old and die where we were born, where we feel at home. Home for me will always be India." Similarly, she says, "I *feel* Indian, I *am* Indian; I spend more time in India than I do in New York, more time in Kampala than anywhere. I am, really, an *Indian* filmmaker, despite the work I have done in America."[12] As Redding and Brownworth state,

> Despite living in the United States and traveling between continents from her late teens through her thirties, Nair has not assimilated into Western culture.... At the heart of most of Nair's films lies India, in all its myriad complexities, to which the filmmaker brings her own prismatic vision.[13]

Nevertheless, in spite of this Indian perspective and Third World frame, *Mississippi Masala*, as its title suggests, remains centered in America and constitutes an important statement and discussion of the meaning of America today. The film's major ideological concern and focus can be discerned by seeing beyond the romanticized perspective that dominates the shooting of the Ugandan landscape as a lush, beautiful, and sensual environment. Flashbacks of this landscape through Jay's consciousness dramatize his melancholic and nostalgic yearning for Uganda.

However, the destruction, disorder, and death that this environment produces dramatically subvert any potential comparison between Uganda and America as natural environments for cultivating democratic societies. The visual perception of a potential garden for new life in the Ugandan landscape immediately becomes a nightmare of chaos and catastrophe, thereby complicating any comparisons with the New World Garden of America. In the beginning of the film, state-sanctioned lawlessness, violence, terror, and discrimination overwhelm the landscape that Jay and his family treasure. At the end, the devastated remnants of Jay's home provide a prism through which to view the lush landscape that the house occupies and overviews. The friendly touch of a black stranger's child and the joy of African music and dance conclude the film on a note of peaceful ambiguity about Uganda's future under a new regime.

Just as the visual splendor of the landscape of Uganda clashes with the verbal and dramatic representation of Amin's ideology and program, so also the title of the film itself articulates an important ideological tension. Discussing her film, Nair says, "*Masala* is an Indian word – it means hot and spicy, a mixing of spices. The film is about the mixing of black, brown, white – *masala*." At first masala, as Nair explains it, seems comparable to the classic imagery of America as a "melting pot," a fusing together of different peoples from all over the world, even to the point of Nair's particularizing the term to New York City, the putative epitome of the quintessential melding of races, cultures, and peoples. She says, "I think this kind of mixing is what we are coming to see all over – here [New York] you see it everywhere."[14] As Freedman further explains:

> One half of the film's title, "masala," refers to a variety of spices in different shades, and to Ms. Nair symbolizes the polyglot culture of Indians who were colonized in their nation by the British and then forced by poverty to seek survival elsewhere. Often they served in those adopted countries as

the mercantile class, comfortable enough to be represented from below, not comfortable enough to be protected from above.[15]

To Freedman, Jay is in "precisely the situation" just described of being a polyglot–Indian surrogate for other people's power.

Of greater importance perhaps, the break between father and daughter in the film, between generations, also dramatizes an incipient ideological and cultural conflict in the term masala, making the word a potent sign of tension and ambiguity throughout the film concerning the clash between American individuality as opposed to an ideology of ethnic and racial continuity and coercion. Freedman convincingly argues that Jay and Kinnu's daughter, Mina, brilliantly played by Sarita Choudhury in her first film performance, "has grown into a self-proclaimed "masala" who wears the traditional smock called a kameez, hangs a John Lennon postcard by her bedside and still remembers a few childhood words of Swahili."[16]

However, the crucial point for the film concerns not Mina's self-styled mixing of culture but the much more difficult and magnificent process of transformation. She becomes an American, meaning more than a mixture or a conglomerate but something new. She says, "This is America, Ma!" Being an American involves more than, as Freedman implies, merely adding another color to the pot – in this case black – in the form of man named Demetrius, played by Denzel Washington. Similarly, Mina's rebellion against her parents involves more than simple adolescent self-assertion. It entails establishing a new identity through her relationship with Demetrius. She literally runs into her future when her car rear-ends the truck Demetrius's uses for his rug cleaning business. In the auto accident, Indian masala collides with a new world ideology. Demetrius becomes a tutor of sorts about America and American values when they fall in love. And, of course, the love story provides the basic narrative thrust for the film. However, at this point it also becomes an American love story. The film literally enacts Whitman's concept of love as the foundation of democracy when he writes in "Song of Myself" that "a kelson of the creation is love."[17] For sure, Nair brilliantly and beautifully portrays the union of the lovers as the merging of black and brown skin colors and cultures. Nair says,

> It is a melding of these two groups, these Indians who have never been to India, who are really Africans, but who have been expelled from the country because they are not black, and these African Americans who were born in

America and know nothing of Africa. So you have that exploration of what home is, of personal and cultural dislocation.[18]

At the same time, the biology that occurs between Mina and Demetrius fuels a kind of chemical change, an original creation, as Whitman suggests. The two people come to embody an idea that transcends biology and descent to redefine themselves as individuals and as a couple. In this regard, the intensity of Mina's transformation may reflect more of the experience and influence of Nair's long-time friend and screenwriter, Sooni Taraporevala, who has known Nair since they were Indian students at Harvard and has worked and collaborated with her since their first film, the critically praised and successful *Salaam Bombay!*, a film with real street people and homeless children.[19]

Transcending mere mixture to seek regeneration and transformation indicates the alternative in the film to the determinism of identifying people primarily in terms of origins, race, and descent. However, the film also dramatizes the challenge to such an ideology of renewal of overcoming ethnic and racial competition and hatred. Jay himself comes to feel the inevitability of racial and ethnic divisions. Toward the end of the film, Jay articulates his acceptance of a view of people based on blood and race when he explains to Mina why, as he sees it, the family really left Uganda. Jay's explanation contains an element of tragedy. He describes an attitude that is anathema to him but one which now seems unavoidable. Reversing the liberalism of his earlier years, he has become conservative and tries to tell Mina as well as Demetrius that things cannot change.

Jay asks Mina, "Do you know why we left Uganda? Do you?"

She responds, "They put you in jail."

He answers: "After thirty-four years, my brother Okelo told me, 'Africa is for Africans. Black Africans.' After thirty-four years that's what it all came down to, the color of my skin. That's why we left. Not because of Idi Amin or anything like that. Mina! Believe me. I'm speaking from experience. People stick to their own kind. You're forced to accept that when you grow older. I'm only trying to spare you the pain."

She protests, "Okelo risked his life to save yours. I don't know what more proof you could have of his love."

He asks, "What do you remember? You were just a child."

And she says, "I remember. I remember his face when he came to say good-bye. And you wouldn't even look at him."

In contrast to Jay's fatalistic pessimism, a prescient comment by Nair summarizes the importance of ideology and belief over blood and biology as a means for defining one's identity and destiny in an historical and cultural context. She told Freedman that "you live between your ears." She continued, "You carry your home within yourself. That's a nice-sounding cerebral concept, but the truth is that you're torn."[20]

Accordingly, in their blending of black and brown, Mina and Demetrius move beyond mere mixing, melding – masala – to the representation of an ideology of individual character and autonomy that breaks with racial roots, geographic groundings, and ethnic determinism. In their union, they seek to construct a future of possibilities that involves an escape from the past and a belief in regeneration. Nair's and Taraporevala's brilliant incorporation of the relationship between Mina and Demetrius into the American idea of regeneration and individual achievement comprises a major aspect of *Mississippi Masala*'s aesthetic success and cultural significance. One academic review complained:

> A fundamental problem with the film, however, is that it contains two different stories which compete for the audience's attention – the romance between Mina and Demetrius, and the more interesting story centered around Mina's father, Jay, and his relationship to Africa.[21]

Arguably, just the opposite of this obtains. The genius of the film involves its intense fusion of the love story and family history in the context of the themes of globalism, colonialism, and the American experience in the 1990s.

In their struggle to find a place in the American Dream, Demetrius and Mina become a kind of colorized George Bailey and Mary Hatch, the couple in Frank Capra's *It's a Wonderful Life* (1946), starring Jimmy Stewart and Donna Reed. Interesting parallels between the stories of the two couples occur throughout the films. Similarities with the Capra classic help explain Mina's and Demetrius's relationship as well as the cultural significance of the couple. Comparable social and psychological moments in the films provide focus and structure for Mina and Demetrius as individuals, as a couple, and as potential icons for America of middle-class values of individuality, self-discipline, work, stability, devotion to family, and community responsibility. Understanding Mina and Demetrius as a new kind of all-American couple suggests the intense American-ness at the core of Nair's Indian perspective of America. Seeing the black man and brown woman as following in the footsteps and fulfilling the cultural and social role of George and Mary helps to identify and bring out the deeper meanings of the film.

Equally significant, relating Nair's Mina and Demetrius to Capra's George and Mary also may help explain the possible disconnect today of this couple and film with the dominant values of a changing contemporary America. At least as much as issues of color and race, matters of values, belief, and behavior may separate Mina and Demetrius, and *Mississippi Masala*, from much of current popular American culture.

At a time of the acceleration of by now familiar social trends – corporate power, overwhelming technology, conformity, mass entertainment, self-indulgence, advertising, consumerism, immediate gratification – Mina and Demetrius represent values of individuality, small entrepreneurship, family, work, and discipline. By trying to live the myth of success for themselves and to reinvent the ideology of renewal, this couple of color counters many of those today who feel disaffected and alienated from the historic American experience. Mina and Demetrius embody, in a new form, the classic conception of the American idea.

Ironically, many other people of color in the film, including Asians, typify superficial American lifestyles and values that dominate the media and popular culture. While Erika Surat Andersen castigates Nair for her portrayal of Asians and finds "many of the Indian characters in *Masala* to be negative and satirized," it could be argued that many of these Indians have become Americanized much too easily and readily into an artificial culture of selfish consumerism and surface relationships.[22] In fact, one Indian, who at the end of the film has been accused by another of becoming "American" for evicting and abandoning Jay and his family, exclaims, "So what! I live here in America. If you don't like it, go back to India."

Thus, examining *Mississippi Masala* in the light of its intertextual connections to *It's a Wonderful Life* can render important insights into Nair's film.[23] Some interesting narrative parallels between the two films eventually suggest consideration of ideological aspects to Mina and Demetrius and the insinuation of important cultural significance into their relationship. Although George Bailey and Mary Hatch have grown up together in the same small town of Bedford Falls, New York, their actual romance begins at a dance. Similarly, Demetrius and Mina start to get involved at a dance. As in the George and Mary relationship, the presence of another woman from the past and a male competitor heats up the chemistry between Mina and Demetrius. Thus, the music and ambience of the scenes are radically and significantly different, but the end result of bringing two people together connects both films.

One of the most powerful and replayed scenes in *It's a Wonderful Life* focuses on the use of a telephone as a prop to intensify the attraction and resistance George and Mary feel for each other. The fetishization of the telephone in the George and Mary scene becomes a blatant suggestion of phone sex between Demetrius and Mina. Mina and Demetrius each talk on their own telephones while lying in bed in the privacy of their own rooms. As they speak softly in sensuous and seductive tones about what they are doing and wearing, the camera concentrates on their bodies and their suggestive hand movements. As in the dancing scene, the camera also seems to emphasize the beauty and difference of their skin colors.

The sexual excitement of this conversation propels the couple, at Demetrius's instigation, to their first and only evening together at a motel in Biloxi, Mississippi for what becomes a sexually graphic scene. *It's a Wonderful Life*, which was made during the era of the production code, offers little that could compare to the explicit love-making between Mina and Demetrius. In *It's a Wonderful Life*, the sexualized tension of the phone conversation as a sign of both connection and separation visually erupts in an explosive cut to George and Mary's wedding that will sanction sexuality and ultimately parenting.

However, the filming of the love-making between Demetrius and Mina should not necessarily offend the sensibilities of George and Mary as representatives of their generation and social situation, if the heavenly director of the Capra film could enable them to see the scene. The filming infuses the love-making with love and tenderness. In a motel that could mean disaster for any genuine emotion, Nair directs the scene with feeling and taste that convincingly suggest the emergence of a genuine relationship between the lovers. Music, touch, speech, expression, lighting turn the motel into a mise-en-scene of feeling and love. An evocative soundtrack of African music accompanies their caresses. The camera concentrates on intertwined parts of their bodies that intimate not only sexuality but also an emotional joining of body and spirit. The initial cut focuses on their hands and fingertips, brown and black. Another cut lights upon a dark male shoulder and a soft brown face. The scene establishes a visual and audial rhythm of sexuality and love. Such detail and sensitivity anticipate Nair's later success in *Kama Sutra: A Tale of Love* (1997).[24]

Thus, while nothing in the love-making of the scene should offend people like George and Mary, one crucial aspect of the scene, of course, might very well prove shocking or at least unsettling to people with George's and Mary's background during this time, namely the issue of race and color. Certainly few in the late 1940s would anticipate a scene of such physical and emotional affection between people of color, and many, including some in today's audiences, might still be shocked by it. Rather than shrink from this issue, Nair emphasizes the mixing of colors in the scene. She relishes the merger of brown and black flesh and bathes the screen in nuanced variations of dark-skinned coloring as signs of passion and love. Also, documentary images in the form of intimate shots of the actors' brown and black bodies meld with the fictional context to reenforce the case for a potential reembodiment of the American idea.

Nair and Taraporevala confront race and color, in part, by engaging the issue through the attitudes of people of color toward each other, thereby further complicating the cultural, psychological, and social dimensions of race relations. On their own brief holiday, some of Mina's relatives and friends discover her with Demetrius. Although no one ever makes a blatantly racist remark, racial concern and superiority are implicit, even in Jay's attitude toward Demetrius's relationship to his daughter. The film suggests that when race again enters Jay's home, as it did in the case of Okelo, his liberalism and open-mindedness fade. Moreover, as in Africa, for Asians it becomes economically, politically, and socially important to distinguish themselves from the darker-skinned African Americans, an irony already noted for Mina whose dark coloration, according to an Indian gossip played by Nair, weakens her potential to marry an eligible Indian bachelor. Demetrius himself forces Jay to face this complexity of conflicting feelings about race. He says to Jay, "I know you and your folks can come down here from God-knows-where and be about as black as the ace of spades, and as soon as you get here you start acting white – and treating us like we're your doormats."

At the same time, significantly, a recurring nightmare awakens Mina when she sleeps with Demetrius. The dream goes back to Uganda and her terror as a little girl over the violence inflicted upon the Indians by blacks. Violence and hatred over race can be mutual, the film argues.

The hostility of both groups, Asians and African Americans, to Mina and Demetrius's love affair triggers a personal and community crisis that initially separates the couple but finally strengthens their relationship. Before their reconciliation, both must confront the active opposition of their families, communities, and the various people who resist any race mixing. For Demetrius, the crisis involves the near loss of his business. His business collapse and personal crisis at this point in the film compare to several similar moments of panic and crisis in the life of George Bailey in *It's a Wonderful Life*. For Bailey such events usually involve his leadership of a small loan company that puts him in extreme opposition to the city's leading economic figure. Similarly, Demetrius must deal with a banker who withdraws his support after learning about the scandal involving Demetrius and Mina. In a wonderful scene, Demetrius and his black partner, Tyrone (Charles S. Dutton), visit the bank to negotiate an extension of the bank's loan. They find the previously helpful banker (Ben Burford) has assumed a supercilious and condescending attitude as he patronizingly advises them about their affairs.

When compared to the opposition that George Bailey must face from his enemy banker, Potter, as played brilliantly by Lionel Barrymore, the scene in *Mississippi Masala* becomes a study in the modern banalization of evil into mindless conformity. Barrymore's Potter becomes the devil incarnate, the personification of brutal fascistic and monopolistic impulses. He epitomizes the death that results from selfish greed. In contrast, the Mississippi banker is all farce, the personification of self-importance based on local ignorance and institutional prejudice. He is what George Bailey could have become if Bailey had sold out to Potter. Demetrius must listen to the man – "Bob at the bank" – lecture about the importance of good economic planning that he characterizes as "character, credit, collateral, capital, and . . ." – only he cannot recall the last "c." Later Demetrius says, "color, that's the one they left out." Personally impotent, the banker's bureaucratic position nevertheless gives him the ability to crush Demetrius for mixing and confusing the color line.

Mina and Demetrius overcome the obstacles and opposition of color and community to attempt to build their own lives. Drawing ironically on the very strength instilled in them by the love and devotion of their parents and families, they find the inner resolve to resist efforts to sever their relationship. Mina especially summons the energy to chase Demetrius down, ostensibly to say good-bye before returning to Uganda, but somehow her farewell turns into an exchange that marks a new beginning for them as a couple in love. Having found Demetrius as he tries to get new customers in neighboring communities

that will help him save his rug cleaning business, Mina's good-bye provokes Demetrius's confession, "I never thought I would fall in love
with you." She persuades him and they convince each other that they
can work together to use their love, youth, and experience to make
a life for themselves. "I could be your partner. I know how to clean
rooms.... It's crazy to stay here."

Mina's assumption of the self-evident reasonableness and legitimacy
of her break with her family and background to start a new life with
Demetrius constitutes a special instance of her Americanization. Of
course, Demetrius must also leave his father. For him, the separation
suggests the completion of a traditional rite of passage as a young man
and an American, who ultimately must make his own independent way
to achieve success.

Nair beautifully parallels and develops these culminating moments
in the concluding portion of the film. Once again, a telephone becomes
a crucial prop to dramatize the tension between separation and connection, between drastic change and continuity. Although Mina and
Demetrius are only in Indianola, a relatively few miles away from their
parents, in terms of psychology and the construction of a new reality,
they could be calling from a different world; and in a sense, they do
metaphorically make a long-distance call from another continent called
America where one generation breaks with another to try to create its
own wonderful life.

First Demetrius calls his father to tell him that he and Mina will be
leaving. It is evening. Several hours have passed since the couple decided
to begin a new life together. Mina and Demetrius have probably been
enjoying the excitement of being together, of thinking about preparing
for the future, of dreaming about that future. They have also been
enjoying the luxury of their freedom from the guilt that will fall upon
them after they inform their parents of their decision. As Demetrius
speaks to his father, Williben (Joe Seneca), the light of the telephone
booth dramatically stands out against the evening darkness. The scene
consists of basic intercuts between Demetrius in the phone booth and
his elderly father in the kitchen of the restaurant where he works.
Demetrius's tears dramatize his sadness and worry over leaving his
widowed father and his younger brother, Dexter (Tico Wells), who
has for too many years relied upon his help. It is an extraordinarily
powerful scene for the way it suggests such deep love between two
men, father and son. It also makes an original and effective statement
about manliness in its emotional expression of unselfishness, concern,

and care. The father wonderfully frees the son from his responsibility, emphasizing that Demetrius has sacrificed enough and that the time has come for him to live his own life.

Although extremely moving, the painful intensity of the conversation between father and son anticipates the even deeper emotion in Mina's call to her parents. For Mina, the separation signifies a truly radical transformation of herself as a woman and individual. She must break not only from her dependence upon her parents but also to some degree from her Indian heritage and identity that her parents embody.

Nair brilliantly builds upon the emotional mise-en-scene established first between Demetrius and Mina and then between Demetrius and his father. In each of these scenes, Taraporevala's compassionately personal screenplay adds considerably to the emotional depth and realism of the characters and situation. Again the telephone and a lonely telephone booth dramatize the conflicting sense of both proximity and distance. However, even more time has passed since Demetrius's call. Mina obviously has delayed telephoning because heavy rain now pours down at both ends of the conversation. The rain adds to the emotional and psychological tension of the conversation between daughter and parents. In such darkness and such weather that evoke feelings of dread and uncertainty, the pain of imminent departure and separation becomes quite palpable.

As in the conversations between the two lovers and between father and son, the basis of Mina's conversation emphasizes the love shared by all the people involved and the concern they feel for each other. However, in this particular conversation, the worry and concern of parents for their only daughter becomes almost operatic. At first, both parents are on different telephones speaking and listening at the same time to Mina. The father, when learning that Mina will be leaving with Demetrius, puts the phone down. Mina, cryingly pleads, "Ma! I'm sorry, I'm really sorry" and then in a voice of continuing despair and frustration says, "Why did he put the phone down?" knowing that it was a gesture of her father's pain and helplessness. "I'll talk to your father," the mother desperately says. "Just come back home now," she adds, obviously hoping to forestall the inevitable dread of not knowing what the future will hold for her daughter with this stranger. Mina says, "Demetrius and I are going to work together. We're leaving Mississippi to see what we can do." The mother in a lifeless voice repeats her impossible plea, "Please talk about it. But come back home now!" Mina answers with the inescapable truth: "I can't. If I don't leave now, I'll never leave. You know that." Kinnu finally concedes defeat with her plea for a promise from Mina "to ring... every two days" so that they will know "where you are." Mina hangs up with, "I'll see you soon, okay. Kiss poppa for me."

This meticulously composed sequence of scenes works so well partly because Nair and Taraporevala so brilliantly place a realistic and emotional story in an important historical and cultural context of the meaning of becoming American. The pain all participants suffer derives directly from the transformational experience of becoming something new and different, of becoming American. The film educates about that pain and difficulty of breaking from a past history and separating from established ties and loves. It makes the pain tangible and personal. Mina's compelling appeal to Kinnu about working with Demetrius to see what kind of future can be created out of nearly nothing except energy, will, dedication, and love not only recalls the story of George and Mary in *It's a Wonderful Life* but also revivifies an ideology of renewal at the core of the American idea. It emphasizes the importance of mind over matter, of ideas and ideology over inherited qualities. Thus, in the earlier conversation about their love and future, Demetrius teases Mina, "You out your mind, you know that?" to which she responds in words worth repeating: "I'm not out of my mind. It's crazy to stay here." Her answer and attitude resonate with Nair's insight that "you live between your ears" and that "you carry your home within yourself," suggesting that every individual must strive to live according to one's idea of one's self. It would be hard to be more American than Mina and Demetrius at this point in the film.

At the same time, the great pain and sense of loss involved in this personal and cultural experiment of newness also demand consideration. As people of color, Mina and Demetrius face an unclear future by following in the footsteps of George Bailey and Mary Hatch in searching for a place in the American Dream. The uncertainty involves not only the reality of being black or brown in America but the question of the continued centrality and relevance of the American idea and vision in the world today. Nair's own profound concerns about globalism, feminism, and the Third World often seem to take precedence over the idea of the meaning of America to the world, although some critics such as Laura U. Marks question the authenticity of her commitment to these issues.[25] Positioning *Mississippi Masala* so carefully within a frame of Indian and Ugandan borders of time, circumstance, and consciousness certainly reenforces the quality in her work of a dialogue that contradicts the absolute domination of a self-perpetuating American ideology. In light of her life experience and commitments, as well as the body of her work to date in film, for Nair it would seem problematic to assume that the classic ideology of America can compete successfully in importance and influence with other ideological and cultural forces in the world today based on gender or Third Worldism.

In terms of such ambiguity and skepticism about the meaning and long-term impact today of the American idea, Nair's position and work contrast dramatically with another Indian artist and thinker, the acclaimed writer Bharati Mukherjee for whom America means "hope." For Mukherjee, America "fuses" people together in a way that not only recreates them but also reinvents the future and invests it with infinite possibility and opportunity as well as danger. She says:

> What America offers me is romanticism and hope. I'm coming out of a continent of cynicism and irony and despair in many ways – a traditional society where you are what you are according to the family that you were born into, the caste, the class, the gender, and suddenly I found myself in a country where I can choose to discard that part of myself that I want and invent a whole new history for myself. In doing that we, of course, very painfully, sometimes very violently murder our old selves and that's an unfortunate, perhaps, inevitable process. I want to think that it is a freeing process in spite of the pain – in spite of the violence – in spite of the bruising of the old self to have that freedom to make mistakes, to choose a whole new history for one's self is exciting.[26]

In *Mississippi Masala*, Nair and Taraporevala question whether America makes the pain, violence, and self-brutalization that Mukherjee describes worthwhile. They ask if America can still come through on the old promise of regeneration, of freedom and equality, of upward mobility and make possible the pursuit of happiness for people of color, for new immigrants, and for future generations born into an increasingly fluid and unstable society of media, corporations, and technology. They wonder if the American idea still has the capacity to capture the imagination and consciousness of the world. Can it continue to persuade peoples of great differences to come together with faith in each other and in the future? In reembodying the American idea in this couple in Mississippi, Nair and Taraporevala have invented two people who offer the hope and put forth the best face for the fulfillment of such possibilities.

CHAPTER TWO

LONE STAR

An Archeology of American Culture and the American Psyche

Visitors to Freud's consulting room and study at Berggasse 19 in Vienna easily could confuse these rooms with the offices of a professional archeologist. In fact, when he visited these offices, the Wolf Man, the subject of one of Freud's most influential case studies, thought, as Peter Gay recounts, not of

> a doctor's office but rather of an archeologist's study. Here were all kinds of statuettes and other unusual objects, which even the layman recognized as archeological finds from ancient Egypt. Here and there on the walls were stone plaques representing various scenes of long-vanished epochs.[1]

Freud explained to the Wolf Man that archeology represented more than a hobby to him; it provided an important analogy to his work in psychoanalysis since

> the psychoanalyst, like the archeologist in his excavations, must uncover layer after layer of the patient's psyche, before coming to the deepest, most valuable treasures.[2]

Throughout his career, Freud persisted in comparing the exploration of the deepest recesses of the psyche with the most important archeology diggings in history such as the discovery of Troy.

Close associates and friends of Freud, such as writer Stefan Zweig and professor of archeology Emanuel Lowy, also noted Freud's fascination with archeology.[3] Freud's famous analysis, as Gay notes, of *Gradiva* (1903), a short novel by German writer Wilhelm Jensen, developed this comparison between archeology and psychoanalysis. Discussing comments by the novel's heroine about the archeologist hero of this work, Freud wrote:

> There is actually no better analogy for repression, which both makes something in the mind inaccessible and preserves it, than the burial that was the

fate of Pompeii and from which the city could reappear through the work of a spade.[4]

For Freud, investigating the Oedipus complex and repression involved a form of scientific excavation of the psyche and history. Apparently, he saw one of his prized treasures, a painting by Ingres of Oedipus questioning the Sphinx, as illustrating such an effort at reconstructive excavation.[5]

Freud's comparison of archeological excavation with psychoanalysis to illustrate his practice of uncovering the inner workings of the mind and the secrets of current and lost civilizations sheds light on the methods and the art of John Sayles's film, *Lone Star* (1996). *Lone Star* literally begins with an excavation activity that quickly establishes the pattern for the film's story of investigation into American culture and the American psyche as represented by Texas. The concept of excavation, of digging for resisting historical, social, and personal truths, operates throughout the film.

From the film's beginning, Sayles creates an elaborate narrative structure and investigative methodology to reconstruct the past in order to understand present events and to anticipate an uncertain future of change. The structure entails the complex intermeshing of individual stories with the reconstruction of historic events. Sayles establishes sets of parallelisms between the stories of individuals and couples with the histories of their particular ethnic and racial groups. He relates and connects these stories and histories to each other and to Texas society as a whole. Individual and historic events often operate in temporal fluidity so that important personal and historic moments interfuse with related moments and events. In its cohesive organization of multiple perspectives on the past, *Lone Star* works as a kind of group psychoanalysis of cultural history and meaning.

Moreover, in developing this methodology of reconstructing events, *Lone Star* at its narrative level creates what could be called a kind of fictionalized documentary of complex multicultural realities and contexts. Sayles delineates an extensive history of extreme diversity and maps the topography of deep social and cultural tensions that comprise the past and present and portend the future of the fictional border city and area of Frontera in the midst of waning Anglo domination. Sayles demonstrates the relationship and contribution of different groups – Anglo, Hispanic, African American, and to some extent Native American – to the history of the region and the formation of the current cultural crisis and conflict at the core of the film. But beyond just intermingling these different particular histories, Sayles maintains a steady focus on classic questions about the meaning of America as exemplified in this Texas narrative. *Lone Star* considers how the changing relationships and histories of these groups influence American culture. The film articulates mythic and ideological ways of thinking about origins, identity, and history to the point of indicating how a siege mentality, symbolized by the Alamo, slips into a comical bartender's ethnic and racist paranoia, a disgruntled parent's anger over Hispanic-based curriculum changes, and even the fanaticism over sports of the hero's ex-wife. Ideologies as ways of interpreting individual and group experience become part of the narrative structure. Thus, *Lone Star* poses questions about changing values, beliefs, and opportunities for all groups and peoples in a dynamic of cultural change.

Lone Star also dramatizes how immigration over generations into Texas from Mexico contributes to the transformation of America through the infusion of people of color into America from all over the world. As in Mira Nair's *Mississippi Masala* (1992), Sayles's *Lone Star* reembodies and revivifies American character and culture through the surging prominence of immigrants and minorities of color. For Sayles, the story and meaning of America entail such mixing of peoples, especially in Texas. Sayles literally reenacts on the Texas frontier, Herman Melville's concept described earlier of an America in which the blood of all peoples mingles. In most of the film's interracial or mixed relationships, Sayles dramatizes an admixture of people and cultures that might shock even the frequently outrageous and unconventional Melville. The film also returns to the questions raised by *Time* in 1993 about how immigration and new minorities, as already noted, are reforming and reshaping the American people and character. Like that issue of the magazine, the film ponders the portents for the future of such a new ethnic dynamism.

In an interview with *Cineaste*, Sayles states that the film represents "pretty much the opposite of Pat Buchanan's idea of this monoculture which is being invaded." Sayles continues:

> English-speaking culture is just one of many cultures. It has become the dominant culture or subculture in certain areas, but it's a subculture just like all the others. American culture is not monolingual or monoracial. It's always been a mix.

Asked if he therefore sees the United States as "an increasingly multicultural society with more and more bicultural couples," Sayles vigorously responds that,

> it's not *increasingly* multicultural, it's always been so. If you go back and turn over a rock, you find out, for example, that maybe a third or more of African-Americans are also Native Americans and a much higher percentage of African-Americans are also white Americans. You know, as they used to do in New Orleans, if you're 1/64th black, you're black, and it doesn't matter what you look like.[6]

At the same time, Sayles emphasizes how this juxtaposition and intermingling of groups involves a history of strife that continues today. For him, Texas accentuates that ethnic strife and racial tension.

> It was a republic formed in a controversial and bloody way. And its struggles didn't end with the Civil War. There is a kind of racial and ethnic war that has continued. That continuing conflict comes into clearest focus around the border between Texas and Mexico.[7]

Moreover, in addition to including this continuing historic battle of ethnic, racial, and national groups, *Lone Star* examines the psychological dynamics of such conflict. In a manner consistent with the comparison of Sayles's narrative method of excavation with Freud's image of psychoanalysis, Sayles explores the inner psychological drama of the external transformation of the American body. For him the borders and boundaries between peoples become a metaphor for boundaries and differences in general. Ideological identifications with groups have a basis in the inner search of the individual for a personal identity. Sex and love propel group identification and complicate personal relationships. Similarly, external conflict and tension relate to inner division. In *Lone Star*, external engagements of the individual and the group with intrusive forces and people have their counterparts in internal psychological insecurities and tensions. For Sayles, an atmosphere of racial and ethnic difference exacerbates the inner anxieties of identity and love, while also providing opportunities for growth and learning. Sayles says:

> In a personal sense, a border is where you draw a line and say "This is where I end and somebody else begins." In a metaphorical sense, it can be any of the symbols that we erect between one another – sex, class, race, age.[8]

Thus, Sayles's narrative method of excavation and reconstruction entails psychological, historical, cultural, ideological, ethnic, and racial explorations that ultimately fuse into one story and search for the meaning of Texas as a metaphor for America. The film documents the history and culture of Texas to authenticate the fiction of one man's search for the truth. The journey turns into a personal quest for identity and salvation. The personal and political merge.

The excavation begins simply enough in the film with two off-duty soldiers pursuing their different hobbies by working over the terrain of scrub flats of an old Army base. Sergeant "Mikey" Hogan (Stephen Lang) uses a metal detector to check the ground for hidden bullets that he later turns into art objects. Sergeant Cliff Potts (Stephen Mendillo), who studies plants and flora, prophetically says, "You live in a place, you should know something about it. Explore – " just before Mikey in close-up hastily interrupts him.[9] Mikey, has uncovered the remains of a dead body. The masonic ring on the skeletal bones of the corpse's hand apparently attracted the metal detector. Mikey also recovers a sheriff's badge near the body. The ensuing criminal investigation by Sheriff Sam Deeds (Chris Cooper) becomes a systematic process of revealing the embarrassments and transgressions of the past.

Discussing the meaning of *Lone Star*, Sayles proposes excavation as symbolic of the search for truth. In his introduction to the screenplay, Sayles says:

> It is Sam Deeds, the white sheriff, who digs the story out for us. The structure of the detective story serves as the vehicle to carry us through the past and present social structure of a Texas border town, with surprises in store for each of the three [main characters]. (*LS* vii)

Sayles elaborates upon the idea of excavating for the truth in language that resonates with Freud's metaphor for exploring psychological and cultural depths. He says, "Sam's action in *Lone Star* was circular, a kind of digging through layers, always moving toward a center of truth." (*LS* viii).

While repeating Freud's image of excavating for the truth, Sayles's view also compares to Freud's in his emphasis on the inevitable intertwining of the individual with the social and cultural. For Sayles, history and individual psychology and character merge. He says, "You know, history has the word *story* in it, and I think the main thing I was thinking about in writing the movie was: 'What do we need history for? What do we use it for?'"[10] Emphasizing the intrinsic relationship of the most personal feelings with group history and identity,

Sayles says:

> Everybody starts with some kind of handicap or advantage, and that's their personal history. And it's also their group history. I was interested in the way those two interact: both the personal, and the social and group history.[11]

The Oedipal theme also connects Sayles to the Freudian conception of the social construction of the person. Reacting to Sayles's ideas about the individual and the group, Gavin Smith notes that *Lone Star* can be read as "a reworking of a classic myth, the myth of Oedipus." And Sayles in turn agrees that "I wanted that idea that you have to be careful of what you look for, because you might find it."[12] Evoking a Freudian version of the Oedipus myth, Smith asserts in his introduction:

> If Sayles has an overarching impulse, it is to investigate the complex, shifting relationship between individuals and their communities and social orders, or put another way, the dynamic between the personal and the political in ordinary life.[13]

Sayles's summary of the film also emphasizes the relationship of the individual to the conventional view of the Oedipally-constructed and defined family that provides the basis for Freud's theory of the Oedipus complex. Sayles says:

> The backbone of *Lone Star* is the definition of personal identity through family history for a white county sheriff, an African-American army colonel and a Chicana high school teacher. The trigger for this is the discovery of the remains of a former sheriff, evidently murdered. (*LS* vii)

Ironically, aspects of the Oedipal theme, such as repression and the prohibition against incest, suggest a contradiction in Sayles's thinking that also relates to Freud's notion of excavation. As related earlier in his comment about Jensen's novel *Gradiva*, Freud associates archeological excavation with denial and repression. Sayles's statements in interviews about the theme of incest in *Lone Star* insinuate some degree of denial in his thinking. At the core of *Lone Star*, the deepest and most painful mystery of all involves the secret blood relationship between the Hispanic teacher Pilar Cruz (Elizabeth Peña) and the investigating sheriff Sam Deeds (Chris Cooper). As teenagers Pilar and Sam became lovers, the Chicana and the Anglo, before realizing that Sam's father, Buddy Deeds (Matthew McConaughey), and her mother, Mercedes (Miriam Colon), once also had been illicit, but devoted, lovers in a long affair that resulted in Pilar's birth. In his discussions of the film, Sayles repeatedly suggests that with all the mysteries solved and revealed to those most concerned, Sam and Pilar somehow can stay together in spite of the incest issue. They can overcome the incest "taboo" just as others in the film must surmount opposition to interracial marriage. Sayles said, "You can do that on a personal level, but probably not on a social one."[14] Similarly, he told *Cineaste* that Sam and Pilar can make "an individual accommodation" and live among strangers unfamiliar with their incestuous ties, but they are "not going to change society."[15] Discussing the last image of the film of Sam and Pilar pondering their future in the daylight of the dilapidated and abandoned outdoor movie that once was the scene of their evening lovemaking, Sayles told Smith:

> There are the ravages of the past. So in that last image, I wanted both the sense that they are going to go forward, something could be projected on that thing. But they're not the fourteen-year-old kids that they were. They've had some damage. Things have fallen away. They're different people. But that doesn't mean that their love is dead.[16]

Perhaps out of a writer-director's fondness for the imaginary couple he created, Sayles refuses to deny them the possibility of a future together, thereby seeming to minimize the full implications of their unintended incest for either themselves or the society. Creating a possible inconsistency with both Freud and Sophocles as to the horrific meaning of incest, Sayles's sanguine vision of the couple's future also puts him in a bind about the relation of the individual to history. By presuming the possible separation of the problem of these two individuals from the problems of history, he seems to subvert the thrust of his own work that so tightly interfuses the personal with the political. He unravels what he had worked so hard to put together. He says:

> They can't stay in Frontera, around her mother and other people who know eventually, the thing is going to get out. So there is also the sense that sometimes what you have to do is just forget history, you have to escape it.[17]

Of course, forgetting and escaping history, as Sayles proposes here, contradict the premises of *Lone Star* and Sayles's other work such as *Matewan* (1987) that maintain the interweaving of the individual into history.

Indeed, the belief in escape ironically belies the depth of the hole into which Sayles digs his characters. Sayles's comments belittle the power and significance of his film's portrayal of the ideology and psychology that feed tensions over American ethnic and racial diversity. In relating Sam and Pilar's story, *Lone Star* unearths themes that go back to the roots of the American experience. Incest in the film between a Chicana and Anglo evokes primal fears in America of ethnic chaos to match the idealism of ethnic melding. In spite of Sayles's hopes for Sam and Pilar, the film marries the personal to the historical.

In *Lone Star*, the intense mixture of races, ethnic groups, and cultures, replicates in Texas an American situation of ethnic and racial fusion that has occurred throughout our history. The incest theme in *Lone Star* emphasizes that in Texas, and all America, the racial or ethnic other could actually be a family member. Thus, incest in the Texas of *Lone Star* becomes a metaphor that strikes at the heart of the American dilemma of the ideal of harmony and consensus and the concomitant and contradictory fears of racial, ethnic, and sexual transgression.

Lone Star also translates the story of America into the Oedipal myth. As noted above, Sayles confirms Gavin Smith's insight about the film as "a reworking" of the myth. The projection of the primal taboo of incest also parallels on a psychological and cultural level *Lone Star*'s narrative foundation of an investigation into a murder. By investigating Wade's murder, Sam also pursues the dreadful possibility of exposing his deceased father as the killer, thereby destroying Buddy's reputation and the town's continued reverence for him. Such public exposure of Buddy would constitute a symbolic slaying of his father. Sam says to Mayor Hollis Pogue (Clifton James), "People have worked this whole big thing up around my father. If it's built on a crime, they deserve to know" (*LS* 142). From a Freudian perspective, the Oedipal impulse behind Sam's pursuit of his dead father relates to ambivalence regarding love, desire, and identity. Sam's animosity toward his father reenforces the tensions of the film's other father-son relationships. Thus, when Sam tells Hollis he appreciates how Hollis "might want to believe" Buddy couldn't kill Charley, Hollis's retort, "And I understand why you might want to think he *could*" (*LS* 143), speaks to the feelings of other sons to their fathers. Sayles's directions follow this remark: "This is a low blow, but accurate enough to shake Sam up" (*LS* 143). In other words, guilt for real and imagined deeds infuses the film. Ironically, the film ultimately reveals young Hollis (Jeff Monahan), a deputy sheriff for both Wade and Buddy Deeds, to be the killer. Buddy only witnessed the act that was committed to prevent Wade's shooting of Young Otis Payne (Gabriel Casseus) for not giving Wade pay-off money on a craps game.

In any case, the issue of incest obviously insinuates into a story about borders the question of constructing the most basic of boundaries involving sexuality. Despite Sayles's apparent insouciance in his interviews about the consequences of Sam and Pilar's incest, *Lone Star* suggests that the democratic goal of withering prohibitions against ethnic and racial crossing and mixing can create a precedent and mindset for the collapse of all borders. The theme of incest insists on the danger of refusing to recognize the importance of differences and demarcations. *Lone Star* indicates that constructed geographic, social, and cultural boundaries continually recur because human beings require them, even while sometimes calling for their demolition.

Accordingly, *Lone Star* constitutes an assiduously systematic exploration of being an American, meaning for some, by definition a mixed breed. Through the guise of a detective story and criminal investigation, Sayles uses his highly diverse set of characters to construct a history lesson about how the past has shaped the present and will influence our future direction as a country and people. He tries to imagine through these character how socially-useful meaning can be derived from past differences to shape a common character and destiny for America. Any potential answer to this contemporary version of the "American Dilemma," he seems to suggest, will relate to the history of how American institutions and values previously have dealt with diversity and consensus. To Sayles, this involves something like the democratic construction of meaningful boundaries for structured self-definition, while also achieving a consensus based on a common and synthetic culture.

In the film, the process of investigation and reinvention begins with a classic Hitchcockian MacGuffin, which is a pretext, device, or gimmick for initiating the action of a story in a startling way that will attract and sustain the audience's attention through the complicated intricacies of dense plot and character development.[18] In *Lone Star*, the discovery of the dead man performs this function of starting the story. As already suggested, the film contains an extremely complex and detailed plot and narrative structure involving many different people in very complicated situations.

To reiterate, several couples with diverse but frequently interlocking backgrounds and circumstances come together in the film. As discussed, the relationship between the current sheriff Sam Deeds (Chris Cooper), and the schoolteacher Pilar Cruz (Elizabeth Peña) propels the film's plot and energy. His investigation of the death of Charley Wade (Kris Kristofferson) not only confirms Wade's corruption and dictatorial brutality as sheriff, it also reveals the truth about Sam's deceased father, Buddy Deeds (Matthew McConaughey), who followed Wade as sheriff and became a political legend in Frontera for helping people. Buddy sanitized and organized corruption, while also conducting an affair with the woman who would become Pilar's mother, Mercedes Cruz (Miriam Colon). Through Buddy's help and her own extraordinary abilities and will, Mercedes became a great business success as a restauranteur.

In addition, Sayles develops the story of a black family. Otis Payne (Ron Canada) owns a bar and restaurant that caters to black soldiers from the area's army base. His son, Delmore (Joe Morton), becomes the base's commanding officer after years of feeling neglected by Otis who had abandoned him and his mother. The beginnings of a reconciliation between Otis and Delmore, "Del," leads to the reconciliation between Delmore and his own son, Chet (Eddie Robinson). LaTanya Richardson, as Sergeant Priscilla Worth, develops the interracial theme through her relationship with Sergeant Cliff Potts (Stephen Mendillo). Of several important supporting characters, Hollis Pogue (Clifton James) has a key role as the current mayor and a former deputy. Frances McDormand plays Bunny in a brief but interesting role as Sam's ex-wife who exemplifies the neurosis of a portion of rich white society that exists in a cultural vacuum of sports and popular culture. Gordon Tootoosis as Wesley Birdsong also personifies marginalization as an Indian who lives off of the reservation because of his dislike for reservation politics. Finally, numerous Hispanic figures dramatize the diverse contribution of Hispanics to the area. As a local reporter, Jesse Borrego (Danny) voices a running commentary on the region's long record of Anglo abuses and Chicano grievances.

A true achievement of *Lone Star* involves the brilliance of Sayles's structuring of the film into a coherent, persuasive, and dynamic art form that enables it to far exceed the complexity and density of most films. He controls the intricacies of narrative detail and the proliferation of important characters in part by framing everything within a spatial structure called Texas. Texas becomes a region of ideas and symbols and a significant geographic space that stabilizes the film's difficult narrative. Keeping the film based solidly on the Texas border, Sayles's story strays only on occasion to maintain Texas and Frontera as the central focus of *Lone Star*. Texas serves as a geographic stage that becomes a mise-en-scene of ideas, history, and personal and social relationships.

Besides developing the spatial unity of Texas for coherence, Sayles, as suggested above, also creates an original temporal structure for

Lone Star. Organizing the complexity of characters and plot detail, Sayles regularly uses flashbacks to reconstruct the past throughout the film, while at the same time rendering the current political and cultural environment of Frontera in intimate detail. These brilliantly contrived and filmed flashbacks integrate the past and present. The temporal dimension of the film remains fluid and dynamic so that the past exists within the present. By avoiding cuts or dissolves that accentuate temporal divisions and fragmentation, Sayles creates what are called by the Wests in the *Cineaste* interview "seamless transitions." Sayles said he wished in the film "to erase that border" of past and present in order to "show that these people are still reacting to things in the past."[19]

In terms of historical and cultural continuity and coherence, *Lone Star* gains much from earlier classic films that geographically and thematically relate to Texas. *Lone Star* advances the influence of two major films of 1956, John Ford's *The Searchers* and George Stevens's *Giant*, that also present Texas as a metaphor for America. In those two films, the focus on Texas, as in *Lone Star*, helps the political and cultural discussion achieve structure, coherence, and depth. Both *Giant* and *The Searchers* also picture Texas as a mythic national arena with boundless horizons for the serious engagement of ideas and values. Anticipating *Lone Star*, in these films Texas provides a stage for dramatizing conflicts over contentious problems involving the nation, especially issues of race and national identity. A Texas perspective on race, ethnicity, and diversity is key to both films, although each film develops these themes in radically different ways. *Giant*, for example, represents the growing importance of liberalism in the mid-1950s.

In contrast, the racism, brutality, and anger of John Wayne's character, Ethan Edwards, in *The Searchers* vaticinate the hatred and violence of Charley Wade in *Lone Star*. However, Kristofferson's character has none of the potentially redeeming qualities of Wayne's heroism, responsibility, leadership, and capacity for change. Charley exaggerates a kind of monomaniacal hatred and aggression that the darker, ominous part of Wayne's character so vividly dramatizes. In *The Searchers*, as Arthur M. Eckstein demonstrates, Ford exposes and condemns the racism of Ethan's character. Eckstein delineates the crucial departures from the original Frank Nugent screenplay that Ford undertook to counter the negative qualities of the Wayne character.[20]

In *The Searchers*, Wayne dominates the screen, scene, and action. As well as being a story of Texas, *The Searchers* also becomes the story of Ethan's alienation and redemption on his journey to find his niece,

Debbie, who has been captured by Comanches.[21] The search for Debbie externalizes the inner search for regeneration. In *Lone Star*, none of the other main male characters – perhaps not even the collection of them – carries the power or authority of Wayne's Ethan Edwards, a testimony to the unique genius of Ford and Wayne in this film that many still consider to be an American masterpiece.

The major male characters in *Lone Star* tend to divide among themselves the conflicting aspects of Wayne's character in *The Searchers*. Kris Kristofferson's Wade embodies evil racism and sadistic violence. His gestures, voice, abrasively ironic language, sarcastic intonation, visual and verbal sneer, and timing all evoke an insidious power and threat. Kristofferson's portrayal gives his character real power and makes him genuinely intimidating, but physically Kristofferson cannot compare with the presence of Wayne on the screen. His size as described in the autopsy of his character in the film at under six feet measures several inches less than Wayne's, while his bulk as a mean but lean man also lessens his physical power in comparison to Wayne's. Wayne's power emanates from his body and presence, while Kristofferson's character derives his strength from his bullying manner and his gun. On the screen, Kristofferson physically shares the frame with the other men rather than dominating it and them. Compared to the complexity, conflicts, and contradictions of Wayne's character, Charley Wade functions as uncompromisingly evil and controlling, a brutal bully and racist, saved from becoming a dismal stereotype by the precision of Kristofferson's effective performance.

The potentially redeeming qualities in Wayne's character carry over to the other major male figures in *Lone Star*, primarily Sam Deeds (Chris Cooper) and his father, Buddy Deeds (Matthew McConaughey). Together with Kristofferson, these two men form a total character and man that approximates the complexity that Ford's direction and imagination and Wayne's acting provide Ethan in *The Searchers*. The Deeds men, father and son, together counter the absolute evil of Charley Wade and complicate the film's representation of Anglo masculinity. Cooper's Sam Deeds and McConaughey's Buddy Deeds dramatize the difficulty of achieving moral responsibility and leadership in a complex world of steadily diminishing individual authority. Cooper especially demonstrates the pain of gaining independence in a modern technological and bureaucratic society.

Lone Star focuses on the social and cultural environment as opposed to concentrating exclusively on one man. The idea of Texas as the "Lone Star State" pervades and dominates the screen and story. As Sayles says, "Texas is the Lone Star state. Texas chose the lone star because they were an individual who wanted to become part of a group."[23] Even upon his return home in *The Searchers*, Wayne, with a famous gesture of his hand and arm that mimics and honors the great actor Harry Carey, remains isolated and alone. Significantly, Sam (Cooper) also remains a loner and outsider in the Lone Star state, as Sayles suggests, but in a way that keeps attention focused on Texas and the "group" rather than Sam's marginality, as in Wayne's case. Sayles sees Sam Deeds as "an individual who stands very much outside of the group, looking at it, and who is supposed to eventually join it, but in this case he decides not to."[23]

In *Lone Star*, the mystery and drama of a police investigation disguise a self-consciously intellectual exploration of Texas as a way of thinking. The film becomes an academic lesson in cinematic and dramatic form of the social, political, and cultural life of Texas as a representation of America. As Sayles says, "One of the reasons why I chose Texas for this thing is because the state of Texas has a compressed history that is like a metaphor for the history of the United States."[24] The film, therefore, seriously examines historic issues about the formation and meaning of American culture. *Lone Star* can be read as a late-twentieth century examination of endemic issues in American history of racism and hatred that were presented so powerfully in the films of the mid-1950s.

Sayles takes his academic and historical role so seriously that Pilar's lesson about the multicultural history of the region becomes a brief but important part of the film. He uses her classroom to develop her character and role but also to emphasize the importance to the film of her history lesson. The scene provides a rare moment in film of portraying the ambience and attitudes of a high school classroom with realism and authenticity. The careful rendering of this academic mise-en-scene imbues her lesson with credibility and conveys the film's high regard for her point of view as a teacher on her subject. The scene provides valuable information and ideas, while also giving stature to Pilar as an important interpretive voice concerning the complexity of cultural, social, and historic forces that shaped and continue to influence the region.

Moreover, the classroom scene comes soon after a brilliantly cast and shot one where teachers, administrators, and parents from different

Figure 3. Chris Cooper and Pilar Cruz confront multiple obstacles when they renew their love in the Santa Barbara Cafe in *Lone Star*. (Museum of Modern Art/Film Still Archives)

ethnic backgrounds confront and challenge each other over curriculum matters involving the same historic and cultural issues that Pilar's lesson will address so cogently. The meeting of school authorities and parents also demonstrates history and education as a process that must be made and constructed as opposed to being realms of inherited and ultimate knowledge and abstract, final truth. The scenes generate serious self-referentiality by drawing attention to the way our understanding of history and culture as a set of ideas and practices grows out of complex negotiations on different levels.

In other words, the heated argument about history and then the presentation by Pilar of that history in an authentic setting show history and culture as living and changing forces. The curriculum debate over history and ethnicity by representative characters from various ethnic groups and social backgrounds followed by Pilar's history lesson illustrates how history and culture shape lives but also grow out of those same lives even in ordinary events such as classes and meetings. Also, the participants in the curriculum meeting demonstrate the ethnic diversity of the community, while their conflicting views vividly personalize the film's core cultural issues. Each group often sees itself as mistreated and endangered. Sayles, therefore, dramatizes many interconnected levels of action and meaning in these brief scenes. He infuses life into the abstract notions of culture and history by dramatizing the intimate connection of these forces to the lives of real, recognizable people, some of whom are ready to engage ethnic differences in the classroom by talking about food and lifestyles but not ideas and conflicts.

Significantly, the combination of scenes sustains the process from *Lone Star*'s beginning of blending fiction and documentary through the authenticity of its articulation of the historical and social tensions and changes that constitute the fictional environment. The film retains its docudrama quality.

It should also be stated that the continuity between the school meeting and the classroom exemplifies Sayles's artistic integrity as a director and screenwriter. He completes the action and meaning of one scene by developing and complicating it in another scene of comparable complexity and difficulty. He follows through by fulfilling his own ideas, images, and issues. A similar example of such continuity, integrity, and self-referentiality involves Sayles's treatment and development of African American characters and themes in the film.

Sayles's approach in *Lone Star* to the situation of African Americans attests to the seriousness of his commitment to examine the issues of race and ethnicity in America with breadth and depth. He purposefully includes the African American Payne family, as well as race-related stories about a black recruit who requires discipline and guidance, and another about interracial relationships. Sayles obviously believed in the necessity of keeping blacks in the story of America. He says:

> I wanted to have these three communities, where we were basically in a part of Mexico that somebody had drawn a line underneath and made into America, but the people hadn't changed. So, the Anglos got to run things, but it was still basically a Mexican town. And where do the blacks fit into that? Well, they're kind of mercenaries in this case.[25]

Sayles appropriately makes the role of the blacks in the military consistent with their minority position and history in civilian society. He reports feelings articulated in the film by, Athena Johnson (Chandra Wilson), a black female private in trouble over drugs. She tells Colonel Delmore (Del) Payne (Joe Morton), the black base commander, that blacks join the army because they are good at fighting other people of color for whites who really own the country. She says, "It's their country. This is one of the best deals they offer" (*LS* 217). In spite of such exploitation, the army offers an alternative to what Del calls the "chaos" outside. Touched by her situation and reflecting on his own family tensions, Del adjusts her cap and describes basic pride, discipline, and group identification to her in the hope that his leniency and example will help her mature and grow into a better soldier and stronger person.

Rather than concentrating upon only this aspect of black military and civilian life, Sayles writes Otis Payne, the elder of the family and the owner of the serviceman's bar, "Big O's Roadhouse," as an amateur authority on the African American history of the Texas border region. The makeshift museum that Otis maintains in the bar to illustrate the history of "Negro-Indian" soldiers and scouts, provides an education for his grandson, Chet, and even, to some extent, his son, Del, the base commander. He advertises the museum with "a hand-lettered sign" that reads: "Black Seminole Exhibit – Rear Entrance" (*LS* 166). Sayles says,

> I started thinking about the Buffalo Soldiers, the Negro-Indian scouts, which I actually knew a bit about before I started writing this, how, yes, they were part Indian, but they were there working for the white people against other red people. How there comes that point where, yes, you can move up as long as you're willing to be the mercenary or the hired gun.[26]

Indicative of the seriousness of Sayles's artistic and social purposes, the rendering of the African American experience in Frontera confirms his commitment to making a film of contemporary America from a perspective of detailed thoroughness.

In some ways, the artistic seriousness, intellectual depth, and social accuracy of Sayles's work resemble in cinematic form the kind of literary consciousness that for generations involved the classic novel of social realism. The rendering in *Lone Star* of an entire community balanced in tension with all of its parts resonates with the work of such writers as William Dean Howells. Sayles strives to present the society in its entirety, while at the same time doing justice to all of the groups that comprise it. Similarly, the aesthetic completeness and balanced form of the film with its reenforcing themes and parallel structures also recall the genius and purpose of writers such as Tolstoy.

Consistent with the egalitarianism of the literary social realists, in *Lone Star* the alphabetic ordering of actors in the opening credits, as opposed to a conventional hierarchical ordering of stars, fully anticipates the film's democratic commitment. At the same time, the credits also blatantly assert the importance of a single creative force behind the film by proclaiming Sayles as the film's director, writer, and editor. As the auteur figure for *Lone Star*, Sayles deserves such credit for the aesthetic brilliance and cinematic ingenuity of the film. The coherence of *Lone Star*'s aesthetic form, with its democratic cultural ideology of ethnic and racial equality, explains its contemporaneity as much as the relevance of its subject matter to current events. The power and brilliance of the film's ideology of cinematic and aesthetic form as much as its discussion of history make the film unique and important.

As part of its cinematic and aesthetic form, *Lone Star*'s direction and style involve the provocative manipulation of the relationship of time and space. As previously suggested, the film strives to reformulate the representation of time so that present and past merge. What have been called "seamless transitions," rather than overlaps and cuts, dramatically emphasize the felt presence of the past in the frame of the present. The past and present occupy the same frame and moment in the film in one early transition to the past when Hollis recalls the argument between Buddy and Charley that resulted in Charley's murder. Brilliant rack focus brings a glaring Mercedes into the visual space and associates her with the time transition.

Thus, in *Lone Star*, the spatialization of time occurs in the spatial juxtaposition and interfusion of the present and the past. Space also transforms time with the potential for personal and cultural renewal through the regenerative power of American space and geography as informed by the American ideology. For Mercedes, language acquisition as a form of ideological expression signifies such renewal. She regularly shouts to her workers about using English, especially to Enrique, variations of "In English, Enrique, in English.... This is the United States." For Mercedes, language ensures her American identity. An immigrant herself, she risked her life crossing the border as a young woman and ends the film helping others do the same thing in spite of her conservative views. At the same time, borders and boundaries in the film also emphasize the inevitability of the wound of spatial and temporal limitation and enclosure.

The manipulation of time and space in overlapping shots and scenes that bring Pilar and Sam back together again signifies rebirth and transformation but also danger and uncertainty. In this sequence, aggressive cuts inventively connect time and space to register tangible emotion, change, and love. In her office, a colleague reminds Pilar about "The old-high-school-heartthrob Sheriff. I thought you were crazy about each other" (*LS* 203). Pilar stares off into space, remembering through a flashback the night at the drive-in movie when Buddy and Hollis noisily disrupted and broke apart Sam and Pilar, the high school lovers. The film then shows Sam in the present at the abandoned drive-in also remembering like Pilar about the past. Spatially separated, they are reunited in time in the form of shared memory. Music and soft cuts of Sam driving at night take him to her at school where she works late. "Follow me," she says (*LS* 207).

In this sequence, color and music also participate in the process of transformation. The cinematography imbues the scene of their meeting with an original and unusual redness that conveys the warmth of the desert night as a visualization of passion and danger. The red tint bathes the scene in a visual sultriness that reenforces their heated reunion after more than 20 years of separation. Just as interesting, the music that plays for Sam and Pilar from the jukebox also entails an auditory fusion of musical forms and sounds that represents the ethnic blending and danger involved in Sam and Pilar's love. About the symbolic implications of this music and scene, Sayles says:

> The jukebox holds some of their past. The song they play, "Since I Met You, Baby," or "Desde que conosco," is also playing on the jukebox when Del walks into Otis's place, a different version of it. That's very subtle, but that's how different cultures use the same song. It was a song that was a hit on black stations, and then it was the first hit for Freddy Fender, the first Hispanic rock-and-roll guy. He took rock and roll, black music that was becoming used by white people, and brought it to Latin America. I don't know whether anybody would have picked that up.[27]

The musical mixture of different ethnic versions of the song inevitably suggests the union of Sam and Pilar as well as other racial and ethnic unions in the film. The slow, sensuous rhythm evokes temptation and excitement.

Similarly, on the night years before when Buddy and Hollis interrupted the young couple's love-making in the car at the drive-in, the movie that Sayles puts on the drive-in screen concerns racially mixed relationships. Sayles explains,

> It was *Black Mama, White Mama*. . . . It was basically *The Defiant Ones* in a women's prison. Pam Grier and Margaret Markow – they're handcuffed together and they escape. Once again, it may be a little literary, but it's about people of different races being chained together whether they want to or not.[28]

Throughout *Lone Star*, the mixing of music, the intense fusion of colors to create mood, the experimentation with time transitions, and the fluidity of spatial and temporal relations all suggest aesthetic blendings that work as a counterpart to the ethnic mixing of peoples. Equally significant, in both scenes involving the restaurant jukebox and the drive-in, the documentary foundation in the social and cultural history of musical and cinematic events testifies to Sayles's documentary mindset and the film's documentary contexts. Documentary reality lends credibility to the fictional argument and to the focus in the film upon interethnic and interracial mixing. In a way, *Lone Star* becomes a series of minidocudramas of sorts on race relations in America, including racial representations on the screen and in music.

Of course, the key example of ethnic and racial mixing concerns the main characters, Sam and Pilar. They personify a commingling that contains a potential for the transformation of American culture and character. As *Mississippi Masala* concentrates on the union of people of color as part of the transformation of the American people, in *Lone Star* Sam and Pilar also represent the reembodying of America in people of color.

However, incest, as discussed above, and the fact that Pilar cannot have any more children complicate the symbolic meaning of Sam's and Pilar's relationship for the national and cultural future as well as their own. She says, "I'm not having any more children. After Amado, I had some complications – I can't get pregnant again, if that's what the rule is about – " (*LS* 244). Although they seem to embody the ethnic and racial transformation of America, they also appear to be at a dead end with what Pilar calls "the rule," meaning the incest taboo against sexual relations between family members. The ambiguity of the couple's future echoes the uncertainty about the country's future.

The personal and cultural symbolism of this uncertainty and ambiguity at the end of the film harkens back to a scene much earlier in the film's screenplay when Charley Wade's skeletal remains undergo examination in the forensics lab. In the published screenplay of the film, the directions for the soundtrack for this scene call for "Hank Williams's gospel song 'I'll Have a New Body (I'll Have a New Life)'" (*LS* 136). The irony of the contrast between these words and the stark visual display of skeletal bones on a laboratory table undermines the potential in the film for personal rebirth and cultural renewal. In the actual film, the Hank Williams song becomes a song in Spanish. The rhythm and intonation mock the sanctity of the dead and minimize any suggestion of individual or group salvation.

The somber mood and words in the last scene of the film emphasize a sense of dread and loss. Sam and Pilar remain together, but their situation epitomizes conflict and ambivalence. Finally realizing her true origins, she implores, "We start from scratch – " and Sam without much animation or seeming determination simply says, "Yeah" (*LS* 244). She continues, "Everything that went before, all that stuff, that history – the hell with it, right?" Her words actually impart a meaning opposed to her apparent intent. At this crucial time, for Pilar her life and history remain inextricably intertwined. Her speech immediately places her tragic personal history in the context of the regional, cultural, and national history that she knows so intimately as a person and teacher. As a history teacher who has lived her professional life inculcating in her students an understanding of how history has helped shape them, the idea of suddenly getting away from history seems like more than a mere contradiction. In response to Sam's sad quiescence and reticence, "Pilar takes Sam's hand, kisses him" and says, "Forget the Alamo" (*LS* 244). Strange words about one's immediate personal situation. The words place her right in the middle of history. They emphasize her historic consciousness. "Forget the Alamo" implies forgetting old wrongs, crimes, and grievances as well as old boundaries and borders. Forget the past. However, her words suggest a psychological internalization of history that makes forgetting the past impossible. Sam and Pilar may stay together but they can not forget or escape the past. The dominant presence in the scene of an empty outdoor movie screen contributes to the mood of uncertainty. The empty screen evokes the nostalgia over lost youth and past times of Peter Bogdanovich's *The Last Picture Show* (1971). It suggests a distant past and projects a fear concerning an unknown future.

At the same time, an alternative combination of symbols and metaphors for understanding *Lone Star* further complicates the film's meaning and conclusion. This alternative also relates to the empty drive-in movie screen and poses the possibility of another reading of *Lone Star* that can be informed by the multiple meanings of still another film. Sayles himself compares the significance of *Lone Star* to the classic *High Noon* (1952). Sayles says:

> A wrong has been done and he's going to right it, even if it costs his father's reputation. It's kind of like *High Noon* – the man against the town, that's how he sees himself. By the end, what you hope is that he doesn't see himself that way anymore. He's starting to reintegrate himself in society.[29]

Like Marshal Will Kane (Gary Cooper) in *High Noon*, Sam Deeds will also reject continuing in office as a lawman, ostensibly to pursue his relationship with a woman. Here too a similarity obtains in that the great age difference between Cooper and the female star who plays his young bride, Grace Kelly, invariably raises questions about the paternalistic nature of their relationship. Visually, the film creates the appearance of a father-daughter affection between the older marshal and his young wife that compares to the incestuousness of Sam and Pillar.

However, a crucial and symbolic difference also occurs between the two films. In *High Noon* a vengeful gang of killers arrives from outside the town to initiate the action and violence. The threat of the gang to kill Marshal Kane for previously imprisoning their leader externalizes the originating and immediate danger. Only as the film progresses does it become clear that cowardice and disloyalty within the town constitute the real threat to the community's survival. The real enemy in the town is some of its citizens. The important story then becomes the contrast between their fear and group inaction as opposed to Kane's courage and individual action.

In *Lone Star*, however, from the very beginning the danger and enemy seem internal. One lawman, in the person of Sheriff Charley Wade, personifies lawlessness, corruption, and violence. The political activities of a new generation of leaders in the area imply the continuation of secret corruption and conniving as the hidden motivation behind political rhetoric and argument. The faces, colors, and ethnic origins of the corrupt will change, but the foundation of self-serving lies and abuse will remain. In addition, the people's veneration of Buddy Deeds obscures aspects of his own frequently questionable actions. As previously noted, Sam's investigation exonerates Buddy from the suspicion of having killed Charley, but the discovery of the body and the subsequent investigation raise the notion that the community still will blame Buddy. With some irony, Sam says, "Buddy's a goddam legend. He can handle it" (*LS* 242). Sam's reaction to the unfairness of mistakenly blaming the deceased Buddy recalls yet another Western, another Ford classic, *The Man Who Shot Liberty Valance* (1962). In that Ford film, a similar question about the contrast between the truth and the legend provokes the famous response by a newspaper editor, "When the legend becomes fact, print the legend." In both cases, legend and factual truth complicate each other, a situation consistent with the interdependence of fiction and documentary in film.

In *Lone Star*, the tensions between legend and fact, truth and fiction reaffirm the difficulty of knowing and explaining the justification for borders in general. In the film, confusion over rationalizing intellectual borders between truth and fiction muddies the clarity of all borders. A Mexican man's comments about the arbitrary nature of national borders summarizes the film's questioning of the meaning of all boundaries. Sam meets the man, Chucho Montoya (Tony Anendola), in Mexico as part of his investigation. Chucho had witnessed Charley's shooting murder years before of Eladio Cruz, Mercedes' husband, for taking immigrants across the border without paying off Charley. Eladio at one time had similarly helped Mercedes, his wife and Pilar's mother. In Mexico, Chucho scorns the "gringo" sheriff and makes a line in the dirt, teasing Sam to step over. Chucho says:

> Bird flying south – you think he sees that line? Rattlesnake, javelina – whatever you got – halfway across that line they don't start thinking different. So why should a man? (*LS* 194)

Sam, who characteristically takes a muted oppositional stance in encounters and conversations, defends the borders and government. He says, "Your government always been pretty happy to have that line. The question's just been where to *draw* it" (*LS* 194). Chucho angrily responds, "My government can go fuck itself, and so can yours" (*LS* 194).

Of course, the argument over the legitimacy of borders problematizes the charged *High Noon* symbolism of drawing lines in the sand and making last stands against real or imagined external enemies. However, as part of the recurrence throughout the film of the question of building and deconstructing borders, the dilemma of *Lone Star*'s ending for the lovers suggests the view that borders and boundaries remain inevitable. Only the process that goes into the construction of borders can change.

The extensive discussion of race and ethnicity in *Lone Star* also suggests the negotiated nature of ethnic and racial definitions as a form of borders and boundaries. Lines in the sand, as Chucho maintains, work as political and cultural constructions that reflect power relations and the victory of groups through history rather than inherent or predetermined absolute truths. For Sam very few "High Noons" exist. He recognizes, as he tells Hollis and Fenton, that the Hispanics now asserting control of Frontera arrived their "first." He also appreciates that before the Hispanics were the Indians.

Thus, in *Lone Star* boundaries, inner and outer spaces, often seem muddled. The lines move according to circumstances and events. Outsiders become insiders, while insiders, like the white minority of Rio County, suddenly find themselves on the outside, often without having physically moved themselves. Some people such as Sam never feel sure exactly where they stand.

However, with all of the film's open-mindedness about open borders and open relationships between races and groups, Pilar's tragic dilemma introduces a crucial dimension to the question of boundaries, one that Sayles obviously intended to present as complicating the ideological and psychological discussion. The incest issue counters the film's theme of the subversion and undermining of structures that separate and divide peoples. Sayles's injection of incest into the narrative accomplishes more than simply a surprise ending.

While Sayles's comments about the couple mitigate their plight by proposing the possibility of their private escape from history, he never suggests that society can execute such an escape. And Pilar's painfully unsuccessful efforts to think around the indomitable meaning of the "rule" about incest confirm its irreversibility. Sayles's personal advocacy of multiculturalism, Sam's defense of minority rights and equal justice, and the film's liberalism must confront Pilar's tragedy as well as the irony that in this case discrimination separates a couple with the same origins as opposed to keeping people with different backgrounds apart. Such ironies concerning the film's cultural and psychological themes gain added poignancy with the suggestion in *Lone Star* that in America people with apparent racial and ethnic differences still can be blood relatives.

However, this theme of incest only disrupts and complicates the film's liberalism in the form of its efforts to articulate the reembodiment of America in new immigrants and people of color. Pilar's plight does not dismantle the film's overall intention. Rather, incest forces consideration of ideas that really sustain the film's focus on internal danger and the need for individual reform and personal integrity. In some ways, the incest theme works as a bad joke by Sayles in that incest fulfills the nightmares of a racist bartender named Cody (Leo Burmester). Sam teases Cody over his half-baked, reactionary notions about race and civilization. However, some of what Cody says about "lines of demarcation" reverberates in Pilar's incestuous situation. The film at the end suggests that lines of demarcation do need to be drawn, although Cody for sure should not be the one to draw them. As in the dichotomy involving fiction and documentary in film, the absence of absolute truth in experience requires a pragmatic fluidity involving the maintenance of real boundaries.

In its dramatizations of individual and social conflict, *Lone Star* proffers a powerful case for self-discipline and self-control, classic attributes and traits not only of stable, middle-class democratic character but also of manly Texas-cowboy independence. The dread of incest reenforces the film's interest in internal boundaries. Potential incest as a manifestation of instinctive psychological disorder necessitates the internalization of parental authority, as described by Freud, to signify individual independence and maturity and ensure a society of laws.

The incest theme returns *Lone Star* to its beginning with an archeological metaphor for the exploration of the individual and cultural psyche. The discovery of incest enacts the "return of the repressed" to reaffirm the inclusion throughout the film of the past in the present. This history of incest in *Lone Star* dramatizes Slavoj Žižek's argument that "the past which was repressed, pushed out of the continuity established by prevailing history" constitutes a failure that can be understood and reconstructed only retroactively as in psychoanalytic theory.[30]

As its concern with incest suggests, *Lone Star*'s liberalism stops well short of anarchy and an attack against all social structure. Social and individual authority remain necessary. However, true democratic negotiation over boundaries and rules also constitutes a serious demand. Such negotation entails basing a society on more than descent and origins. As Otis Payne tells his grandson after informing him about his Indian blood, "But blood only means what you let it" (*LS* 216). Character and culture must contribute to determining destiny.

Thus, *Lone Star* welcomes the reembodiment of America in people of color and minorities as a means for working toward a just and fair democratic society that will strive to ameliorate racial and cultural enmities that have divided peoples for centuries. Throughout *Lone Star*, Sayles maintains a democratic aesthetic, meaning an artistic ideology of cinematic direction and construction that works with its democratic ideology of equality and freedom. Such an aesthetic assumes the participation of a thinking audience that must make up its own mind. This also usually requires a degree of Brechtian alienation, a process of separation from the work that allows for critical thinking, aesthetic judgment, and self-examination. Pilar's incest forces such objectification and alienation from the audience.

Maintaining *Lone Star*'s persistent complexity and intelligence, Sayles resists the temptation to end his film with a false feeling of resolution that belies the difficulty of overcoming the intrinsic obstacles to making a true community. He declines to preach or indoctrinate or obscure the true "state of crisis" in Texas. He rejects "Lone Star" chauvinism. Instead, he opts for ambiguity and contemplation over the fate of America as represented by the couple, Pilar and Sam, who dramatize the importance of loving others for their differences instead of simply accepting and tolerating those differences. For Sayles, a call for such opennness presents a profound challenge but one that seems worthy of the cultural imagination of his film's resilient main subject, "Lone Star" as a metaphor for America and for us, all of us.

PART TWO

GREAT FIGHTS FOR THE CENTURY

CHAPTER THREE

RAGING BULL

Revisioning the Body, Soul, and Cinema

The opening scene of Martin Scorsese's *Raging Bull* (1980) continues to impress and startle. A moment of intense abstraction, it immediately conveys a deep sense of both ambiguity and inevitability. Like the rhythm and movement of a Beethoven symphony or the rhyme and meter of a Blake poem, we can know the scene by heart and still wonder at its transforming power. No matter how often we see this long take of a hooded, robed, and ghostly boxer dancing in slow motion by himself in an unspecified ring, time, and place, we still are impressed by the originality of this cinematic representation of this fighter's mental state and the ambiguity and complexity of emotions it arouses in us toward him. The abstractness of Scorsese's mise-en-scene becomes a cinematic metaphor that blends the film's contending forces of grace and violence, courage and fear, isolation and spectatorship, myth and fact. The slow motion operatic ballet of a graceful figure shadow boxing in the ring to the refrains of Pietro Mascagni's *Cavalleria Rusticana* initiates a special tone and feeling for the entire film. The dancing motion and soft music, the muted and impressionistic colors, the dreamy and foggy atmosphere, the imperceptible face of the boxer that remains hidden within the darkness of the hood, the absence of a discernible audience and crowd around the ring all proclaim an abstraction and distance to the scene that nevertheless assert a palpable tension and immediacy through the scene's persistent uncertainty and incipient violence. The abstraction of the cinematic composition and imagery in Scorsese's rendering of the boxing mise-en-scene gives the individual figure in the ring a universal and mythic dimension.

However, preceding the abstract ring scene, credits emerge out of blackness in white print with the names of the producers Robert Chartoff and Irwin Winkler. A following frame announces "A Martin

Scorsese Picture," while another title informs, "Robert De Niro in." The film then cuts dramatically and disruptively to the abstractness of the opening ring scene with the ropes foregrounded as a symbolic enclosure that imprisons the dancing fighter in the background. The muted operatic music erupts in volume and intensity with the appearance of the film's title as ensuing credits impose written elements of concrete specificity into the frame that contrast dramatically with the scene's abstractness. While Scorsese's abstract rendering of the boxer's domain transcends classic realism, the inscribed text introduces real, specific content and subject matter in a concretely informative way. The opening quickly indicates an auteur's work and style that will synthesize documentary sensibility and a self-conscious awareness of film as an art form.

Accordingly, the opening frames of the film incorporate within the art form and artistic medium a tension between abstraction and realism. This tension pervades *Raging Bull*, giving it structure and organizing its divisions and conflicts into a coherent film and aesthetic triumph. Moreover, the tension quickly distinguishes *Raging Bull* from a tradition of earlier boxing films to which it nevertheless belongs. The opening's abstraction and aestheticization of violence immediately mark a break from the film noir realism of earlier boxing films. At the same time, the information on the screen, "Based on the book by Jake La Motta with Joseph Carter and Peter Savage," announces the film's foundation in actual events and history that dramatically offsets the initial abstraction. This information suggests a rootedness in documentary realism for the film that maintains a continuity with earlier boxing films in spite of the opening's self-conscious and innovative abstraction.

The works that provide the cinematic background and cultural context for *Raging Bull* are significant films by serious directors, producers, and actors. *Raging Bull* evidences considerable artistic and thematic debts to these films for their boxing sequences, their carefully choreographed violence, their intense individual characterizations in the context of assiduously detailed boxing environments. These films include Rouben Mamoulian's film of Clifford Odets's play *Golden Boy* (1939) with William Holden; Abraham Polonsky and Robert Rossen's left-wing *Body and Soul* (1947) with John Garfield; Stanley Kramer and Mark Robson's *Champion* (1949) with Kirk Douglas; Robert Wise's *The Set-Up* (1949), featuring Robert Ryan, followed by Wise's

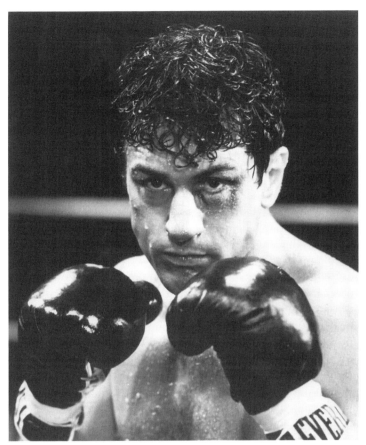

Figure 4. Robert DeNiro fights himself and the world in *Raging Bull.* (Museum of Modern Art/Film Still Archives)

second boxing classic *Somebody Up There Likes Me* (1956), the story of middleweight champion Rocky Graziano (Paul Newman); John Huston's painfully naturalistic *Fat City* (1972) with Stacy Keach; and even Elia Kazan's *On the Waterfront* (1954), starring Marlon Brando; and, more recently Norman Jewison's *The Hurricane* (1999) about "Hurricane" Carter, starring Denzel Washington.

Raging Bull echoes the ethnicity, urban setting, and documentary stylistics that characterize most of these films. Certainly, *Raging Bull*, as David Bordwell and Kristin Thompson suggest, continues the use of boxing as a complex and multilayered metaphor for the violence of the individual's engagement with a brutal and corrupt world.[1] In all of these films, including, to a degree, *Raging Bull*, the boxer as an individual warrior lives and fights as an underdog, frequently becoming a victim, often of himself. Using Paul Schrader's script about La Motta's story, Scorsese's film reiterates the post–World War II and Cold War mindset of many of these films. The fatalism of these years translates into a desperate boxing mise-en-scene.

Nevertheless, Scorsese views this world from the perspective of a very different generation with a markedly dissimilar set of experiences. He imbues the classic and popular film noir and documentary style and vision of La Motta's era with a radical contemporary consciousness of strong modernistic sensibilities. From the very beginning of *Raging Bull*, Scorsese uses the heterogeneous elements of film – visual imagery, cinematography, diverse sound, and inscription – to cultivate profound dichotomies of subject matter and artistic form into an intricate cinematic design that suggests La Motta's potential redemption. *Raging Bull* becomes a film about how cinema art manipulates time and space to convey complex experience. The film dramatizes the transformation of interior space, meaning Jake's inner character and identity, through its revisualization of external space, primarily Jake's body as a field of interior and exterior battle. In the boxing films of the earlier generation, the boxer achieves heroism by becoming an independent man in his personal battles with overwhelming forces. In *Raging Bull*, the protagonist with brutal animalistic impulses becomes humanized through the chaos and destruction of recognizing and accepting softer, more feminine, masochistic, and passive elements of his character.

The focus on Jake's body as a visual spectacle and field of contending inner and outer forces helps structure the film. The initial abstraction of Jake's body in the opening seconds of the film immediately projects and personifies the aesthetic and cultural tensions of the film onto him. Rather than separating Jake from the conflicts he represents, the opening scene of abstraction anticipates the placement of moral and psychological aggressions and defenses onto Jake. Abstraction as a form of idealization or dehumanization aestheticizes and solidifies in Jake the psychic anxieties of the film.

Embodying these tensions in Jake enables Scorsese and De Niro, who won an Academy Award for his performance, to turn the boxer's body into a physical and visual machine for rhetorical engagement. As such, the body serves as a source for initiating a campaign for Jake's spiritual, psychological, and physical transformation. The rhetorical purpose of the film's development of complex film aesthetics and cultural ideologies concerns making Scorsese's and De Niro's case for Jake's redemption as, in part, a transmogrification of his body from a fortress of violence to a cushion of flab. This hope for redemption in the film affirms La Motta's own somewhat tentative suggestion in his book of some form of redemption for himself.

La Motta's book, *Raging Bull* describes a psychological dysfunctionalism that pursued him from childhood to ruin as an adult in his personal and professional life. Somewhat like Rocky Graziano's own youthful past and colorful story, La Motta's highly-publicized life and career included violent crimes, incarceration, street violence, official suspension from boxing for throwing a fight, domestic violence, troubled marriages, and public testimony on corruption in boxing. In his book, La Motta actually admits to believing throughout his life that he had killed a neighborhood bookie in an assault and robbery and to raping his best friend's girlfriend and ruining her life. In the case of the assault and robbery victim, La Motta was stupefied when the man later turned up.[2] Perhaps it should be noted again that La Motta's story involves a collaborative effort with the late Joseph Carter, a scholarly journalist with a Boston and Harvard background, and Peter Savage, who had been Jake's childhood friend and appears in the book as a crucial character, Jake's best friend, Peter Petrella. Savage, an interesting figure in his own right, provides the basis for a composite figure in the film and becomes Jake's brother Joey, played famously and brilliantly by Joe Pesci.[3]

In the opening pages of his book, La Motta describes a horrible childhood in the slums of New York's Lower East Side. He tells a story of poverty, abuse, and violence that could form the basis for a sentimental and conventional film about a hero overcoming overwhelming odds to achieve ultimate personal success and moral triumph. Contributing to this impression, La Motta actually remembers his life almost as though it were a movie, a personal documentary of suffering and struggle. He says, "Now, sometimes, at night, when I think back, I feel like I'm looking at an old black-and-white movie of myself." La Motta's self-representation as a figure in a film seems credible for a person of his background who also has worked in films (for example, a cameo appearance as a bartender in Robert Rossen's *The Hustler* in 1961 with Paul Newman, George C. Scott, Piper Laurie, and Jackie Gleason) as well as in television and nightclubs. However, the vividness and graphic detail of his descriptions give his story a feeling of authenticity.

Also, given La Motta's temperament and character, the first person, tough-guy journalistic style of narration seems quite appropriate. He writes:

> What I remember about the tenement as much as anything else is the smell. It's impossible to describe the smell of a tenement to someone who's never lived in one. You can't just put your head in the door and sniff. You have to live there, day and night, summer and winter, so the smell gets a chance to sink into your soul. There's all the dirt that the super never really manages to get clean even on the days when he does an hour's work, and this dirt has a smell, gray and dry and, after you've smelled it it long enough, suffocating. And diapers. The slobs who live in tenements are always having kids, and naturally they don't have the money for any diaper service, so the old lady is always boiling diapers on the back of the stove and after a while the smell gets into the walls.
>
> And the food you eat when you're poor. All it does is keep you alive, and it has a smell, too, because it's food like corned beef and cabbage, or food that's cooked in heavy grease, and the smell of it cooking goes all through the building.
>
> And there was the heat in the summer, when I'd try to spend all the time I could out in the street or on the roof or the fire escapes, and the cold in the winter. It seems like I was always cold winters when I was a kid.[4]

While the details of smell, sound, touch, childhood anxiety and oppression give this rendition of his background the quality of felt experience, his combination of irony and insouciance over his experiences also contributes to the story's sense of genuineness. His line, "Being on home relief doesn't do much to keep you warm" sounds quite authentic. Similarly, he says with considerable dramatic expression:

> And the rats! What's a real tenement without rats? Not the kind of rats you probably know that turn if they hear a sound. These were rats as big as goddamned alley cats, and if you met them at night you got out of their way. You could hear them at night, too, in the walls, squealing and slamming around, afraid of nothing. *Zoccolas*, we called them, which is Italian slang for a dirty vicious whore.[5]

Granted, Jake La Motta's *Raging Bull* will not displace Richard Wright's *Native Son* as a story of victimization in urban poverty and misery. Nevertheless, his story provides a context for the formation in the film of a character of rage and violence.

The most damaging and powerful individual influence on La Motta's personality apparently was his father, a rough and ruthless immigrant from Messina who worked on a horse-and-wagon as a peddler. From his father he learned the lesson of the streets "that if you want to survive

in this world, you got to be tough." La Motta describes how his father gave him only one important present in his life, an ice pick to use
as a weapon to defend himself. After pounding young Jake for crying
over a street beating he received earlier from neighborhood toughs,
the father gave him the ice pick. "It was the only good thing I ever
got from my father. . . . I never let go of that ice pick after that."[6] The
brutality, anger, and alienation of the father provided the basic model
of manhood and fatherhood for La Motta. Even when the father ultimately abandoned the family to return to Italy as a relatively substantial man of importance with money gotten through Jake's success, Jake
seemed to respect the man's independence and toughness. "In a funny
way, I got respect for the old bum, even though he was never more
than a peddler and he used to beat up my mother and us kids all the
time."[7]

These experiences of violence and danger and denial culminate in
Jake's talking about himself in a way that anticipates Scorsese's vision of
abstraction and alienation in *Raging Bull*. La Motta seems to dissociate
himself from any sense of true, personal identity. He separates his body
from his inner self. Indeed, his use of film as a means to describe himself
and to convey his memories becomes a way to present his sense of
isolation and separation from himself and his surroundings. He sees
himself as a stranger. He says, "Like I said, when I look back to then
it's like looking at a movie. And the strange thing is that it doesn't even
seem to be about me."[8] Seen in this context of La Motta's background
and personal history, Scorsese's opening abstraction of the "Raging
Bull" becomes less of a romanticization or glamorization of La Motta's
lonely violence and independent manhood than a form of dramatizing
psychological idealization and separation.

The psychological and moral conflicts embodied in Jake's figure im-
bue *Raging Bull* with the aesthetic and moral mission of humanizing
Jake's body, of returning Jake to an innocence he immediately lost in
childhood. The film wants Jake to find himself, to see himself in his
own psychological home movie of introspective self-reflection. He must
move from psychic abstraction and the aestheticization of violence to
a transformation of the body that will help him find peace and achieve
a liveable identity. From a Freudian or psychoanalytical perspective,
one that occasionally actually enters La Motta's own language in a
popularized form, La Motta's story involves a process of healing the
originating division in his personality between his body and the psychic ego.[9] This process of seeking psychic wholeness involves a parallel

process of synthesizing the abstraction of the film's subjective aesthetic with its realistic documentation of Jake's life and world. Ironically, in *Raging Bull* a sequence of home videos depicting the domesticity of Jake's first years of marriage to Vickie (Cathy Moriarity) are self-consciously shown in color. The home videos in color starkly contrast with the black and white film. The color suggests a romanticized nostalgia for an unreal past, a continued abstraction for Jake through a process of separation that has become institutionalized in his marriage as well as in the film itself so as to perpetuate deep divisions and assure ultimate breakups of many kinds. Colorized home movies that document domestic scenes are fiction, while the black and white fiction entails a documentary of violence, rage, and strife.

The movement of the narrative along parallel tracks of subjective aestheticism and documentary realism reenforces the psychic division between idealized separation and inner pain and needs. Thus, after presenting the credits, the film quickly cuts to La Motta (De Niro), backstage in a New York nightclub in 1964. The rough backstage realism provides a countermovement to the abstraction and nonreferentiality of the opening. A grotesque La Motta with his bulging body in tight-fitting clothes, puffy cheeks, gravelly voice grounds the initial abstraction in tangible reality. Having gained at least 60 pounds to portray La Motta during this phase of his life, De Niro's self-sacrifice for the role makes the realism of the scene palpable as he literally embodies a marriage of documentary and fiction in film performance. In this cramped dressing room, La Motta awkwardly rehearses his lines, while his pudgy fingers toy with a cigar that reenforces the sliminess. A naked lightbulb hangs from the ceiling and rests above a narrow dressing-room mirror, visually reflecting shabby emptiness. Such harsh reality distances La Motta from the spectator, indicating Scorsese's Brechtian stimulation of his audience's critical thought and detachment.

Scorsese further complicates the situation, condensing into the opening moments innovative narrative and cinematic techniques that make *Raging Bull* a revolutionary film for America, one that integrates new cinematic forms and ideologies into classic cinema to create, in Leo Braudy's term, a new aesthetic.[10] Thus, the backstage scene indicates considerable aesthetic and thematic complexity on many levels. The script suggests some depth to La Motta and raises fresh questions about his character and the ideological meaning of the narrative. La Motta's monologue, in attempted parody, invokes Shakespeare and Laurence Olivier, while the sign on the street advertising the program includes readings from Tennessee Williams and Budd Schulberg, names that challenge stereotypical expectations of the average boxer. At the end of the film, of course, rather than foolishly parodying Shakespeare, Jake seriously attempts to speak Marlon Brando's lines from *On the Waterfront* about how he once had yearned to be a "contender" rather than a "bum," realistically paraphrasing much of the speech. The backstage scene indicates, as Lizzie Borden insists, that Jake hopes to find a language off of the streets to create a new identity for himself.[11] The scene suggests that language as a means for growth and rebirth remains crucial in the film.

And yet, the puerility of his parody and acting contributes to Jake's humiliation. Equally important, by suggesting Jake's division and alienation, the editing and timing of the shots, like the bad humor, contradict the monologue's project of supporting the program of rebirth for Jake. Jake says: "The thing ain't the ring; it's the play. So give me a stage, where this bull here can rage. And though I can fight, I'd much rather recite, 'That's entertainment.'" Upon first saying, "That's entertainment," La Motta extends his arms out in a rather fainthearted gesture toward acting. He then drops his hands, takes the cigar out of his mouth, and looks at it as the title appears under his chin, "Jake La Motta 1964." The camera then cuts, as Robert Kolker also notes, to De Niro as a young and thin La Motta in the ring in a boxing stance with another title once again under his chin, "Jake La Motta 1941," and we hear the overlapping sound of the backstage 1964 Jake repeating, "That's entertainment."[12]

The cut in this scene to the boxing ring and the repetition of the words "That's entertainment" suggest a complexity and contradiction of meanings that demonstrate Scorsese's ability to use the diverse elements of film to create a complex cinema. Overlapping titles and the drastic switch in time periods in the sequence dramatize both continuity and radical disruption. The past continues into the present and seems inescapable. At the same time, the break asserts the great distance between the past and present as demonstrated by the ravages of time on La Motta's body, the sense of loss in his fallen condition compared to his previous strength and potential, and the ironic overtones of the language that equate Jake the former-champion with entertainment and show business, as opposed to the athletic challenge of boxing. The two scenes emphasize boxing as a commodity and spectacle that destroy the manhood and independence of its fighters. The difference between the immediacy of the felt presence of the past versus alienation from past hopes accentuates the enormous challenge for Jake to achieve forgiveness and future redemption.

In the cut to the ring and the posture of compressed intensity of the fighting Jake La Motta, the camera shot of Jake in the corner anticipates a powerful combination of blows to his head delivered immediately by his opponent, Jimmy Reeves. This scene establishes the basic pattern for the film of boxing sequences as studiously designed spectacles of blood-and-guts brutality that structure difficult issues of psychology and personality, power and ideology. It is a carefully choreographed complexity of physical action, camera movement, and sound unmatched by previous fight films. The fight becomes a kind of cinematic synecdoche for the whole film, making blows comparable to camera shots and turning boxers into targets and attackers. This combination of scenes cogently compresses technical moves and narrative themes into a cinematic prologue that prefaces the film and compactly contains many of its elements.[13]

The opening scenes of *Raging Bull*, climaxing in the 1941 Reeves fight in Cleveland, dramatically demonstrate how the film will not only move freely in and out of different time dimensions and historical sequences, it will move just as freely between subjective psychological states of mind and portraits of urban and ethnic life that are rendered with sociological and documentary authenticity. In achieving this fluidity, Scorsese integrates old and new cinematic forms and ideologies into a new aesthetic and ideology. He accomplishes in *Raging Bull* his own expectation of film as a fulfillment of "all the arts." He says:

> I've always believed all the arts culminate in film. Camera movement is dance, lighting is painting. Camera movement is also a lot like painting – and like music. I feel it's always a combination of lighting, camera movement, the use of music and the impact of the actors on the screen.[14]

Of course, not everyone has viewed *Raging Bull* this favorably. The film has aroused the ire of established critics, including Rex Reed and John Simon.[15] Concerning Scorsese's own view of the film's meaning for his career, he said, "It ends everything. I've got to start all over again." As Morris Dickstein's account suggests, Scorsese's word "everything" attests to how much of his personal and artistic life went into the film, an effort rewarded with an Academy Award for Thelma Schoonmaker for editing in addition to De Niro's Award as well as nominations for best director and picture.[16]

Behind such success, a major achievement for Scorsese concerns *Raging Bull*'s intersection, as suggested above, of two historical periods and perspectives. The first concerns the time of La Motta's boxing career, primarily the era of the early 1940s through the 1950s, ending with a brief retrospective in the mid-1960s. The continual flashing of bulbs by visible and invisible news photographers self-consciously suggests the documentary-style recreation of the Second World War and the Cold War eras. Scorsese used black and white cinematography, partly because "it would also help us with the period look of the film" as well as distinguishing it from other more commercial boxing films, while avoiding the difficulties of using fragile Eastman color stock. He said: "We had an idea of making the film look like a tabloid, like the *Daily News*, like Weegee photographs."[17] Although the film emphasizes the life of Italian-Americans in the Bronx and in New York, the film also positions this ethnic group within the complex history of the time. La Motta and his family are part of the American dream as he achieves success and wealth. They participate in the rise of the American middle class. Their ethnicity intensifies their modern Americanism. They are part of the American way, just as "Bugsy" Siegel's Jewishness contributes to his particular American identity in Barry Levinson's *Bugsy* (1991). A shot of the back sports page of the *Daily News* introduces this theme of Italians in sports, and their relation to America at this time. The shot occurs in the movie after La Motta's suspension for throwing the Billy Fox fight on November 14, 1947, an act for which the mob enabled him to fight Marcel Cerdan for the championship two years later. The headline announces La Motta's suspension, but the key picture on the page shows Joe DiMaggio in a highly favorable way with a baby and young child. If here La Motta symbolizes the corruption of boxing, he remains no less American than the "Yankee Clipper" as he also strives toward and ultimately achieves success.

The form and ideology of this history of Jake's career and domestic life compare to classic national and cultural historic narrative: continuous, linear, patriarchal, masculine in perspective, referential in providing detailed documentation of real history and events, and progressive in its assumption of a steady improvement of life. Using various cinematic techniques and innovations, Scorsese privileges this historical reconstruction of events, emphasizing its sense of authority and legitimacy as an historical record. The history of La Motta's time and place in *Raging Bull* provides a narrative foundation for the whole film. Here, art, ideology, and history remain consistent.

However, even while privileging this documentary-style rendering of Jake's self and culture, Scorsese questions its authority by bringing attention to its processes. This self-consciousness relates to an alternative modernistic view of narrative in the film, a form of Brechtian alienation and self-reflexivity that became a pervasive academic and intellectual ideology at least since the beginning of Scorsese's career in the early 1970s.[18] While giving us one documentary narrative of historical continuity and linearity, the film relates this classic historical narrative to a second historical context of self-reflexivity and alienation that effectively challenges the progressive assumptions of the linear narrative. In this self-reflexive historical narrative, Scorsese presents what Sumiko Higashi categorizes in other films as a "postmodern" theory of history that pronounces the end of history and the emergence of synchronicity, the spatialization of time, nonreferentiality, and in Fredric Jameson's term, "perpetual presents."[19]

Scorsese makes such self-reflexive history the encompassing framework for the interior linear narrative of family and success. He encloses the classic masculine narrative of Jake La Motta and the America of the 1940s and 1950s within a contemporary consciousness that chooses, in Higashi's phrase, to "eschew any attempt at illusionist narrative, play fast and loose with the facts, and collapse past and present tense by telescoping events." In presenting such a contrast between classic continuity and radical spatialization of time, *Raging Bull* adheres to Higashi's prescription for a needed balance between, in her terms, "postmodernist historical representations" and "traditional notions about history" in film.[20]

This balance obtains from the beginning of *Raging Bull*. The abrupt breaks in and out of conventional historical narrative in the opening scenes and throughout the film and the presentation of the Reeves fight typify an extremely self-reflexive manipulation of time and space. In the fight a furious tempo of close-ups, medium shots, and long shots matches the accelerated ferocity of the boxers' contact. An especially sensitive use of sound, including pregnant silences, conveys the chaotic atmosphere as well as the pain of the punches. Most impressive, the camera moves with amazing vigor and agility to manipulate time and space and evoke the feeling and psychology of the battle. All of the elements of film function to present extraordinary physical and emotional intensity.

In *Raging Bull* boxing becomes a paradigm of balancing differing conceptions of time and history. As in classic narrative structure, time organizes boxing. However, the experience of boxing exists in a time and world all its own. Joyce Carol Oates describes this relationship between different orders of time and boxing in *On Boxing*:

> The fighters in the ring are time-bound – surely nothing is so excruciatingly long as a fiercely contested three-minute round – but the fight itself is time-less. In a sense, it becomes all fights, as the boxers are all boxers. By way of films, tapes, and photographs it quickly becomes history for us, even, at times, art. Time, like the possibility of death, is the invisible adversary of which the boxers – and the referee, the seconds, the spectators – are keenly aware. When a boxer is "knocked out" it does not mean, as it's commonly thought, that he has been knocked unconscious, or even incapacitated; it means rather more poetically that he has been knocked out of Time. (The referee's dramatic count of ten constitutes a metaphysical parenthesis of a kind through which the fallen boxer must penetrate if he hopes to continue in Time.) There are in a sense two dimensions of Time abruptly operant: while the standing boxer is *in time* the fallen boxer is *out of time*. Counted out, he is counted "dead" – in symbolic mimicry of the sport's ancient tradition in which he would very likely be dead.[21]

Oates's discussion of time and boxing recalls Paul Tillich's existential theory of *kairos* as "time fulfilled" in contrast to *chronos* or ordinary time.[22] For La Motta moments of fulfillment remain rare, but the life-or-death encounter with time in the form of the existential challenge against inner demons and real or imagined external enemies constantly recurs. The interaction between self-reflexive and conventional modes of history creates a living present. Through this intersection of two kinds of time, Scorsese's and De Niro's La Motta achieves unique in-dividuality while at the same time being firmly ensconced within a broader flow of history. Time itself becomes part of Jake's battle.

The vigor of temporal and thematic fluidity in the initial sequence and organization of shots in *Raging Bull* propels the dualism of doc-umentary realism and self-reflexivity throughout the film. In terms of modernistic realism, the cut to the scene after the Reeves fight in the beginning of the film suggests more documentary-style representation, this time of urban life. Words again provide the fact of place: "The Bronx New York City 1941." A low angle establishing shot focuses on the symmetry of fire escapes that form a kind of scaffolding for a Bronx building, a signature Scorsese touch of artistic intervention to convey realism. A marvelous tracking shot follows Jake's brother, Joey (Joe Pesci), as he walks with a neighborhood thug. The details of urban life fill the foreground and background: garbage cans, the shoul-der and head of an iceman carrying a huge block on his back, a fruit cart, various activities on neighborhood stoops, mothers and children, a woman sitting on a ground-floor window sill, an old man leaning out of another window, crates neatly stacked for garbage collection, a thin tree maintained by the city with two ties to two posts, classic 1940s sedans parked on the street between the camera and the walking men. Following the temporal chaos of the Reeves fight, the scene indeed resembles urban documentary realism, thereby perpetuating the film's dynamic dialogue between different forms of historical narrative.

Scorsese's intellectual and ideological drama of history as documentary realism versus the radical manipulation of time and space matches his cinematic aesthetic. Discussions about realism, narrative, and the representations of history relate to the construction and criticism of films in general. Just as Scorsese contrasts realistic referentiality with the foregrounding of historical process and simultaneity in *Raging Bull*, he also balances the illusionism and continuity of classic Hollywood cinema with what D. N. Rodowick calls "countercinema." Rodowick succinctly summarizes the difference between both approaches to cinema:

> The idea of "code" here is allied with all those stylistic devices of Hollywood films that present an illusionistic "impression of reality" as opposed to the reflexive devices of countercinema that criticize or deconstruct this illusion by promoting a critical awareness of the materiality of the film medium: flatness of picture plane instead of depth illusion; elimination of continuity to stress the formal integrity of each shot; nonlinear exposition to undercut narrative coherence; and the rejection of verisimilitude to burst the illusion of a believable fictional world, complete in itself.[23]

While this contrast between two kinds of cinema describes the aesthetic dialogue and synthesis that occurs within *Raging Bull*, Rodowick's definition of countercinema also pertains to the film:

> Discontinuities inherent in the movement within and between shots can be emphasized rather than suppressed, calling the spectator's attention to the work of film form and its construction of norms of realism, coherence, and continuity.[24]

Throughout *Raging Bull*, Scorsese practices such countercinema that contests classic Hollywood cinema.

As in his balance of classic and self-reflexive history, Scorsese's style incorporates countercinema within traditional American cinema. In addition to the scenes and shots already discussed, one relatively minor scene demonstrates Scorsese's penchant for countercinematic self-reflexivity within classic cinema, a pattern that occurs throughout the film. Jake goes to a neighborhood party. The chaos compares to Frank Capra's scene in *It's a Wonderful Life* when Jimmy Stewart and Donna Reed dance together at a high school party. In *Raging Bull*, similar chaos surrounds Jake. When he sees Vickie with Salvy (Frank Vincent), the external activity enacts his inner anxiety. However, beautifully timed slow motion, sound, and editing involve the viewer in Jake's lonely sensibility while self-reflexively bringing attention to the materiality of the filmic processes and concomitantly propelling the narrative. Nondiegetic jazz suggests Jake's mood and reenforces the frenetic action around him. Jake follows Vickie and her friends as they go down a flight of stairs to leave the party. A brilliant shot catches Jake looking down the stairs and captures his abandonment by switching to slow motion. Apparently unaware of his look upon them, Vickie and her group move steadily beyond his vision and grasp. The camera cuts rapidly between group shots and Jake's isolation. On the street outside the club, Jake watches Vickie and her companions in their convertible. He stares at them from a slightly elevated position on a step above the street. While people scream, curse, and fight and fists fly, the camera goes to slow motion as Jake watches Vickie drive off with the despised Salvy. Scorsese adds one more brilliant touch. In slow motion a burning cigarette butt forms a flying arch as it is flicked out of the departing convertible, beautifully conveying Jake's emotions: a blonde and flying butt signal the emptiness of his life and the yearning for meaning. The self-reflexive camera, sound, and editing unmistakably bring attention to themselves. However, even with this self-conscious countercinema, the film's narrative thrust incorporates classic American cinema.

The dual impulses of self-reflexivity and countercinema converge for Jake's redemption. They create a visual syntax of self-reflexive fluidity and discontinuity that renegotiates the relationship of gender to spectacle and power. The early scenes of the movie contain the seeds for Jake's rebirth by immediately problematizing Jake's position as a man and as a spectacle. As a fighter/entertainer, Jake lives as a spectacle. In spite of wishing to be "the boss," Jake survives within the scopic domination of others, as when he responds defensively to the Mafia boss's probing question about Jake's weight gain. Jake as spectacle compares to what Ina Rae Hark perceives for Spartacus, the Roman slave played in 1960 by Kirk Douglas, who also battles a black gladiator, Woody Strode. Hark writes, "Rome maintains and enforces its power through making spectacles of those it dominates."[25] In writing about Spartacus in Rome, Hark could be describing La Motta as a modern gladiator facing the mob. Both Spartacus and the Raging Bull proclaim, "I am not an animal." Jake and Spartacus could also proclaim, "I am not a woman," since, as Hark says, the position of spectacle in Rome involves symbolic castration to equate the male slave to the fetishized woman who assures the oppressor's dominance.

Just as interesting as the connection between two gladiators from different eras, Jake also compares to the situation of women in pornography. Boxing and pornography certainly compare in the sense of spectacle, exposure, ritual, repetition, timing, the use of the body as an instrument, and the potential for victimization. Even in *Spartacus*, scenes with pornographic implications occur, including the scene just alluded to of the forced exposure of Douglas and Jean Simmons and another scene of the exhibition of gladiators before lascivious Roman women of the slave-holding class. Like the gladiators played by Douglas and Strode, Jake La Motta will have to reverse the enslavement of specularity and visual oppression to achieve control over his own body and being. The process of liberating his body aligns him ironically with the feminist program of turning exploitation of the body into a weapon for freedom.

Thus, some feminist writers have linked the body, pornography, and empowerment. Linda Williams, who has written the most influential film book on this subject, writes elsewhere about pornography and the dilemma of achieving independence in repressive situations. She asks how one turns around "the discourses in which he or she is situated" given the reality that "there is no subjectivity prior to discourse"? She also asks "if subjects are constructed in and by an already existing cultural field," how do they gain agency and control over themselves? Referring to the work of feminist postmodern theorist Judith Butler, Williams asserts "agency needs to be reformulated as a question of how agents construct their identities through *resignification*." The rules for resignifying or redefining the terms of one's life operate, she says, through "repetition."[26] For Williams, pornography has the potential for such repetition. *Raging Bull* suggests that so does boxing.

For Jake to achieve control requires the reversal of the film's visual syntax of exploiting and oppressing human bodies through their objectification. As in the situation for women, this reversal obtains not only for boxers like Jake but for black fighters in particular. Interestingly, in his book, La Motta expresses special respect and regard, and for him, a rare degree of sensitivity for black fighters.[27]

The goal for Jake to gain visual assertion as a boxer and man relates to the comparable need for him to achieve his voice and identity
through an accession to the importance of language and speech. A
program for feminist empowerment in the face of misogynist culture,
William's case for feminist discourse can also be seen to apply to La
Motta's crippled manhood. Discourse and subjectivity relate directly
to Jake's verbal performances that frame *Raging Bull* and to the general issue of language in the film. In spite of Jake's desire to be his own
man, his voice and independence often get subsumed by others – the
mob, the culture of the streets, official authorities. Thus, profanity as a
form of profound linguistic impoverishment dominates the film to the
point of perversion so that even Jake ludicrously complains about his
brother's speech, while at another point, Joey, without realizing that
his brother Jake is on the other end of a phone call, swears horribly
about the caller's mother. When imprisoned in Florida toward the end
of the film, Jake can only curse at his jailers and their absent mothers.

Jake's alliance with the feminine position, with the need for voice and
articulation, and with liberated specularity involves other compelling
issues. For David Bordwell and Kristin Thompson, Jake's difficulties re-
side in "a strain of repressed homosexuality" and an "unacknowledged
homosexual urge" that account for his "aggressiveness" and unhappy
"domestic life."[28] However, in Jake repressed homosexuality relates
to both masochism and the feminine. Kaja Silverman's theory of the
relationship of homosexuality to moral masochism and the feminine
maintains that moral masochism and the feminine often merge in some
homosexuals, thereby embodying "corporeal pleasure-in-pain."[29] In
an argument that renders insight into *Raging Bull*, Silverman says this
amalgam of the feminine, the sexual, and the masochist in the homosexual entails a "sexual territorialization of the body" that compares
"the male mouth with the female genitals."[30] Punishment for repressed
feminine desires and the association of love with guilt and pain comprise this form of masochism.

Silverman's theory, which will be discussed in greater depth and detail in a later chapter, helps to rationalize and explain the frequent
appearance and association in *Raging Bull* of the feminine, the homosexual, and the masochistic. Examples of this repeated pattern of association abound. Early in the film, Jake confesses to Joey that he hates
his body and that he has hands "like a little girl's." When Joey calls him
"crazy" for grieving over not being big enough as a middleweight to
fight Joe Louis, Jake demands to be punched in the face and calls Joey

"a faggot" for hesitating. After a loss to Robinson, Jake calls himself a "jinx," meaning a man wracked with guilt over the kinds of criminal acts described in his book. In this scene, Jake sits alone, staring at his bruised face in the mirror and soaking his hand in a bucket of ice to reduce the swelling from his fight just as he also uses ice to drown desire for Vickie. The frozen fist serves as a metonymy for his body and symbolizes icy self-mutilation, an external expression of a mindset of brutal internal aggression and ceaseless self-punishment. With Tommy, the mobster boss who comments on Jake's weight gain, Jake talks in brutal and repugnant homosexual terms about his next fight with a handsome boxer, Tony Janiro, who has aroused Jake's ire and jealousy because of Vickie's inadvertent praise of his looks. Silverman's theory of masochism and the feminine, therefore, helps to explain Jake's pathological behavior and to account for the marginalization and abuse of women, especially mothers, in the film, figures internalized and buried in Jake, swallowed up so to speak.

Equally important, Silverman's theory of marginalized masculinity, masochism, the feminine, and the homosexual also rationalizes the psychology of Jake's potential spiritual rebirth. It describes the way masochism becomes a program for renewal and the feminine a hope for strength. Clearly, both Scorsese and De Niro believe in Jake's moral regeneration. Scorsese insists on calling Jake's recitation of Brando's speech from *On the Waterfront* the "redemption scene."[31] "I wanted to show there was hope for the resolution of the soul, to show it simply with an unsympathetic character; that is, to take all the unsympathetic things from myself and throw them up on the screen."[32] He also says, "*Raging Bull* is about a man who loses everything and then regains it spiritually."[33] Scorsese further insists that *Raging Bull* "wasn't about boxing" and supports De Niro's defense of La Motta when he was called a "cockroach."[34]

Jake's liberation and resurrection will occur through his body, a rewriting and revisioning of that body which has been the very vehicle of his pain and punishment. For Jake resurrection will not occur through supernatural intervention as in *It's a Wonderful Life*, given the film's mixed messages about organized religion. Instead, a key instrument of salvation comes from a punishing human force: Sugar Ray Robinson. The film portrays Jake's beating in the last fight as a crucifixion with blood dripping from the rope that supports Jake, just as the cross holds Christ in Scorsese's *The Last Temptation of Christ* (1988). News photographs of this moment in the actual fight verify the brilliant visual accuracy of Scorsese's representation of the match's horrible conclusion. In the psychology of the film, Jake's punishment prefigures eventual regeneration. In this battle, Sugar Ray's blackness relates to Jake's feminine masochism. Race and gender cross and transpose each other, enabling Jake the masochist to displace Sugar Ray the black fighter as victim. As Robyn Wiegman writes, in a racist culture the black male becomes constructed as feminine, suggesting "not simply an aversion to racial differences but a profound attempt to negate *masculine sameness*, a sameness so terrifying to the cultural position of the white masculine that only castration can provide the necessary disavowal."[35] Jake's inner needs as manifested in his masochism open him for punishment from Sugar Ray, the one individual in the film he genuinely respects as his equal, as the ringside broadcaster Don Dunphy repeatedly states. Ironically, by refusing to be knocked out, Jake's masochism counters Sugar Ray's punishment.

This fight as well as his downfall in Florida open the door for Jake's rebirth. Jake's redemption occurs in part through his acceptance at last of language as a sign of symbolic castration. Falling far short of becoming a saint, Jake needs to settle for becoming a man by finally overcoming his resistance to accepting his multiple vulnerabilities and his emotional needs for love and affection. How interesting that to gain himself and his redemption, the Raging Bull as presented by Scorsese and De Niro, assumes the mask and mantle of weakness and vulnerability so universally condemned and loathed in our society: FAT.[36] Exterior increase as an indication of self-inflation and egoism marks La Motta's connection to his internal self. Fat as a sign of an inner compulsive need, an obvious eating disorder for him, also signifies his acceptance of what he would consider to be the feminine part of himself, the weaker, more vulnerable aspect of his character. Through Jake, the film makes a force for renewal what some writers, such as Susan Bordo, see as a special crisis for women in our culture concerning body ego and weight. The promotional language for one book about women and fat could apply to the feminization of Jake in *Raging Bull* but from the perspective of a man accepting his emotional vulnerability in the form of getting fat as less dangerous behavior than other kinds of past self-abuse. The book asserts:

> Fat is about protection, sex, mothering, strength, assertion and love. Fat is a response to the way you are seen by your husband, your mother, your boss – and yourself. You can *change* that response by learning the difference between "mouth hunger" and "stomach hunger," by seeing weight loss as a good thing rather than a punishment, and by realizing that food is not your enemy.[37]

Like some of the women who gain weight "at first, as they learn to accept and like themselves," Jake by growing heavy finally comes closer to being the boss over himself. He gains some subjectivity through his body as a signifying process that informs and articulates. In Jake's case, fat means a necessary surrender to his own weakness to end his suicidal battle against that weakness. Jake disarms death by accepting it in himself as the fear for him of the feminine and the vulnerable. In Jake's case, the fat represents progress, but it also indicates the continuing pain of internal disorder and unhappiness. By dealing with his body and identity through the alternative extreme of obesity, Jake replicates the achievement Hark attributes to Spartacus by making his "mediating body" and "spectacularized body" into "the signifier that authorizes his discourse, a signifier of the revolutionary Other."[38] In turn, De Niro, the actor and star, transmogrifies his body into the visual and corporeal fulfillment of the interaction in film of the documentary of performance and the fiction of a documentary of the real.

The controversial quote from the New English Bible, John IX: 24–26, at the conclusion of *Raging Bull* proclaims the film's view that Jake has finally achieved vision. Now he sees clearly with his own eyes and spirit free from those who would exploit him. As his attempted reconciliation with his brother suggests, he strives to love and to accept human fallibility. His insistence upon hugging, embracing, and even kissing his brother at the end of the film dramatizes a radical change in psychology and position for Jake. "Come on, gimme a kiss," he says to Joey. Such love enables the resurrection of the body and the acceptance of the flesh in all its weakness. Those who deny this aspect of the film because La Motta remains a bullish figure, miss the point of Scorsese's artistry. Working from Schrader's script and in collaboration with such people as editor Thelma Schoonmaker, who received an Academy Award, and cinematographer Michael Chapman, who earned a nomination for an Academy Award, the real Raging Bulls, of course, are Scorsese, De Niro, and Pesci, three Italian-Americans from New York, who have transformed how we view film in America today:

> So for the second time, [the Pharisees] summoned the man who had been blind and said: "Speak the truth before God. We know this fellow is a sinner." "Whether or not he is a sinner, I do not know," the man replied. "All I know is this: Once I was blind and now I can see."

CHAPTER FOUR

THE BLACK GLADIATOR AND
THE SPARTACUS SYNDROME

Race, Redemption, and the Ring

Sugar Ray Robinson ended Jake La Motta's boxing career as a champion and serious contender on February 14, 1951, in Chicago when referee Frank Sikora stopped their middleweight championship fight in the thirteenth round. La Motta compared the defeat and his beating to the St. Valentine's Day massacre of 1929. La Motta writes in his autobiography, "Well, Robinson didn't have a submachine gun and there was only one victim but it was still a massacre."[1] After fighting Robinson for nine years through an amazing six bouts, the competition finally ended in this brutal middleweight championship fight. La Motta recalls: "Well, Robinson couldn't hit me hard enough to put me down, but the only thing that was holding me up in the thirteenth round . . . was the fact that I had one arm wrapped around the ropes." To be fair, La Motta also explains that his strength had been greatly diminished because he had been forced during training in the weeks before the fight to go from weighing 187 pounds to the limit for a middleweight of 160 pounds. He says, "Christ, I was even above the weight limit for a light heavy, and I was going to fight middleweight! I swear to God, never had I gone through the hell I did then."[2]

Winning the middleweight title for what would be the first of five times after already being welterweight champion from 1946–1949 marked one of the many extraordinary peaks and triumphs in Robinson's truly exceptional career. In his foreword to the Robinson story that he wrote with the champion, Dave Anderson of the *New York Times* reminds us that Robinson remains for many "pound for pound the best boxer in history." Anderson says:

> Over a quarter of a century, from 1940 to 1965, he had 175 victories against 19 losses, but five of those losses occurred in the last six months of his career after he had turned 44.

He registered 110 knockouts, but he was never knocked out and he was stopped only once. . . .

To appreciate Sugar Ray's reign, consider that he was undefeated in his first 40 bouts with 29 knockouts, lost a 10-round decision to Jake La Motta in 1943, then extended his record to 128–1–2 with 84 knockouts while holding the welterweight and middleweight titles.[3]

At a time when African Americans were just beginning the modern Civil Rights Movement for true equality and full citizenship, Robinson represented a new and special level of power, success, and independence for a black man. Following in the footsteps of his childhood hero from Detroit, heavyweight champion Joe Louis, Robinson's greatness as a fighter gave him a unique position of strength, not only within American sports but American culture as a whole. In contrast to Jackie Robinson, who became the first black man to play in Major League Baseball when Branch Rickie signed him on to play for the Brooklyn Dodgers in the late 1940s, Sugar Ray Robinson as a prizefighter fought alone without having to worry about getting along with his own teammates or suffering racial abuse from opponents.[4]

At the same time, black fighters, of course, still faced obstacles in boxing in line with the discrimination African Americans encountered in other areas of American life. Indeed, La Motta's awareness of this situation, as previously noted, awakened in him a sensitivity to black fighters as underdogs that sharpened his appreciation for the greatness and achievements of fighters like Sugar Ray and Joe Louis. Speaking of this issue of race during his early years as a fighter, La Motta remembers:

> Most of the guys that I fought then were colored and they weren't able to get many bouts. A colored fighter could starve in those days because if a manager had a white kid who seemed to have potential he would baby him and try to build him on stumblebums or used-up names who were just looking for a payday.
>
> In those early days, even though, Louis and Robinson had broken through, just the fact that they were so great made everyone leery of colored fighters. And some of them were great, believe me. Many of those colored six-round fighters would have chased some high-priced top-notchers right out of the ring. A lot of them would have to fight with handcuffs on just to get a pay night here and there.[5]

In a way, consistent with the extreme individuality of being a prizefighter, Sugar Ray saw himself as a "gladiator," the archetype for the isolated and singular fighter. He says, "As a boy, I wanted to be a doctor, but that dream ended when I quit school in the ninth grade. Another dream began: to be a gladiator. And like a true gladiator, I never lost."[6] Indicating a sense of religious mission to his life and triumphs, he also compares La Motta to a gladiator, thereby adding to the significance and value of his ultimate victory over him. "Jake La Motta was a gladiator, too, when he wanted to be."[7]

In spite of his self-confidence and sense of purpose, Robinson suggests a deeper meaning behind La Motta's loss to him in their championship fight. "Jake La Motta hadn't lost. Something had happened to keep him from winning."[8] Of course, in *Raging Bull*, Martin Scorsese dramatizes, as already discussed, these deeper forces of masochism and crucifixion that dramatize and complicate La Motta's own story. Emphasizing the psychological and spiritual dimensions of the combat between La Motta and Robinson, Scorsese's film suggests that the 1951 championship bout initiates a process of potential redemption for La Motta.

In making Robinson so instrumental in La Motta's psychological development and regeneration, *Raging Bull* follows a persistent pattern in American boxing films in which black boxers develop stature and significance by becoming savior figures for troubled, deficient white fighters. Such use of blacks as sacrificial figures takes place to varying degrees in fight films from *Golden Boy* (1939) and *Body and Soul* (1947), to *Rocky* (1976) where even Rocky Balboa's (Sylvester Stallone) triumph of endurance supersedes in importance the black champion's (Carl Weathers) win. Although Sugar Ray Robinson's victory and success break the customary fictional pattern of black defeat, his major purpose in *Raging Bull* centers on his relationship to La Motta rather than upon his own identity as a character and leading sports figure.

One of the clearest expressions of this theme of the black fighter as a savior and moral figure for whites occurs in a now classic film that merges the symbolism of the gladiator and the modern prizefighter, *Spartacus* (1960). Using his own money, Kirk Douglas took an option on the the book *Spartacus* by Howard Fast. At one time a member of the Communist party, Fast apparently wrote much of the novel while serving a prison term for his Communist associations. For Fast, writing the novel constituted an act of rebellion since Spartacus, a Roman slave who led about 90,000 slaves in a revolt that defeated two Roman armies around 73 B.C., had become a hero to German Communists, inspiring an antifascist "Spartakist" movement during the period of the

First World War.[9] Contributing to the controversy, Douglas enlisted Dalton Trumbo, a Hollywood writer on the notorious blacklist for his Communist sympathies, to do the screenplay. Douglas made history when he broke the blacklist by crediting Trumbo for his work.[10] This left-wing orientation and background to the film infuriated conservatives such as the columnist Hedda Hopper and the American Legion. However, the film in fact really epitomizes conventional liberal politics of the time in emphasizing and popularizing an ideology of individual and group freedom against the oppressive and dictatorial Roman state. As evidence of the film's basic liberalism, President John F. Kennedy displayed his interest in the film by going to a public showing of it.[11] Included in the stellar cast of Peter Ustinov, Jean Simmons, Charles Laughton, Nina Foch, Tony Curtis, John Gavin, John Ireland, and Herbert Lom, was Laurence Olivier, who played Crassus, the Roman general who ultimately acts with Pompey to defeat Spartacus.

Douglas, of course, plays the lead of Spartacus. At one point relatively early in the 196-minute film, Spartacus, who has been made into a gladiator, must fight another slave-gladiator, Draba, a black man played by Woody Strode. The gladiators engage in mortal combat for the amusement of Crassus and his entourage. Spartacus uses a sword, while Draba fights with a trident. After a prolonged fight, Draba overcomes Spartacus. The Romans, including the women, call for Draba to execute Spartacus. Spartacus waits for his death with a look that mixes dread and fear with something approximating the anticipation of relief from his life of misery and enslavement. Instead of killing him, however, Draba hurls his trident at the Romans above him, trying to assassinate Crassus, who cuts his throat when the gladiator climbs to the elevated seats of the Roman rulers.

Woody Strode personifies the situation of an array of black performers who gained recognition for their talents during the decades from the late 1930s to mid-1950s but never achieved true independence or the pinnacle of stardom because of race. They were marginalized in their work and careers. However, they still struggled to the forefront of the steadily developing movement of blacks into mainstream America in all fields of endeavor. Such figures as varied as Canada Lee, Juanita Moore, and even Dorothy Dandridge achieved fame and success but still found their roles restricted and careers compartmentalized by race and the expectations of white audiences. Arguably, a figure as talented and promising as Dandridge was destroyed by limitations imposed upon her by race.[12]

Figure 5. Gladiator Woody Strode personifies "The Black Spartacus," a figure of strength and sacrifice, as he considers the thumbs-down verdict by Romans Laurence Olivier and Nina Foch to execute another slave-gladiator, Spartacus, played by Kirk Douglas in *Spartacus*. (Museum of Modern Art/Film Still Archives)

Even in this pantheon of neglected black figures of enormous talent and genius, Woody Strode stands out because of his intelligence, dignified bearing, extraordinary personal appearance, and genuine physical power. Strode was a natural athlete. Along with Jackie Robinson and Kenny Washington, he was a football star at UCLA. He received increased attention when he and Washington became the first African Americans to play in the National Football League.[13]

Strode's charisma and truly dynamic and domineering physical presence both in person and on the screen attracted the attention and admiration of one of Hollywood's most celebrated and powerful figures, John Ford. Strode's genuine achievements as an athlete, performer, war veteran, and personality earned the respect and admiration of Ford, who was notorious for being grudging in providing such support to actors. Conceivably, part of Ford's feeling for Strode derived from the director's growing desire to compensate personally for decades of his own insensitivity toward the situation of both blacks and Native Americans, not only in his own films but in American history as well.[14] Ford became something of a mentor to Strode by starring him in *Sergeant Rutledge* (1960), a film about an heroic black soldier in the black Ninth Cavalry who suffered persecution and discrimination over a false charge of rape, a situation that resonates with the insecurity and plight of African Americans throughout American history and culture. Ford also cast Strode as John Wayne's helper in *The Man Who Shot Liberty Valance* (1962), dubbing him Pompey, a name with gladiatorial associations with *Spartacus* that also relates ironically to Strode's near-slavish dependence upon Wayne's character in the film.

As an example of his authentic appreciation and respect for Strode as well as his own cantankerous personality, Ford relished using Strode to goad and tease John Wayne, who apparently could not match Strode in both natural athletic ability nor in military experience. Although Ford helped to create Wayne's masculine and heroic image by directing him in many of the great movies that ultimately established Wayne's career and stardom, Ford could not help but display his notorious maliciousness in denigrating Wayne by elevating Strode. Thus, Gary Wills reports:

> Ford also took the opportunity to renew his sardonic references to Wayne's lack of military service, contrasting his record with that of his new star, Woody Strode, who had played a military hero in *Sergeant Rutledge*, but had also been a real serviceman in World War II. Ford made the contrast between Wayne's short period on the USC bench and Strode's career as a star end at UCLA. The riding of Wayne rubbed his nerves so raw that he started a fight with Strode – which Ford had to end with hasty pleas to Strode not to hurt the older, weaker man because "We need him."[15]

Strode brings and fulfills all of this authority, power, and dignity to his role as the black gladiator and slave in *Spartacus*. Even though he appears very briefly in the film, his impact stands as unforgettable. Vincent LoBrutto describes Strode and his scenes with Douglas in his biography of the film's director, Stanley Kubrick, who was brought in by Douglas after the original director, Anthony Mann, was fired.

> Actor Woody Strode didn't have a stunt double. There were black stunt men available, but none who matched his physique. So the stuntmen worked with Strode, who was a fine natural athlete. For the fight to the death between Strode and Douglas, the stuntmen worked with both actors, teaching them how to fight.[16]

In addition, a friend of Kubrick's on the set also described Strode in impressive terms. Alexander Singer said of him, "Woody Strode was a man of innate dignity. When you just turned the camera on him there was something rather special."[17]

As a gladiator engaged in mortal combat, Strode in *Spartacus* wonderfully epitomizes the physical and personal heroism that Sugar Ray advocates as the standard for a boxer. Strode's combative role also relates to Douglas's and Kubrick's boxing experiences. Douglas, of course, played a boxer in Mark Robson's *Champion* (1949), although not one necessarily involved in racial concerns. Kubrick also was deeply interested in boxing, achieving one of his earliest professional triumphs as a young photographer for *Look* magazine with a series on boxing that evidenced, as LoBrutto says, "his abiding passion for boxing." LoBrutto says:

> In January 1949 Stanley Kubrick came of age as a photojournalist with a mature study of a boxer titled "Prizefighter." Kubrick received the credit "Photographed by Stanley Kubrick" on the first page of the article. The assignment came his way because of his abiding passion for boxing.

LoBrutto goes on to explain:

> The forties were a vital time for the sport, and men like Joe Louis, Gus Lesnevich, Tony Zale, Rocky Graziano, Marcel Cerdan, "Sugar" Ray Robinson, Willie Pep, and Jake La Motta were urban heroes.
> Kubrick saw great drama in boxing and aimed to investigate beyond the gloss of the sports pages. He wanted to penetrate the human and mythic areas that boxing occupied for many young men who idolized the warriors of the ring.[18]

The title and focus of this particular piece of Kubrick's early photojournalism on boxing was "The Day of a Fight." Discussing this work, LoBrutto makes the connection between boxing and gladiators by describing the boxer featured in Kubrick's piece, twenty-four-year-old New Yorker Walter Cartier, as having "the strong body of a gladiator."[19] LoBrutto describes the care Kubrick put into telling and showing the fighter's story.

Significantly, this piece of photojournalism evolved into Kubrick's first film. The article "The Day of a Fight" turned into a short film called *Day of the Fight* (1951). To make his first, short film, Kubrick developed a documentary style that mixed strong realism with fiction. As LoBrutto says, "The text poses as documentary fact, but it is filled with noir poetry."[20] LoBrutto even argues that the film anticipates *Raging Bull*.

> The fight is shot hand-held, a restless, moving camera peering outside the ropes, inside the ropes, and from the point of view of the canvas, looking up at the fighters as they flail at each other, a moment recaptured by Martin Scorsese in *Raging Bull*. It's hard not to think of *Raging Bull* while watching *Day of the Fight*, a film that looks back on the history of boxing in film and points toward its future.[21]

Obviously, Kubrick brought his experiences with photojournalism and early filmmaking as well as his genuine interest in boxing to his filming of *Spartacus*.

In *Spartacus*, the spectacle of the battle between gladiators becomes a meaningful political event. The vision of Strode, this amazing black figure, hurling himself and his weapon against a Roman tyrant dramatizes an individual and group demand for freedom. At the dawn of a new era of historic civil rights activism that would be led by figures such as Martin Luther King, Jr., Strode embodies the readiness of African Americans to lead their fight for equality. He achieves a kind of architectural stature as a living symbol of the drive for freedom. In his actions and presence, he embodies one expression of a new moment in American civil rights history.

Strode's heroic role makes him an example of fighting for freedom, and puts him in the position of a leader and model. He suggests not only the sympathy and support of the film for the situation of blacks in America at the time, his character achieves a form of political authority that derives from the actual condition of inequality of people of color in America. He assumes a special status in the film, exercising his right to speak for freedom. His character instructs Douglas and the other slaves about their unrealized strength and potential power. Personifying the film's theme of freedom, Strode performs a kind of nondiegetic ideological function that enriches his character's significance by transferring contemporary realities of discrimination and racism onto the back of the black gladiator who fights Spartacus. Strode's gladiator renegotiates the relationship of history and fiction.

However, while dramatizing the liberal ideology of the early 1960s, *Spartacus* also represents and embodies many contradictions and conflicts in that ideology. If Strode embodies a liberal drive toward equality and justice, he also dramatizes the situation of the African American within the liberal creed during this period of the Cold War. The same ideology that extolls Strode's cause also contains him. He dies. He becomes a sacrifice for what the film makes into a greater cause, the lesson of freedom that Spartacus learns from him about freeing white slaves. The film transforms a potential argument for including blacks in a story of freedom into a political program for Spartacus to lead a white revolt.

As striking as this example of racial exploitation and liberal neglect is in the film's narrative and ideology, Douglas and Kubrick appear indifferent and dismissive in their attitude toward Strode and the potential significance of his role for blacks in America. Building on Trumbo's screenplay, the film clearly uses Strode for a visual and cinematic statement for freedom. However, the film's ultimate neglect of freedom and civil rights for blacks seems confirmed in the way Douglas and Kubrick so readily withdraw from any discussion of the racial question. Douglas fails to discuss Strode in his chapter on the film in his book.[22] Kubrick similarly seems generally unconcerned with developing this aspect of Strode's role and function in the film.[23] In spite of the film's leftist orientation, Douglas's major concerns center on making the production a hit, while Kubrick strives for some independence as the director facing artistic challenges. In the final analysis, both seem to take Strode and his importance to the film for granted.

Strode's awesome physical power and undaunting moral presence as the black gladiator make him a truly impressive symbol for a pattern of sacrifice by a black gladiator for a white one that goes back to *Golden Boy*. However, another film, *Body and Soul*, most famously and authoritatively asserts the relationship of a black gladiator of conscience and integrity who teaches a white fighter about honor, honesty, and courage. The New York and Jewish origins and backgrounds of many of those associated with *Spartacus* – Douglas, Kubrick, and Curtis, among others – provide a political and cultural subtext to the film. In *Body and Soul*, Jewishness, left-wing ideology, and New York constitute the very foundation and fabric of the movie. The hero of *Body and Soul*, John Garfield, born Julie Garfinkle on New York's Lower East

Side, plays a Jewish boxer. Also born on the Jewish Lower East Side, the film's director, Robert Rossen was himself a professional boxer. Abraham Polonsky, another New Yorker, wrote the screenplay. These figures, as well as the film's other leading actors, New Yorkers Canada Lee, the black boxer, and Anne Revere, who plays Garfield's mother, were known for their left-wing views and activism and faced attack by conservatives, especially the House Un-American Activities Committee. Even with this strong commitment to left-wing social causes, the film nevertheless precedes *Spartacus* in sacrificing the black fighter to save the white man. In an extremely close and detailed reading and analysis of the film along these racial and political lines, Michael Rogin in *Blackface, White Noise* says that "*Body and Soul* fails to free the African American actor from inheriting the sacrifical role" from an even earlier tradition of exploitation of blacks, Jewish blackface.[24] Rogin explains:

> *Body and Soul* insists on what *The Jazz Singer* shows in spite of itself: that, the black face represents the sacrificed immigrant Jewish community. The left-wing film takes the pariah side against the upwardly mobile Jewish son.[25]

For Rogin, Jewish success with blackface in the first talking movie, Al Jolson's *Jazz Singer* (1927), involves very little gain or advancement for blacks and anticipates the subsequent sacrifice of blacks in the boxing film. As with *Spartacus*, in *Body and Soul*, as Rogin says, "Only one body is resurrected, however; in this film's spiritual miscegenation, Ben [Canada Lee, the black man] has died to save Charley's [John Garfield] soul."[26]

Rogin sedulously constructs a case to demonstrate the occurrence of an oppositional and exploitive relationship in which Jews in blackface or Jews in the ring emerge victorious. He sees no sense of unity or common purpose in the mirror scene in *The Jazz Singer* when a blackfaced Jolson merges images of the Jewish prayer of *Kol Nidre* on Yom Kippur, the Day of Atonement, with the mirror image of himself as a black man. He also diminishes the significance of the common cause in *Body and Soul* between the Jewish and black fighters, Garfield and Lee, in struggling for survival and success, while dealing with the mob, crime, and violence. Although Rogin remains correct about black sacrifice and the foregrounding of Jewish characters, it can be argued fairly that especially from the perspective of their respective historic moments, both Canada Lee and Strode, as representative figures, gained much from their roles in *Body and Soul* and *Spartacus*.

Thus, in contrast to Rogin, some students of black film see Lee's work in *Body and Soul* as a triumph for the actor and a major gain for blacks in general. In the film, the black fighter, Ben Chaplin (Lee), becomes the trainer for the Jewish fighter, Charley Davis (Garfield) after being severely injured in a boxing match between the two men. When Ben in a scene in training camp melodramatically protests Charley's plan to throw a fight to win a bet against himself, Ben also challenges the mob leader's efforts to get rid of him. As Thomas Cripps reports, "Ben refuses to leave, but under the stress he cracks and begins fighting a snarling shadow bout with himself and some long-gone opponent, until he sets loose in his brain the embolus that will kill him." To Cripps, Canada Lee's performance in this scene perhaps stole the film from Garfield and gained the attention of both critics and the public. He writes:

> Obviously it was Garfield's movie, but at its moral and dramatic center was the chiaroscuro performance by Canada Lee as Ben, dancing his ballet of death, the clarity of which provided the ethical bridge between the complaisant Charley and the resolute Charley. Without the sacrificial presence of the trainer, *Body and Soul* would have been only another prize ring melodrama. But a black role had made a movie *work*. What is more, moviegoers noticed.[27]

Both Cripps and Donald Bogle note how the influential film critic for the *New York Times*, Bosley Crowther, also saw Lee as making a major success of this role for himself as an actor and probably for African Americans as well. Crowther wrote:

> It is Canada Lee who brings to focus the horrible pathos of the cruelly exploited prize-fighter. As a Negro ex-champion who is meanly shoved aside, until one night he finally dies slugging in a deserted ring, he shows through great dignity and reticence the full measure of his inarticulate scorn for the greed of shrewder men who have enslaved him, sapped his strength, and then tossed him out to die. The inclusion of this portrait is one of the finer things in the film.[28]

Obviously, much of this language today seems dated and patronizing. Similarly, the sympathy *Body and Soul* expresses for Ben also comes across today as offensive in its manner of presenting a physically and psychologically damaged black man. In its own way, this attitude is as unfortunate in *Body and Soul* as *Spartacus*'s abandonment of Strode, despite the advances for blacks that Cripps, Bogle, and others see in the film.

Interestingly, even Rogin, who also asks, "Was a different relation imaginable in 1947 between African American and Jew?" notes how both Polonsky the screenwriter and Garfield the star fought to keep Canada Lee's role as Ben in the film.[29]

> Polonsky had resisted an early effort to eliminate the black fighter from his film. As he put it half a century later, "There is an obvious deep relationship between people held not so much in contempt but in deep antipathy by society. Garfield ... refused to be part of the betrayal."[30]

In repeating this comment by Polonsky, Rogin remains uncertain if Polonsky's allusion to Garfield was "referring to the actor who stood up for the script or the character who stood up for Ben."

In any case, the quote suggests that Polonsky answers Rogin's question about possible alternative relations between Jews and blacks with the idea that both Jews and blacks faced extraordinary obstacles to genuine racial and ethnic equality but gained from the relationship dramatized in the film. Also interesting, a year after *Body and Soul*, director Robert Wise felt he could not cast a black actor, James Edwards, as the lead in another fight film, *The Set-Up* (1949) and instead turned to Robert Ryan, a Dartmouth boxing champion for the lead, saving the secondary role for the black actor in a way that repeats to a certain extent the situation and relationship in *Body and Soul*.[31]

The ideology and imagery that dramatize the "Spartacus Syndrome" of a black boxer sacrificing himself for whites had its counterpart in the actual world of boxing. Barely two years after the release of *Spartacus*, on September 25, 1962, Floyd Patterson defended his heavyweight title against Charles (Sonny) Liston in Chicago going into the match with the burden of American liberalism on his shoulders. The elite of white America from President John F. Kennedy to Frank Sinatra along with the entire sportswriting establishment presumed the redemption of liberal America in the widely-anticipated victory by Patterson over Liston, who was a notorious thug with a criminal record and a reputation for unsavory associations and actions. Evincing a certain quality of boyishness and fighting with a flashy intelligence, Patterson was generally seen as a positive African American image since winning the Olympic middleweight championship in 1952. Succeeding the legendary Rocky Marciano to the heavyweight title, Patterson became champion on November 30, 1956 after upsetting the favored Archie Moore. The youngest heavyweight champion in history, Patterson's somewhat unconventional career made him seem different and more interesting than the usual fighter. For example, after his stunning loss of the title to the Swedish Ingemar Johansson, he became the first heavyweight to regain the title when he triumphed in the fifth round of a return match with Johannson on June 22, 1960 at New York's Polo Grounds.[32]

By the time of his epochal encounter with the infamous Liston, Patterson had attained a reputation as a unique figure in the world of boxing. He also had become a symbol, especially for whites, of respectable blackness. He was widely seen as an exemplary black man striving to accommodate himself to white middle-class values and demands. Known to some reporters as *"Freud* Patterson," Patterson gained admiration and respect for the intensity of his introspection. David Remnick writes:

> There had never been a heavyweight champion as sensitive, and as honest about his fears, as Floyd Patterson. He was the first professional athlete to receive what would become the modern treatment, a form of Freudian sportswriting that went beyond the ring and into the psyche.[33]

Similarly, one of the most creative and interesting chroniclers of boxing in the second half of this century, Norman Mailer, also was intrigued by the symbolism connected to Patterson, especially the political symbolism. Discussing the Patterson–Liston fight of 1962, Mailer, the acclaimed and prize-winning novelist and commentator, writes:

> And Patterson was exhausted before the fight began. Lonely as a monk for years, his daily gym work the stuff of his meditation, he was the first of the black fighters to be considered, then used, as a political force. He was one of the liberal elite, an Eleanor Roosevelt darling, he was political mileage for the NAACP. Violent, conceivably to the point of murder if he had not been a fighter, he was a gentleman in public, more, he was a man of the nicest, quietest, most private good manners. But monastic by inclination. Now, all but uneducated, he was appealed to by political blacks to win the Liston fight for the image of the Negro. Responsiblity sat upon him like a comic cutback in a silent film where we return now and again to one poor man who has been left to hold a beam across his shoulders. There he stands, hardly able to move. At the end of the film he collapses. That was the weight put on Patterson. The responsibility to beat Liston was too great to bear. Patterson, a fighter of incorruptible honesty, was knocked out by punches hardly anybody saw. He fell in open air as if seized by a stroke. The age of surrealistic battles had begun.[34]

Part of that weight, that cross, that was too great for Patterson to bear was placed upon him by President Kennedy, who reportedly informed the champion, "Well, you've *got* to beat this guy," meaning Liston.[35] While all of this symbolism may have been heavy on Patterson's shoulders, and may even test the patience and credulity of the reader, it also should be remembered that in the final analysis, Liston himself was simply too much for Patterson. As Nat Fleischer and Sam Andre wrote, "At 212, he outweighed Patterson by 25 pounds and outreached him thirteen inches."[36] Indeed, Patterson went on to lose the rematch on July 22, 1963 in Las Vegas and was later devastated by Muhammad Ali in a fight that took place on the second anniversary of the Kennedy Assassination, November 22, 1965 in Las Vegas. In this fight, as Fleischer and Andre describe it,

> the ex-champion received a merciless beating from a younger, taller, heavier, and sharper opponent. Ali, at 210 pounds, bewildered the 194-pound contender with left jabs and jolting rights to the body. The one-sided affair was halted at 2:18 of the twelfth round by referee Harry Krause.[37]

Disregarding such disadvantages against stronger opponents, Patterson seems to have imposed on his own body and internalized in his psyche the willingness of a real Black Spartacus figure to withstand punishment and to sacrifice himself for a cultural force greater than himself. The late 1950s and early 1960s New York and Hollywood liberalism that the film *Spartacus* represents indeed was embodied in Patterson, a Spartacus hero so devotedly bearing a burden of political and cultural beliefs that he apparently truly believed in his mission to fulfill the hopes so many had placed on him. Concerning Patterson's fight with Muhammad Ali, who of course was known by his birth name of Cassius Clay before becoming a Black Muslim, Remnick writes:

> And yet what was remarkable about Patterson was the degree to which he felt he was on a mission to beat Ali, not simply to prove his boxing superiority to a dubious public, but to prove the superiority of a religion and the liberal rhetoric of equal opportunity.... Patterson even offered to fight Ali for nothing and turn his purse over to the NAACP. One had the feeling that his offer was only half in jest. Patterson actually said that beating Ali – beating *Clay*, as he insisted on calling him – "would be my contribution to civil rights."[38]

Patterson said a victory over Ali was "both a personal goal and a moral crusade."[39] Fighting against Ali as what Remnick terms "the champion of accommodation," Patterson's representation of the liberalism of the

time aroused the contempt and derision of Mailer.[40] Discussing the
Patterson–Liston fight in Chicago, Mailer said that Patterson

> was a liberal's liberal. The worst to be said about Patterson is that he spoke
> with the same cow's cud as other liberals. Think what happens to a man with
> Patterson's reflexes when his brain starts to depend on the sounds of "intro-
> spective," "obligation," "responsibility," "inspiration," "commendation,"
> "frustrated," "seclusion" – one could name a dozen others from his book.
> They are part of his pride; he is a boy from the slums of Bedford-Stuyvesant
> who has acquired these words like stocks and bonds and income-bearing
> properties. There is no one to tell him it would be better to keep the psy-
> chology of the streets than to cultivate the contradictory desire to be a great
> fighter and a great, healthy, mature, autonomous, related, integrated indi-
> vidual. What a shabby gentility there has been to Patterson's endeavor. . . . [41]

Of course, someone besides Mailer promulgated a lesson about
Patterson's situation as the liberal Spartacus figure – Ali himself, the
man who overturns the Spartacus syndrome and, through the strength
of his mind, body, and soul, revolutionizes the role and position of the
black fighter by becoming what could be called the anti-Spartacus, the
man who would not sacrifice himself, who said, "I had to prove you
could be a new kind of black man. I had to show that to the world." In
contrast to Patterson's liberalism, accommodation, and self-sacrifice,
Ali after making his own sacrifices by refusing to be drafted during
the Vietnam War, declared, "I was determined to be one nigger that
the white man didn't get. One nigger that you didn't get, white man.
You understand? One nigger you ain't going to get."[42] He refused on
April 28, 1967 to be inducted into the army on the grounds of being
"exempt as a minister of the religion of Islam" and because, "Man, I
ain't got no quarrel with them Vietcong."[43] Because of this action, Ali
was stripped of his title and could "not fight for three and half years,
the prime of his boxing life." Sentenced to five years in prison and fined
$10,000, Ali's appeal resulted in a unanimous decision in June 1971
by the Supreme Court that sided with him.

However, it would not be until October 29, 1974 at the age of thirty-
two that Ali would become the second man in boxing after Patterson
to regain the heavyweight title by winning it for a second time in his
fight with George Foreman in Kinshasa, Zaire.[44] An important event
for boxing and cultural history, it also marks a transformation of the
black boxer on film as the representation of African Americans. It took
director/producer Leon Gast twenty-three years to complete *When We*

Were Kings (1996), the Oscar-winning documentary of this event, the so-called "Rumble in the Jungle" of Zaire. In the context of previous representations of black fighters, Gast's documentary demonstrates the demise of the sacrificial Spartacus figure and the emergence of new kind of hero in the person of Ali. Having proclaimed, "I am the king! I am the king! King of the world! Eat your words! Eat! Eat your words!" after beating Liston the first time, Ali would embody what Toni Morrison terms "a new posture for a black man."[45] Remnick describes this shift:

> But whether the press understood it or not, he had quietly foresaken the image of the unthreatening black fighter established by Joe Louis and then imitated by Jersey Joe Walcott and Floyd Patterson and dozens of others. Clay was declaring that he would not fit any stereotypes, he would not follow any set standard of behavior.[46]

Remnick goes on to emphasize the political and cultural nature of the differences between Ali's form of independence and the kind of undirected rebellion typical of Liston.

> And while Liston had also declared his independence from convention (through sheer don't-give-a-shit truculence), Clay's message was political. He and not Jimmy Cannon [the influential sportswriter] or the NAACP would define his blackness, his religion, his history. He was a vocal member of an American fringe group and America would soon be learning about it.[47]

Thus, Gast's film makes the importance of Ali's influence upon America a relevant development for film as well.

With the insight of a major writer and student of culture, Mailer in his coverage of the Ali–Foreman fight declared boxing to be an important key to understanding the black man and described the drama of the battle in the ring as an extension and intensification of the struggles in the society. He writes:

> For Heavyweight boxing was almost all black, black as Bantu [certain languages and peoples of Africa]. So boxing had become another key to revelations of Black, one more key to black emotion, black psychology, black love. Heavyweight boxing might also lead to the room in the underground of the world where Black kings were installed: what was Black emotion, Black psychology, Black love?[48]

Mailer's little shift in capitalizing the letter "b" humorously makes the point in a visual way of how this boxing event came to signify the emerging prominence and authority of African Americans as an independent and powerful force to challenge the establishment.

Figure 6. A sweating Muhammad Ali engulfed in thought after working out for the "Rumble in the Jungle," his 1974 heavyweight championship fight against George Foreman in *When We Were Kings.* (Museum of Modern Art/Film Still Archives)

A crucial quality of Gast's documentary film concerns the way *When We Were Kings* covers the fighters and the event as part of a celebration of blackness in general. It advocates an ideology of color, of blackness that goes beyond the lines of traditional national and economic ideologies. With Mailer and writer George Plimpton as informed participants and commentators, the film glorifies all things black from America as well as Africa. Singers James Brown and B. B. King, boxing promoter Don King, music that originates in African American culture, and music from Africa become nearly as important as the fighters. Blackness suffuses the film as it covers the origins and the surroundings of the boxing match, including the planning and promotional phases in America and the transition to Africa.

At the same time, the film undoubtedly extolls not only Ali's particular and unique greatness but also his embodiment and personification of blackness. In this sense, *When We Were Kings* exemplifies a form of documentary that develops a position and point of view as much it presents an event. It shows Ali as hero, almost Ali as a god, which is how some in the film literally describe him. Ali takes center stage in a powerful mise-en-scene of blackness, leaving Foreman as a brooding and distant figure, in spite of scenes in the film indicating Foreman's qualities of mature reserve, patience, and stolidity.

Of course, this element of Ali advocacy and promotion in the film derives primarily from the magnificent force of Ali's personality and presence, his language, humor, antics, charisma, especially in contrast to the usual reticence and remoteness of Foreman during this stage of his life. However, in a commentary that follows the film on the videotape, Gast provides some insight into the events involved in the film and how it was made. He offers one piece of information that can be interpreted upon reflection as important evidence of the need to remember, as Bill Nichols and Gilberto Perez proclaim, that documentary realism, like fiction, entails artistic construction and human intervention. Gast notes how cooperative and even enthusiastic Ali was about the presence and intrusion of the filming crew throughout the prolonged period preceding the fight that had been seriously delayed because of an injury above Foreman's right eye.

In other words, part of Ali's dominance of the film involves not just the popularity of his aggressive and dynamic personality but also his availability for the camera. The film becomes so much of his story because he made it that way, while Foreman tended to be reclusive and reserved. The film favored what it could see, focus on, and shoot, and

Figure 7. Muhammad Ali, who eradicated the Black Spartacus image and became an American Hero, with admirers of different generations in Zaire in *When We Were Kings*. (Museum of Modern Art/Film Still Archieves)

this just happened to be a lot of Ali, who would let Gast and his crew know when and where to find him. Some of the documentary truth-testing and examination of the film's characters and themes that could have added depth and texture to the film never occurred. Ironically for a documentary film about blackness, it relies heavily upon commentary from white writers and intellectuals, Mailer and Plimpton, for various perspectives that the film itself might have explored and analyzed with greater energy and imagination.

Accordingly, because of both the film's proclivity to favor Ali as a subject and figure as well as its concentration on him during the filming and production processes, it creates a distorted view of Foreman. It, therefore, takes the creative and restless intelligence and imagination of a Mailer to suggest the enormous potential of Foreman as a fighter and character. Mailer writes:

> Taken directly, Foreman was no small representative of vital force....He did not look like a man so much as a lion standing just as erectly as a man. He appeared sleepy but in the way of a lion digesting a carcass. His broad handsome face (not unreminiscent of a mask of Clark Gable somewhat flattened) was neither friendly nor unfriendly, rather, it was alert in the way a boxer is in some part of him alert no matter how sleepy he looks, a heightening common, perhaps, to all good athletes, so that they can pick an insect out of the air with their fingers but as easily notice the expression on some friend in the thirtieth row from ringside.[49]

Nichols's concern, as discussed earlier, about recognizing the boundary between fiction and documentary especially obtains in *When We Were Kings* on this issue of racial symbolism as embodied by Foreman and Ali.[50] This award-winning creative documentary that synthesizes race and ethnicity, music, global and international politics and cultures, sports, social and cultural history, and journalism, nevertheless still epitomizes in certain ways the dangers involved in not adequately considering, for whatever reasons, this boundary between fiction and documentary. The physical and emotional poetry of Ali and the cultural richness and power of blackness and Africa overwhelm the visual representation and narratival participation of Foreman and diminish his significance at the time as a black man and prizefighter. The complexity of documentary suffers a sacrifice to a form of cinematic, cultural, and racial fictionalizing and myth making.

Accordingly, on the issue of race and culture, an important problem emerges in the film related to the general neglect and misrepresentation of Foreman. The controversial issue concerns the meaning of blackness as a force for identity and culture. The problem does not disappear with the recognition that the film's proclivity to proclaim Ali as the representative black man of the new age acquires strong confirmation in the attitudes of the Africans themselves. Individual Africans repeatedly appear stating a blatant bias toward Ali as being more black than Foreman, while the crowds of adulating followers clearly venerate Ali. Ali, of course, from the beginning of his career and well before ever getting to Africa, cultivated such a view of himself as more black than his opponents. Remnick says:

> One of the less entertaining components of the Ali act was the way he tried to "outblack" someone like [Joe] Frazier, call him an Uncle Tom, an "honorary white," when in fact Frazier had grown up dirt poor in South Carolina. If Ali was joking, Frazier never found it funny.[51]

Ironically, on both race and background, Ali misled. Ali's family recognized that on his mother's side "the blood was mixed."[52] Also, in contrast to the truly impoverished and disadvantaged backgrounds of Ali's opponents, as well as the conditions of poverty for blacks in general in the South at the time, Ali grew up in Louisville, Kentucky relatively comfortably, although still well below economic standards for whites.

Saying that the fight in Zaire "would then be a religious war," Mailer contests Ali's image, making what could be seen as his own stereotypical assumptions about blackness. He says:

> The paradox, however, on meeting the Champion was that Foreman seemed more black. Ali was not without white blood, not without a lot of it. Something in his personality was cheerfully even exuberantly white in the way of a six-foot two-inch president of a Southern college fraternity. At times Ali was like nothing so much as a white actor who had put on too little makeup for the part and so was not wholly convincing as a Black, just one of eight hundred small contradictions in Ali, but Foreman was *deep*. Foreman could be mistaken for African long before Ali.[53]

In spite of such contradictions and paradoxes that indicate the subjective nature of the difficult and complex issue of differences based on color and race, efforts persist, including in academic and critical circles, in proclaiming Ali's greater blackness, even when emphasizing blackness as an ideological position and cultural construction. Thus, in an article about the black genius Paul Robeson, Jeffrey C. Stewart uses the putative blackness of Ali in *When We Were Kings* to emphasize the greatness of Robeson in making his own body and character a statement for blackness from the late 1920s to the 1950s. Stewart says that Robeson's "posture of defiance connects him with the contemporary manifestations of the Black body as a site of resistance, one which is captured in the 1996 documentary film *When We Were Kings*."[54]

Before Ali was born, Robeson, a great athlete, Phi Beta Kappa scholar, intellectual, and world-acclaimed singer, was a dominant black figure of genius on the stage and screen. When Ali was still young, Robeson had the personal courage and fortitude to continue his life-long fight against racism and for labor and human rights, while trying to defend his own rights of free speech as a committed Communist and Soviet sympathizer. Regardless of history's judgement about the perspicacity of Robeson's allegiance to communism and the wisdom of his political actions at the beginning of the Cold War, few would challenge his genius or question his strength and courage. Yet Stewart feels compelled to enhance Robeson's stature and status by seeing *When We Were Kings* as "a discourse on Muhammad Ali and the Black body" in which Robeson anticipates Ali's role as being more black than each man's contemporaries. Stewart writes of Ali:

> Ali is the talking, specifying, intellectualizing, African-bonding Black man from America who constantly displays his body for popular consumption and constantly refers to himself as pretty. Indeed, his performance points up how far we have come in one sense from Robeson's time, since being the Black body no longer requires dark skin color. Being black is talking Black, having a Black consciousness, a Black identity, something that Foreman lacks in the movie (and in the 1970s) even though he is bigger and darker skinned. He is merely a Black body, simply a Black physical mass. Foreman's massiveness narcotizes the white media, who believe he will pound Ali, the intellectual body into the floor of that Zairian ring. But while we might want to equate Robeson with Foreman, the real connection is with Ali.[55]

Ironically, Stewart's argument reverses and undoes to a considerable extent the work of *When We Were Kings* in transforming the Spartacus figure into a hero of independence and authority. Instead of affirming Ali as an anti-Spartacus hero and a serious force for change, Stewart helps create another dehumanized black figure and potential stereotype by basing black identity on a new orthodoxy of imposed and determined racial meanings. Whereas Remnick lauded Ali for fighting stereotypes and resisting the imposition of other people's categories and definitions, Stewart's ideological position takes an absolutist stance toward color and culture that creates new straitjackets of forced identity that vitiate individuality. Much of the greatness of Robeson derived from the multiplicity of his various expressions of genius from acting to singing to political heroism. The power and importance of Ali and Foreman together involve their diversity and differences that complicate and individualize the meaning of blackness. By resisting absolute categories and definitions, the combination of the two men humanizes and particularizes the meaning of blackness.

Moreover, the popularity and success of *When We Were Kings* suggest how blackness steadily has become a heroic term for much of American culture as a whole as opposed to remaining a term of isolation and exclusion. The marginalization of what Remnick calls Ali's position on the "fringe" of American culture has changed so that the movement from Spartacus to anti-Spartacus perhaps has undergone yet another transforming development in which the Black Spartacus instead of being forgotten, neglected or sacrificed becomes a true national hero and representative. The very subtitle of Remnick's book makes this suggestion. Remnick's subtitle asserts: *Muhammad Ali and the Rise of an American Hero.* Proclaiming Ali such a hero seems a big step from marginalization and liminality. Another example of Ali's Americanization in a society that steadily blackens itself, so to speak, for inclusion and incorporation as opposed to promoting racial sacrifice involves quite a transformational figure in himself, Governor Jesse Ventura of Minnesota, the Reform/Independent political figure and wrestler. Asked by Chris Matthews on his television program *Hardball* to name his heroes, Ventura immediately responded, Muhammad Ali:

> Because he was a man that totally stood up for his convictions. He gave up his world title because he wouldn't go to war. He had no fight with the Vietnamese. And for a man to give up the world heavyweight title, not in the ring. Oh, Muhammad Ali is my hero.

Ventura, a Vietnam veteran and a former Navy Seal, insisted:

> Oh, I've been with him since he beat Sonny Liston. My quote, "I shocked the world," I took that from him, when he beat Sonny Liston for the world title. He looked at Howard Cosell and said "I shocked the world."[56]

In a somewhat similar vein, as another example of political and cultural change, a full-page advertisement for Amnesty International, the human rights organization, in the *New York Times* of June 7, 1999, features Muhammad Ali standing over Liston and proclaims in four rows of headlines: 25 TIMES IN HIS CAREER, MUHAMMAD ALI, FOUGHT FOR A BELT. NOW HE'S FIGHTING AGAINST ONE. The advertisement calls for a

ban on the use by police and guards of "stun belts," which it describes
as electroshock weapons of up to 50,000 volts. "Please join Amnesty
International and Muhammad Ali to Ban the Belt."[57] Given his explosive and controversial past and personality, Ali's role in this campaign
suggests great change in institutional and popular representations of
American character and leadership.

Without exaggerating the significance of either an advertising strategy to advance a cause or the endorsement of a convert to politics from
wrestling, both the advertisement and the governor's endorsement indicate how much Ali has become a part of mainstream America. The
idealization of Ali as a man of independence, authority, and power
represents an enormous change in the culture. Indeed, the celebration
and veneration of Ali has become embedded so deeply and firmly in
a modern orthodoxy about race and boxing in America that a book
by veteran sports writer Mark Kram makes news because it challenges
the conventional wisdom that Ali automatically signifies "the greatest."
Thus, Richard Sandomir writes in the *New York Times*:

> Mark Kram is preparing for the barrage of critical response to his revisionist
> view of Muhammad Ali. In *Ghosts of Manila: The Fateful Blood Feud Be-
> tween Muhammad Ali and Joe Frazier*, which examines the divergent lives of
> Ali and Joe Frazier through the prism of their three fights, Kram demystifies
> Ali's often deified public image.[58]

Nevertheless, even in the face of such revisionist controversy, in the
context of our discussion of the Black Spartacus Syndrome, it seems appropriate to suggest that Ali's symbolism in the culture today provides
further evidence of the reembodiment of the American idea to include
people of color. Rather than acquiesce to dominant-culture demands
for sacrifice, Ali insisted throughout his life and career on personal self-
assertion and group identity. He, therefore, stands today, as Remnick
claims, as a new American hero, a view Remnick defends when asked
about Kram's claims.[59] Ali's achievement suggests the transitional nature of the symbolism of the Black Spartacus Syndrome. Self-sacrifice
by African Americans for marginal gains in the ring, other sports, entertainment or in the wider culture no longer works as a program
to justify and excuse white privilege and dominance. Thus, in Ridley
Scott's *Gladiator* (2000), the black slave-gladiator, played by Djimon
Hounsou, not only does not serve as a sacrificial figure, he becomes
a surviving voice and oracle for the white hero, as played by Russell
Crowe.

Michael Mann's *Ali* (2001) starring Will Smith becomes a climactic moment in the story of the American hero as a man of color. The film culminates several movements and themes in American culture and cinema. In *The Last of the Mohicans* (1992), Mann directed Daniel Day-Lewis and Madeleine Stowe as epitomizing individual and cultural rebirth in the new American wilderness. In the film, Mann celebrates the myth of America as a wilderness garden that cultivates the regeneration of European settlers into a new mongrel breed of people – Americans. In a period of nearly a decade that also involves the transition into a new century and a new millenium, Mann transforms the myth to dramatize a revivified American ideology of equality and freedom to include people of color. As in *The Last of the Mohicans*, Mann positions *Ali* at the center of a cultural consciousness in revolution as he recreates and reenacts the spirit and events of Ali's era: the music of Sam Cooke, the assassinations of Malcolm X and Martin Luther King, Jr. racial turmoil, and Vietnam protest. Out of this chaos and crisis in *Ali*, Muhammad Ali emerges as the new mythic American hero, the symbol and agent of regeneration. Like others in recent history who found their careers and prospects resurrected by appealing to the Supreme Court, Ali, his family, and his entourage learn from Howard Cosell (Jon Voight) that the court has overturned Ali's conviction for draft evasion. The scene in the film suggests both Ali's vindication as a hero of conscience and the vindication of American institutions of justice and fairness. Moreover, Ali's triumph over George Foreman to regain the title in Zaire concludes the film as a sign of his own and of national redemption. American flags appear in the crowd while a flag waves vigorously in the center of the frame with an energy and emotion that evoke the events of September 11, 2001, and their aftermath.

Accordingly, *Ali* highlights the transformation of the sacrificial black hero of the Black Spartacus Syndrome into the American hero. At one point as Ali trains and prepares to face Foreman, he finds himself accused by his second wife of being willing to sacrifice himself, of putting himself on the cross, for corrupt forces in both the boxing world and the Black Muslim movement. In spite of arguments to the contrary, Ali persists in proclaiming that he defines himself and makes his own decisions.

As part of its work of developing the myth of the Black Spartacus, *Ali* inevitably also perpetuates the sub-genre of the boxing film. The camera work and cinematography in the amazing boxing sequences, the presentation of the world of boxing, the theme of redemption distinctly recall the great boxing films of the past, including *Body and Soul, On the Waterfront,* and *Raging Bull.* One scene in particular connects to *Raging Bull* when Ali walks briskly through the inner channels of the stadium in Zaire to appear before the crowd. Similarly, Mann's use of shots, angles, cuts, speed changes, music, and diverse sound establishes rhythms and movements that build on the work of Martin Scorsese, Robert Rossen, and Robert Wise.

Mann's and Smith's *Ali* would suggest that today the broader and deeper meanings of Spartacus the gladiator, leader, and revolutionary, seem closer to realization in America. *Ali* opened in late-December 2001 when this book was at the end of the editing stage of an extensive production process. The critical and popular reaction to the film had not yet registered. One could assume, however, that many would see the film as a celebration of Ali's symbolism in bringing together America, African Americans, and Africa. For some, *Ali* confirms that partly because of Muhammad Ali's achievements, the ending of *Spartacus* now resonates with clearer and greater truth. The transformation of the Black Spartacus into mature and heroic independence suggests that we have moved closer to being able to proclaim, as do Spartacus's people and followers, that indeed we are all Spartacus.

PART THREE

THE IMAGE AND THE WORD: LITERATURE AND FILM

CHAPTER FIVE

"FRESH STARTS"

Bugsy, The Great Gatsby, and the American Dream

The dichotomy and tension in film between fiction and documentary of so much interest to Gilberto Perez can achieve a new twist and dimension in the relationship of literature to film. When a literary work translates into film, the film can become a form of literary documentary that seemingly must adhere as closely as possible to the literary work. In the case of classic Hollywood films, especially during the great studio era, the novel, it can be argued, often acquired the status of a governing reality or dominant text that served as a rigid guide for evaluating, criticizing, and appreciating the film. Hollywood studios often would proclaim their great achievement in bringing an acknowledged classic or popular novel to the screen in a serious almost studious way that accurately replicated the original literature, thereby suggesting an immediate transfer of the literary form to the accessible film medium. Examples of books that were treated in this manner include David O. Selznick's productions of Margaret Mitchell's *Gone With the Wind* (1939), Daphne du Maurier's *Rebecca* (1940), Charles Dickens's *David Copperfield* (1935), and Samuel Goldwyn's production of Emily Brontë's *Wuthering Heights* (1939).[1]

However, serious modern film scholars readily recognize the inherent difficulties involved in making the transition from literature to film, an important example among these being George Bluestone in an early work on the subject. Arguing that "the film becomes a different *thing* in the same sense that a historical painting becomes a different thing from the historical event which it illustrates," Bluestone emphasizes essential aesthetic differences between the two forms based on their relationship to time and space:

> Both novel and film are time arts, but whereas the formative principle in the novel is time, the formative principle in the film is space. Where the novel takes its space for granted and forms its narrative in a complex of time values, the film takes its time for granted and forms its narrative arrangements of space.[2]

Despite early critical and scholarly recognition of important aesthetic, cognitive, and structural differences between film and literature, provocative, historically informed, and critically astute studies of film and literature continue to demand strict conversion from one form to the other. As James Naremore says:

> Even when academic writing on the topic is not directly concerned with a given film's artistic adequacy or fidelity to a beloved source, it tends to be narrow in range, inherently respectful of the "precursor text," and constitutive of a series of binary oppositions that poststructuralist theory has taught us to deconstruct: literature versus cinema, high culture versus mass culture, original versus copy.[3]

One "academic" view of making classic novels into films occurs in a recent essay by Jeffrey Walker who brilliantly synthesizes history, literature, and culture studies as well as film history and theory in his vehement attack on Michael Mann's film version of James Fenimore Cooper's *The Last of the Mohicans* (1992). Walker organizes impressive scholarship along with considerable critical intelligence into a major assault against Mann's film. He takes strong exception to Mann's profound violations of the Cooper novel, while also noting differences with earlier film versions. Of course, Mann's most egregious changes demand notice and consideration – switching the roles of the Munro sisters, Cora (Madeleine Stowe) and Alice (Jodhi May); transforming Hawkeye (Daniel Day-Lewis) into a romantic hero; and inventing a romance between Cora and Hawkeye. Still, arguing as a literary purist and Cooper apologist, Walker might lighten up a bit and take both Mark Twain's famous humorous attack on Cooper as well as Cooper himself less seriously.[4] To me who finds Mann's film to be a powerful achievement of modern filmmaking in which all the elements of film cohere, Walker fails to see the cinematic forest for the specificity of the literary trees. As Bluestone's argument suggests, Mann made a film as its own work of art, not a filming of a book. Working assiduously to achieve historical accuracy and cultural dynamism, Mann evokes the most profound and lasting elements of Cooper's tale, especially as interpreted over many decades by writers such as D. H. Lawrence, Henry Nash Smith, and Richard Slotkin – violence, the transformative powers of the landscape, cultural exchange between whites and Native Americans, the Puritan mission in the wilderness, the shaping of a unique colonial and national character and culture through the interaction of ideology, experience, and environment.[5] Rather than berating Mann for straying from Cooper's text, Walker probably should work from his area of expertise and brilliance of relating historical and cultural contexts to the aesthetic and cultural meanings of film production, as when he describes Cooper's real interest in Native Americans, including their plight during the dreadful Federal Indian Removal Policy.[6] Even when representing Cooper, fiction film should not be compelled to become a form of pure documentary that must adhere rigidly to primary literary sources.

Many of these issues concerning literary fiction, documentary, and myth obtain in comparing Barry Levinson's film *Bugsy* (1991) to F. Scott Fitzgerald's *The Great Gatsby* (1925). When *Bugsy* came out, most reviewers, reflecting the tastes of much of the public, saw the film primarily as a vehicle for Warren Beatty, a superstar whose frequent lengthy absences from the screen during his career up to that point apparently intensified the desires of his fans to see him. More selective in choosing films than many other comparable stars, Beatty's appearance in *Bugsy* with co-star Annette Bening, his off-screen love who was pregnant with his child at the time of the film's release, fermented additional interest among both critics and the general public.

Newsweek, however, broke the pattern and pursued its own literary instincts and imagination, presciently emphasizing the resemblance of Fitzgerald's *The Great Gatsby* to the film's subject, Benjamin "Bugsy" Siegel, the notorious Jewish gangster from New York who conceived of modern-day Las Vegas. In a brief review, *Newsweek* wondered: "If Gatsby Had Been a Goodfella," a play on Martin Scorsese's great film about the mafia in New York.

> *Bugsy*. Barry Levinson's swank, moody evocation of the life of mobster Benjamin (Bugsy) Siegel, is a gangster movie with some heady ambitions up its nattily tailored sleeve. The movie's view of the mercurial Siegel – played by Warren Beatty with a vigor he hasn't displayed in years – is charged with ambiguity. Partly visionary (he virtually invented Las Vegas when he built the Flamingo Hotel), part psychotic, he's depicted as a lethal Gatsbyesque dreamer, equally charming and chilling.[7]

Although a rather basic point expressed in a somewhat typical "newsspeak" manner, *Newsweek* nevertheless stood alone in making this critical stretch from *Bugsy* to *Gatsby*, a connection that apparently neither director Levinson nor screenwriter James Toback either especially appreciate or emphasize.[8] In spite of the neglect by most of this connection, the parallels between *Bugsy* and *The Great Gatsby* deserve elaboration. A comparison between *Bugsy* and *The Great Gatsby* necessarily involves the relationship of film form to the novel. On the level of ideology, it also concerns how the film and the novel compare and contrast in their expressions of the American myth and ideology of renewal. Levinson's film revisits Gatsby's myth of rebirth to suggest startling continuities with the past as well as crucial new patterns of thought and life. In ways that are unique to film form and art, *Bugsy* vividly constructs complex conceptualizations that relate directly to *Gatsby*. Thus, *Bugsy* provides insight into how film works as both an art form and a medium of cultural and historic negotiation and continuity.

Rather than trivializing serious questions of cultural and cinematic criticism, the glamour surrounding the film sustains the deeper connection between Bugsy Siegel and Jay Gatsby. The conflation in the public mind and the media of Beatty and Bening with the film's characters, Bugsy Siegel and his sexually vagarious lover, Virginia Hill, contributes to the film's meaning and effectiveness. This convergence of actors and characters provides an example of how documentary images of actors influence both the aesthetic and cultural significance of a film, an issue to be discussed in greater detail in a later chapter. The documentary images of the actors Bening and Beatty infuse the very form and ideology of the film with significance. Thus, a *Time* headline – "A Playboy Meets Miss Right" – very well could be referring to both sets of actors and characters.

> For three decades he was Hollywood's ideal bachelor, a handsome, self-assured man who retained just enough boyish shyness to melt a woman's heart. . . . Then last summer came the shocking announcement. No he wasn't marrying (at least not yet), but he was having a child with intelligent, glamorous Annette Bening.[9]

Thus, similarities in the glamorously unconventional lifestyles of Beatty and Bugsy Siegel attracted the attention of some critics and writers who saw the parallels between the celebrity status of Siegel and Beatty as suggestive of the crucial influence in modern cinema of an actor's

personna and image upon a role. Indeed, Beatty dramatizes the interaction between the real life of the actor and the reel life on the screen.

Accordingly, in their commentary and criticism, most magazines and
journals reflected popular film's tendency to concentrate upon the major star lead and, usually, his rather than her development of the basic
plot and thematic complication. They, therefore, focused on Beatty
himself and his involvement with both the film and filmmaking in
general.[10] In the case of *Bugsy*, the obsession with stardom seems especially justified because of the origins of the film in Beatty's mind.
Toback reports that "Warren Beatty . . . approached me with an offer.
He would provide me with some much needed front money in return
for an original screenplay about Benjamin 'Bugsy' Siegel" (*Bugsy* 8).

Perhaps fear of association with the relatively unsuccessful film versions of *The Great Gatsby* (most notably the 1949 version with Alan
Ladd and the much publicized Robert Redford–Mia Farrow effort in
1974) helps explain the absence in Toback's public comments of a connection between Gatsby and Bugsy. The apparent difficulty of turning
The Great Gatsby into a successful film deserves some discussion. At
first glance, *The Great Gatsby* appears readily accessible to the ambitions and inventions of a potential director or screenwriter. F. Scott
Fitzgerald's classic novel of the 1920s certainly has all of the elements
of the Hollywood romance: an unrequited love that barely touches the
horizon of attainment against all obstacles just before its inevitable
tragic end; a glamorous setting filled with colorful and interesting people; a brilliantly constructed narrative that converges directly with
America's rags-to-riches myth; violence, danger, and mystery, along-
with social, cultural, and class conflict. From the perspective of the
characteristics of classic Hollywood cinema, the novel also seems perfect. The characters are so classic – the mysterious, self-made hero
of low origins, the brutal and contemptible rich husband, the goddess
waiting to be rescued. And the mise-en-scene and plot are so formulaic –
parties, roadsters, Long Island mansions, gangsters and the under-
world, socialites and playboys, music and dance, Southern nostalgia.
With all of these elements, *The Great Gatsby* seems ready-made for
Hollywood's standard camera and system of continuity and illusion.

However, like Melville's *Moby Dick*, which John Huston made
into a film in 1956, *The Great Gatsby* ultimately has overwhelmed
Hollywood. Both are about ideas and abstract constructions of identity.
They are metaphors for the American experience and American identity, extended symbolic renderings of a national state of mind and way

of being. As such they defy easy visualization and demonstrate the potential difficulty of transforming the literary and linguistic into a popular visual form. They suggest the conflict proposed by Jean-Luc Godard and Peter Wollen between the literary and painterly traditions in cinema.[11] The continuing commitment of much of Hollywood cinema to formulaic realism, referentiality, and clear causality countermands the demands of *The Great Gatsby* to contrive visual metaphors and scopic strategies for representing the complexity of the novel's literary and cultural symbolism. Ingmar Bergman's visual metaphors, such as his personification of death in *The Seventh Seal* (1957) or Luis Buñuel's subjective moods and fantasy in *Belle de Jour* (1967), remain foreign to the thinking of some in Hollywood who still rely largely upon narrative and the illusion of realism for thematic complexity.

In contrast to such visual metaphors, the melodrama of the Gatsby–Daisy relationship would seem to be easily adaptable to Hollywood-style film. However, in the novel, the metaphoric complexity that conveys Gatsby's character incorporates the psychological and sexual implications as well as the social and cultural conditions of his relationship with Daisy. This literary complexity resists the tendency in much of Hollywood to trivialize the ambiguous and ineffable into romantic melodrama.

Some novels, of course, lend themselves more easily to becoming popular films and seem more amenable to the adaptation process involved in transforming literary works into cinetexts of visual image, sound, music, writing, mise-en-scene. In contrast to the symbolism and metaphor of *The Great Gatsby*, the rich surface texture and detail of Edith Wharton's *Age of Innocence* (1920) provided a fertile field for film adaptation for Martin Scorsese. Temporarily leaving his mean streets culture for the meanness of the upper class, Scorsese makes his film of the *Age of Innocence* (1993) into a semiotic orgy of visual signs of elite social life and activity. Wharton, of course, describes the existence of New York's well-born in terms of a "hieroglyphic world," a system of visible signs that codifies and organizes experience based upon external representation as opposed to emphasizing hidden interior meaning.[12] Scorsese turns this extraordinary density of protective detail into a visual articulation of manners that functions literally as a psychic screen of desire. His dynamic, moving camera goes from intimate close-ups to tracking shots and long shots to document with realistic exactitude the minutiae of his understanding of how the rich of

New York lived and functioned during the Victorian age. Whether portraying the setting of a table, the costume of an evening's entertainment, or exhibiting the decoration of a home, the extensive range of external details forms a visual surface that becomes a visual language connecting feeling with experience. This language intensifies desire throughout the film by suggesting displacement as opposed to fulfillment and satisfaction. Interestingly, Scorsese's work in this film remains consistent with his efforts in other films to balance and synthesize realistic detail and documentary exactitude with visual and cinematic abstraction, as in the opening long take of *Raging Bull* (1980) or scenes in *The Last Temptation of Christ* (1988) that strive to suggest the mystery and wonder of Jesus.

Similarly, Toback thinks of *Bugsy* in personal terms as a project that related directly to his processes of creativity, processes that enabled him to connect deep feelings and emotions to very concrete elements of film production. He says, "*Bugsy* lived in my consciousness and my system. I had written him, however belatedly, from the inside out, and no one could direct my vision, my script, except me" (*Bugsy* 10). Other comments by both Toback and Levinson about the production of the film confirm their concentration upon the specific elements of narration, plot, and character as opposed to abstractions regarding culture and society, interests that might tend to characterize more intellectual, self-reflexive or self-conscious creators such as Godard, Cocteau, Bergman, or Woody Allen. Toback writes:

> Over a four month preproduction period, I wrote seven new drafts and then rewrote and invented new lines, moments and scenes daily during the three months of shooting. Characters who had seemed integral were banished into oblivion; the opening section, in New York (before Bugsy comes to Hollywood and then dreams up Las Vegas), was radically condensed. Connections between personality and fate, humor and tragedy, romance and death, were heightened and refined. There was a wonderful edge of anticipation every day, an intuition that each revision was moving us into an ever darker, wilder, funnier world. (*Bugsy* 10)

Levinson's comments about the film are consistent with Toback's in that his major concerns involve his feelings about the project and production details as opposed to abstract ideas. Levinson expressed special doubts about directing a so-called "romantic" film. "With *Bugsy*, what intrigued me was that I had never done anything termed 'romantic,' and I wasn't sure that I could make it work, that I wouldn't fall on my face trying to do it" (*Levinson* 124). At the same time, he realized his debt to both Toback and Beatty for all the effort that had gone into planning for the film.

> Both Toback and Beatty had done a lot of research during all those years they had spent on it, so what I tried to do was pick up on some details and say, "Hey, what if I was to do this?" You can't be faithful to every date and place and all the events that took place. We collapsed the whole story into a much shorter time frame, because otherwise the film would have spanned ten or fifteen years, and that didn't suit what we wanted to do. (*Levinson* 125)

For Toback, the final product validated what he says Beatty calls "The Third Intelligence Theory of Moviemaking" (*Bugsy* 9) that requires the involvement of at least three people for a production, thereby supposedly assuring a true synthesis of efforts rather than the domination of any one individual (*Bugsy* 11). According to Toback, something of a mystical symbiosis of creative efforts occurred to commingle the work of all three men to produce a great success.

The film opens with a sequence of shots that demonstrates classic Hollywood continuity and ideology in combination with an equally classic ideology of masculine domination. The opening narrative reflects Bugsy's point of view and establishes him at the center of the film. It also proceeds systematically and clearly in a continuous and coherent way of providing immediate facts about the character and story. We get a continuity of various exposures of Bugsy's life – family, murder, romance, sexual adventurism. These shots provide a prolegomenon to his character and to the film. Rapid and clear cuts propel the story line forward and brilliantly establish character and setting.

At the same time, subtly immersed within the visual texture of these opening shots are some suggestive images that later will resonate through the film with rich cultural meaning. These images constitute a parallel narrative and ideological structure for the film, one that initially exists as relatively distinct from the main thrust of the film during its early moments. This second pattern forms a visual and cinematic articulation of cultural and historical meanings that can be found in one of American culture's most pervasive myths – the Gatsby myth of rebirth based on the most corrupt and commercial foundations of American enterprise.

Accordingly, the main impulse of the film clearly reflects the attempt to construct Bugsy's story along classic Hollywood lines, while the second movement dramatizes a constellation of mythic and ideological

Figure 8. Annette Bening and Warren Beatty as Virginia Hill and "Bugsy" Siegel first engage each other in a world of images, violence, sexuality, desire, and renewel on the set of "Manpower" in *Bugsy*. (Museum of Modern Art/Film still Archives)

notions and values to be found throughout American history and culture. Both strains, the classic Hollywood masculinist style and the Gatsby ideology of desire and renewal, soon merge, thereby succeeding in making the film an original contribution to the American ideology of regeneration and consensus. In other words, the Beatty–Levinson–Toback enterprise begins clearly and certainly with Bugsy, but from the very opening it introduces a kind of countertheme of Gatsby-like notions until both the Bugsy and Gatsby lines of narrative and ideology converge into an impressive, ambitious, and successful cinematic achievement.

In a matter of just a few opening moments of the film, we see Bugsy leave a picture-perfect family in suburban Scarsdale, enter a major city hotel, pick-up and seduce a younger woman in an exciting interlude, and murder a man in cold blood as part of a spectacle to impress and intimidate others who might want to cheat him and his associates. In effect, this part of the opening sequence informs the viewer of *Bugsy*'s place within the genre of the gangster film, while also signaling through its interesting editing, cinematography, and narration a serious, creative intelligence involved in the film's direction and presentation. This opening sequence offers dramatically contrasting shots that sustain the dynamic vision of the story and demand the spectator's attention and involvement.

In this opening, Levinson demonstrates a sophisticated cinematic and directorial language that conveys through the cinetext of sight and sound the information and emotion that a writer such as Fitzgerald presents through the written word. This opening proffers a pattern and flow of shots and editing that move from openness and an expansive feeling of security and comfort to ever more restricted and confined spaces of secrecy, intimidation, and fear. In the opening long shot of Bugsy's Scarsdale home, the branches of a tree neatly frame the children and their mother sending Bugsy off to work in the city, almost a Currier and Ives cliché of suburban comfort and complacency. This spacious feeling of rustic reassurance contrasts powerfully with the confined spaces of the hotel and the elevator where the pick-up occurs. The shots progress from the openness of the suburbs to the interior spaces of the hotel, culminating in a series of sexual and violent climaxes, the first in the subsequent love-making scene when we hear but do not see Bugsy and his pick-up. "Is it hurting?" Bugsy asks, interrupting the woman's moans. Not seeing the lovers but only hearing them contributes to the sense of secrecy and danger.

The second critical point in the opening sequence involves the execution scene in which Bugsy kills a man who had been stealing from him, Meyer Lansky, and Charles Luciano. In showing this killing, Levinson's camera follows Bugsy into the steamy interior spaces of a dry cleaning establishment that provides a cover for a bookmaking parlor. The movement from openness to the tangible intensity of illicit love and then murder stops suddenly when the camera shows the actual shooting behind the glass of an inner office while others in the bookmaking parlor observe the shooting. Thus, the camera punctuates the visual movement from openness to enclosure with a slight countermovement of detachment to display and emphasize Bugsy's volatile and unpredictable character and behavior. On the level of action, the film's opening sequence represents classic Hollywood.

At the same time, ensconced within this compelling opening are some elements that do not intrude upon the visual and narrative drama but promise the potential for meaningful development of character and theme along the lines of the Gatsby myth and ideology. The film immediately plants the seeds for cultural themes that exceed the usual expectations and boundaries of the classic gangster genre. Parallel to the film's vision of Siegel the historic gangster-killer, *Bugsy* also develops Siegel the Gatsby-like figure of transcendent vision and renewal. Without drastically upsetting classic Hollywood transparency and illusion, Levinson incorporates this Gatsby pattern and theme in the film, demonstrating ingenuity in creating a cohesion of cinematic form and style with cultural and historic ideology.

As an example of such cinematic innovation, in a Gatsby-like gesture toward self-improvement, Bugsy repeatedly utters a phrase from a book on proper speech:

> In order to speak properly one must enunciate every syllable correctly: Twenty dwarves took turns doing handstands on the carpet...Twenty dwarves took turns doing handstands on the carpet (*Bugsy* 14).

As Bugsy repeats these lines in transit from his Scarsdale home to his business as a gangster and killer, the camera shows his Cadillac in the distance on Henry Hudson Parkway moving past a lake. The combination of the view of a snow-covered suburb and the lake, the repetition of the dwarves phrase in a strained voiceover, and the rapidly unfolding sequence of shots quickly creates a tension not yet totally explained by the story itself at this point. However, Bugsy's drive for self-improvement and domestic security in the face of a life of absolute ruthlessness portends serious tensions and conflicts. As Levinson says:

> Now Bugsy was trying to invent himself, and dissociate himself from his background. He did work periodically on his elocution to that end. So we opened the film with him practising this phrase...(*Levinson* 125).

Another early insertion of a Gatsby theme concerns something that appears prominently on the screen but does not occur in Toback's written screenplay – the shirts display. Even the most uninvolved undergraduate in a modern American novel class probably will recall the much discussed significance of the famous shirt scene in *The Great Gatsby* when Daisy Buchanan's emotions find their external outlet in her response to all of the expensive shirts that Gatsby has bought during the years of their separation. Signs of wealth and success to impress Daisy, the shirts embody the ostentatious commodification of American identity in an age of conspicuous consumption. Fitzgerald describes their reunion in Gatsby's Long Island mansion:

> Recovering himself in a minute he opened for us two hulking patent cabinets which held his massed suits and dressing-gowns and ties, and his shirts, piled like bricks in stacks a dozen high.
> "I've got a man in England who buys me clothes. He sends over a selection of things at the beginning of each season, spring and fall."[13]

Daisy responds:

> "They're such beautiful shirts...It makes me sad because I've never seen such – such beautiful shirts before" (*Gatsby* 93–94).

During the opening shots of the film, the camera emphasizes Bugsy checking over and then purchasing an elaborate display of beautiful shirts and ties from an expensive store. Beatty uses the shirts as a prop that complicates both characterization and action during the scene when he kills the bookie. The shirts, therefore, carry complex connotations. In combination with the elocution program for personal improvement, the shirts concretely suggest the danger involved in Bugsy's Gatsbyish passion for what Levinson calls reinvention.

Furthermore, during these opening moments, the film also reveals a complex aspect of Bugsy's character as a dreamer and believer. While waiting for Bugsy to conclude the execution of the bookie, his childhood friend and current mob associate, Meyer Lansky, played brilliantly by Ben Kingsley, tells Luciano: "The way I see it, Charlie, Ben has only one problem . . . the same problem he's had since we were all kids together stickin' up crap games on the street – he doesn't respect money" (*Bugsy* 22). This early speech anticipates Meyer's later explanation to the mob of Bugsy's actions when he repeats to Luciano and others: "He's always had one basic problem. He doesn't *respect money*. The truth is he's not even *interested* in money for himself off this deal: he's interested in the *idea*" (*Bugsy* 191). In the earlier scene, Luciano responds by wanting to take a nap, while at the end of the movie, the assembled gangsters are merely contemptuous. "*What* idea?" asks Joey A. and Meyer answers: "The idea of building something. Making something. Benny's a dreamer" (*Bugsy* 191). The continued "skepticism" and "cynical contempt" of the group emphasize the contrast between the money-driven gangsters and Bugsy's passion for new opportunities for self-invention. What Meyer terms Bugsy's "idea" and quality as a dreamer compares to the distinction Gatsby makes between his love for Daisy and her husband's love. Referring to Tom's attitude, Gatsby says, "In any case . . . it was just personal" (*Gatsby* 152), suggesting, of course, that his transcendent love for Daisy supersedes mere personal concerns. Like Bugsy, Gatsy has a sense of mission.

In spite of these examples of Gatsby-like enthusiasm at the opening of *Bugsy*, the two narrative and ideological threads really do not merge completely into one integrated film until Virginia Hill enters the action, immediately becoming a focal point for merging all of the elements of the film, just as Daisy serves as the emotional and psychological center for Gatsby and his story. Most important from the perspective of cinematic aesthetics, Levinson bridges the Bugsy and Gatsby themes by using the strengths of the multisemiotic nature of film as opposed to merely imposing a contrived concoction of literary, symbolic, and cultural ideas upon the cinematic material. By the time Virginia Hill appears in the film, Levinson already had established his narrative and cinematic perspective, so he was able to fuse together neatly and coherently both the Bugsy and the Gatsby movements. Interestingly, this blending often occurs in scenes of cinematic self-reflexivity.

In Bening's and Beatty's first scene together, Levinson reconstructed the setting on the Warner Brothers lot of a 1941 film, *Manpower*, which starred George Raft and Marlene Dietrich. On the lot visiting Raft (Joe Mantegna), Bugsy meets Virginia. Apparently Levinson intuited rather than intellectualized the need to evoke a special atmosphere for the meeting of the two lovers that would set up the drama and anticipate the explosiveness of their relationship. Levinson recalls:

> For the big scene on the sound stage where Virginia Hill meets Bugsy for the first time and says to him, "Why don't you go outside and jerk yourself a soda?" I said to the production designer Dennis Gassner, "This conversation has a real spin to it but the setting seems boring." As I saw it, he wants to be a movie star, and neither of them ever became that.... As we were running a tape of the movie, at the end there is a scene on a hill by a gas station, and I put the image on freeze and said, "Dennis, look at this. Let's take the gas station on the hill, and everybody would be going over it to get to their dressing rooms. She would be going in that direction, Bugsy would stop her, and then we can play the scene on the movie set." Playing it against that fake world would be like giving them a glamorous surrounding which they're not actually part of. It would give it a little bit of an edge. And this was early on in the discussions. Sometimes you have a set which you know will be there, and you'll find something in the shooting of it that will add to a scene (*Levinson* 132).

Levinson's comments here are fascinating and deserve some discussion. As he recalls the situation, he merely wanted to avoid being "boring." After almost inadvertently catching an unusual moment with the couple on a hill, Levinson froze the image and found "something" through a second look "like...a glamorous surrounding" that gave Beatty and Bening and the scene "a little bit of an edge." Ironically, while Levinson apparently saw this scene primarily in technical terms of its effect, the scene can be interpreted as visually and critically indispensable to the ultimate meaning and importance of the film. What transpires in this scene involves more than the building of a romantic mise-en-scene with an "edge."

Rather, in the context of the film's development, Levinson in this scene constructs a world of the imaginary that fuses desire and ideology.

The internal, psychological drive for transcendence beyond traditional self-identity and the American ideology of the possibility for regeneration begin to merge here in the scene between Bugsy and Virginia. Elsewhere, I have tried to show how in *The Great Gatsby* desire in the form of the ego's impossible wish for total happiness and security along with the search for a society of unity and consensus help explain Gatsby and the novel.[14] Similarly, Bugsy and Virginia emerge anew in this cinematic environment in which internal psychological and external cultural and ideological forces converge for individual renewal. Bugsy and Virginia create their own world and lives.

The scene is constructed in two parts. First, we have the *Manpower* set, current Hollywood's depiction of an earlier world of artificial images, and we realize Virginia's innocuous part in it as the receiving end of a prop from Raft (Mantegna). Thus, just as Bugsy was introduced to us in terms of language as a sign of renewal through his repetition of lines for improved pronunciation, Virginia's first words in her scene with Raft are about speech and convey her powerlessness as a woman in *Manpower*, as she complains almost pathetically about having no lines, no voice. "I think I need a line here" (*Bugsy* 36) she says to no one in particular but a faceless camera and an unresponsive director and actor. Like Bugsy, she still needs to find a new voice and identity. Virginia and Bugsy meet each other here at a time in their lives when they both already have nationwide reputations, in a sense scripts that define them and speak for them. Together they must learn to write new scripts for each other.

Virginia's frustration and isolation infuse the second part of the scene with desire and the quest for fulfillment. The camera isolates them on a pretend hill on the set in a two shot with a bluish gray background of a fake sky. The set visually and psychologically presents an external representation of their inner, private world of the imagination. They begin to recreate and transform each other. Here we are not far from Gatsby's memory of his evening with Daisy when:

> They stopped here and turned toward each other. Now it was a cool night with that mysterious excitement in it which comes at the two changes of the year.... Out of the corner of his eye Gatsby saw that the blocks of the sidewalk really formed a ladder and mounted to a secret place above the trees – he could climb to it, if he climbed alone, and once there he could suck on the pap of life, gulp down the incomparable milk of wonder. (*Gatsby* 112)

In *Bugsy*, music, image, and acting on the set convey an imaginary mise-en-scene of desire to initiate a similar metamorphosis.

Figure 9. Annette Bening and Warren Beatty with director Barry Levinson and producer Mark Johnson discuss how to film Beatty's transforming moment of envisioning a new paradise for American dreamers on the desert of Nevada. (Museum of Modern Art/Film Still Archives)

In another scene, the screen again becomes a realm for the imaginary relationship of the self and desire. This occurs when Virginia arrives at Bugsy's house while he has been observing his screen test on his home projector. With only the living room light on in the house, the projection light beaming forth on Bugsy's screen, and a powerfully evocative soundtrack playing ever more erotically, Levinson creates a world of what could be termed the "imaginary signifier."[15] The scene expresses again an inner state of Bugsy's desire that Virginia will share with him. As "Light flickers on the blank screen" (*Bugsy* 70), Bugsy and Virginia form a silhouette, and the visual space on the screen becomes a mental world they simultaneously inhabit and embody. Virginia's warning to Bugsy about the danger they are for each other sums up the theme of desire. He asks, "Why would we have to bring each other misery and torment?" She answers, "Because we both want to get whatever we want whenever we want it and we both want everything" (*Bugsy* 71).

In yet another scene, Levinson moves from cinematic realism to the psychological intensity of the imaginary. Following a vicious fight between Bugsy and Virginia concerning Bugsy's jealousy over Virginia's promiscuous past, she waits alone in the hallway for him to complete a

brutal verbal and psychological assault on a Los Angeles gangster who
has robbed him. The camera alternates between Bugsy's room with the
gangster and the growing intensity of Virginia's reaction to the violence. Just as the fight between Bugsy and Virginia greatens anxiety,
so the pattern of shots and sound in this scene creates extraordinary
intensity as we move from hearing and watching Bugsy to hearing and
watching Bugsy through Virginia's visible reaction. The movement of
the camera and the music again generate great excitement. Moreover,
the power of Bugsy's speech surpasses mere brutal assertion. Bugsy
screams hysterically at the gangster, "Did you think you would get
away with it or not? Did you or not? Did you or not?" (*Bugsy* 89) The
tempo and sound of his speech convey not simply sheer power and
intimidation but, in fact, the cadences of a mother screaming angrily
at a child. The man's childlike plea, "I'll never do it again. I promise"
(*Bugsy* 89) adds to the sense of parental assault. Bugsy also injects
a sexual charge with unconscious implications into the fight with an
obscene and superficially nonsensical comment and comparison: "You
stole from me. Stealing is a form of rape. You wanted to rape me and
humiliate me!" (*Bugsy* 88) Referring to himself as the feminine object
of sexual assault evokes a horror and disgust that at the same time
accentuate the maternal threat in his voice and speech.

In the aftermath of her fight with Bugsy, Virginia becomes consumed
by Bugsy's sadistic attack on the man. Overhearing Bugsy's assault
and the gangster's begging, her face and her look as she listens express the situation she now enacts of female masochism. Her face and
look suggest a woman's masochistic sexualization of aggression as described by Freud in such works as "A Child is Being Beaten."[16] The
intense love-making that culminates the scene confirms her sexual reaction to his violence and brutality. The scene also epitomizes the psychological turmoil and sexual struggle at the core of their relationship.

The psychological intensity of their desire fuels Bugsy's faith in his
powers of renewal. Gatsby, of course, establishes the modern model for
the myth of renewal and regeneration. He says to Carraway, the novel's
narrator, "Can't repeat the past? . . . Why of course you can!" (*Gatsby*
111) Bugsy's version of that theme involves his repetition throughout
the film that everyone deserves the opportunity for "fresh starts." He
insists to George Raft that even Virginia can change: "I don't go by
what other people have done. I believe in fresh starts" (*Bugsy* 81).
Bugsy puts this belief in historical and cultural context by referring

to his Jewish origins on the streets and recalling at times the fate of European Jewry. He says, "Hey, without fresh starts, you and I would have been history before we were nineteen" (*Bugsy* 82).

Accordingly, Bugsy's language for his vision of "The Flamingo" casino in Las Vegas exceeds idealism to the point of approaching religious faith. Conceived in his mind in a kind of epiphany while seeking a spot in the desert to urinate, Bugsy's idea of an Eden of gambling rests like Gatsby's upon an understanding of the depths of human corruption and a faith in the power to transform evil into a transcendent experience of redemption. Seeing America itself as a kind of gamble and trying to sell Lansky on his idea for the casino, he argues that "The Flamingo" will give new meaning to "the word *transcendent*!" He says, "I found the answer to the dreams of America." His dreams, of course, mean "building a monument" to "sex, romance, money, and adventure" (*Bugsy* 116).

Although the ultimate moral implications of his utopian vision remain ambiguous, the depth and fanaticism of his faith repeat Gatsby's insistence upon justifying and maintaining the value and validity of his dream through his own sacrifice.

Thus, both the novel and film play with the theme of "nothing" to dramatize Gatsby's and Bugsy's existential devotion, while at the same time continuing to question the true significance of their dreams. At the end of the film, Meyer reminds Bugsy that because of the financial difficulties of their project and the extent of Bugsy's financial commitment to it, "You'll end up with nothing. After all this . . . Nothing" (*Bugsy* 181). Like Gatsby, who at one point watches "over nothing" on his quixotic "vigil" (*Gatsby* 146) to protect Daisy, Bugsy also protests the disbelief of others: "But the Flamingo will be there. That's not nothing" (*Bugsy* 181).

Considering how Bugsy has used Virginia's nickname for his hotel, his reference to the Flamingo being there compares to how in *The Great Gatsby* the vision of Daisy, the symbolism of the "green light," and the myth of the Garden of America all become one. For both Gatsby and Bugsy "nothing" means the power of the idea and vision over the material. For each as well, the quest for transcendence suggests deep guilt over their own evil. Thus, Gatsby looks like a murderer (*Gatsby* 44), while Bugsy looks guilty throughout the film as the man who tries to be all things to all people, as when he fails to make his children happy, and when he must finally admit his wish for a divorce to be with Virginia.

In *The Great Gatsby* vision as ideal and as image, as utopian hope and as advertising sign represents moral and cultural complexity and ambiguity. As a work of cinematic vision, *Bugsy* also continually demonstrates the interaction between image and ideal, nowhere more importantly than in the film's transformation of Virginia into a woman of substance and character. As Lansky notices, Virginia becomes a woman of power and responsibility. After making a mistake of stealing from Bugsy, she overcomes great fear and resolves to fly with Bugsy as a sign of her love. In contrast to Daisy, who never really exists for Gatsby outside of his imagination, Virginia gains independence, making her a figure for our own times and fulfilling the cultural and spiritual implications of her name. In transforming Virginia, the female object of male desire, ambition, and idealism, into a being of power and feeling, *Bugsy* helps reinvent the Gatbsy myth for new meaning in a new century. By implanting the Gatsby myth of regeneration in a Jewish gangster and a sexually liberated woman, *Bugsy* assumes the myth and ideology of America can continue to thrive through the inclusion of outsiders. A Jew and his mistress seek redemption in the American idea, envisioning America as a modern paradise transported to and blossoming in the deserts of the West, still offering boundless hope but to a different kind of tired and restless freedom seeker.

Dealing with race and politics in *Bulworth* (1998), Beatty continues to suggest the potential for reembodying the American idea in minorities and outsiders. However, in the next chapter, a work by Saul Bellow suggests the endless quest for renewal and success can turn the body into a prison and sign of inner pain, thereby creating a nightmare for any potential director and actor hoping to find ways to visualize such complex ideas.

CHAPTER SIX

IMAGING MASOCHISM AND THE POLITICS OF PAIN

"Facing" the Word in the Cinetext of *Seize the Day*

The image of Saint Sebastian as painted by Mantegna graces the cover of Kaja Silverman's *Male Subjectivity at the Margins*, an important and original study of masochism's power to complicate and multiply representations of masculinity in cinema, literature, and society. Bloodied arrows pierce his tormented body. His eyes and face appeal to heaven. This search for love and recognition from an invisible but omniscient deity suggests his pleasure in pain and suffering. So passive to physical abuse and so eager for fatherly approbation, the Saint does not advance any traditional model of manly aggression or power. In fact, some could see in his exposed state a reembodiment of the American male that differs considerably from our discussion so far, an alternative figure of impotence who finds only sacrifice and humiliation on the road toward redemption and regeneration.

Significantly, the painting of Saint Sebastian on the cover of Silverman's *Male Subjectivity* personifies the mental state and character of Tommy Wilhelm, the miserably masochistic protagonist in Saul Bellow's *Seize the Day*. Moreover, Silverman's study of masochism and multiple masculinities in film and literature provides a useful model for analyzing both the literary text and the significance of turning Bellow's brief novel into the visual form of film. In *Seize the Day*, moving from the written word to the specular text of its cinematic version starring Robin Williams sheds light upon the politics of masochism and pain as delineated by Bellow and as espoused by Silverman. While Bellow gives us a character type for the post–World War II era, Silverman presents a program for individual psychological and collective social change. Released in 1986, three decades after the novel's publication, the film, as Gerhard Bach suggests, puts a visible face on Tommy's problems.[1] However, this attempt by director Fielder Cook and screenwriter Ronald Ribman to visualize Tommy's weakness and limitations suggests difficulties in reconstructing masculinity. Turning *Seize the Day* into a film examines the consequences of visualizing masculinity as a form of male subjectivity in film and theory.

Tommy's moral masochism has been analyzed by Daniel Weiss, who transforms the novel into a case history of classic Freudian masochism and neurosis. Weiss writes, "The broadest psychoanalytic category within which Tommy Wilhelm operates is that of the moral masochist, the victim, for whom suffering is a *modus vivendi*, a means of self-justification."[2] Weiss reconstructs Tommy's psyche as a moral masochist:

> The ultimate sacrifice of the moral masochist to the love object accounts for his greatest paradox, his perverse refusal to "please" the parent in any rational sense of the word. The masochist identifies himself with the hating love object. He turns against himself, not his own sadism but the sadism of the parent. His guilt becomes the guilt the hating parent should feel if his cruelties are unjust.
>
> Since the parent cannot be wrong, the child must then feel guilty for him. He must be the bad child who deserves such chastisement.[3]

In *Male Subjectivity at the Margins*, Silverman incorporates moral masochism into her theory of male subjectivity and marginality that builds upon Lacan's transformation of Freud's original paradigm of the individual in culture. In Silverman's theory of masculinity and gender, Freud's dynamic interactive agencies of id, ego, and superego become a Lacanian semiotic and psychoanalytic construction of the self. She emphasizes the relationship of the subjective "I" of nothingness and potentiality to the socially constructed "moi" of the imaginary and fantasy. For Silverman all objects of vision appear to the subject on a screen of cultural and historical context. In addition, Freud, of course, emphasizes the determining influence of the "primal scene" of parental sexuality as well as the structuring of sexuality and psychic development through the resolution of the Oedipal and castration complexes. In contrast, for Lacan as Silverman interprets him, more attention needs to be given to the specular basis of sexuality and identity in which the mirror stage and body image initiate the subject's self-reflection as the psychic foundation of all sexuality. The alignment of what Silverman calls the subject's unconscious fantasy of desire with its body ego and self-image helps to form the subject's identity and position within the cultural and ideological order.[4]

Moreover, the concentration in Freud upon the psychological implications of biological differences evolves into Silverman's emphasis upon the merger of specularity with castration, difference, otherness. Maintaining that subjects are constructed within specularity as well as being determined by biological and psychological forces, Silverman distinguishes between the look and the gaze in cinema, describing the look as a visual statement of desire and absence and the gaze as a kind of transcendent visual moment of self-recognition comparable to the formation of the linguistic "moi" or self-image. The interaction between the look and gaze engenders a visual or specular text for the relationship of specularity and subjectivity. In addition, for Silverman specularity structures and signifies the psychic organization of masochism. The relationship of specularity and masochism, which will be discussed later, provides the foundation for gender reconstruction and cultural transformation *(MSM* 1–12).

The focus throughout *Seize the Day* upon vision, appearance, spectacle, acting, and self-image suggests the novel's relevance to Silverman's thesis concerning the significance of specularity to the construction of male subjectivity. Indeed, from the very first line of the novel, Bellow establishes the connection between external appearance and Tommy Wilhelm's masochistic interior psyche as mediated by his desire to be an actor – to present a contrived performance of the self to the world.

> When it came to concealing his troubles, Tommy Wilhelm was not less capable than the next fellow. So at least he thought, and there was a certain amount of evidence to back him up. He had once been an actor – no, not quite, an extra – and he knew what acting should be.[5]

This opening line should be taken ironically, as Tommy himself later realizes *(SD* 14). The psychology behind the statement contradicts its apparent meaning. Tommy yearns to reveal his deepest weaknesses and most intense emotions to all who can see. He dedicates himself to such self-exposure.

For Bellow the tension between appearance and inner feelings raises the issue of the construction of vision. He proposes that our understanding of what we see stems from psychic and cultural structures and predispositions. It concerns a semiotics of facial and physical gesture, as in acting, and it relates to an interior domain of ambivalence that has been occupied by psychoanalysis. Thus, Tommy describes the man at the newsstand in a way that complicates the meaning of vision.

> Rubin, the man at the newsstand, had poor eyes. They may not have been actually weak but they were poor in expression, with lacy lids that furled down at the corners. He dressed well. It didn't seem necessary – he was behind the counter most of the time – but he dressed very well. (*SD* 5)

"Poor eyes" problematizes the notion of vision. Bellow allows the idea of bad eyesight to remain by not totally refuting the usual meaning of "poor eyes" as suggesting bad vision. "They may not have been actually weak . . ." keeps the question of eyesight open and emphasizes the psychological and social complexity of vision. The man "behind the counter" dresses "well" but remains partially hidden. Who sees, who cares, Bellow seems to ask.

Bellow immediately compounds the complexity regarding vision by adding a sexual dimension to what and how we see. Rubin comments on Tommy's shirt: "That's a real knocked-out shirt you got on. Where's it from, Saks?" Tommy answers, "No, it's a Jack Fagman – Chicago" (*SD* 5). This remark instantly impugns the structure and direction of Tommy's sexuality. The shirt and the statement by Tommy function as signs of unconscious ambiguity and incoherence.

After this exchange, Bellow articulates how Tommy sees himself. Besides exhibiting Tommy's insecurity and split psyche, Bellow's style here also warrants special attention because of its cinematic quality. He describes a kind of interior camera in Tommy's mind, an internal mirror that anticipates contemporary criticism's fascination with the look and the gaze, specularity and psyche. His self-consciousness compares to the gaze of otherness that goes beyond a singular look.

> Even when his spirits were low, Wilhelm could still wrinkle his forehead in a pleasing way. Some of the slow, silent movements of his face were very attractive. He went back a step, as if to stand away from himself and get a better look at his shirt. His glance was comic, a comment upon his untidiness. He liked to wear good clothes, but once he had put it on each article appeared to go its own way. Wilhelm, laughing, panted a little; his teeth were small; his cheeks when he laughed and puffed grew round, and he looked much younger than his years. In the old days when he was a college freshman and wore a racoon coat and a beanie on his large blond head his father used to say that, big as he was, he could charm a bird out of a tree. Wilhelm had great charm still. (*SD* 5–6)

The visionary process embedded in Wilhelm's mind in this paragraph dramatizes Silverman's elucidation of the look and gaze in

Male Subjectivity at the Margins. She also points to the sexual complexity of vision. Silverman writes:

> [W]e are all dependent for our identity upon the "clicking" of an imaginary camera. This metaphoric apparatus is what Lacan calls the "gaze." The gaze does not "photo-graph" the subject directly, but only through the mediation of the screen, i.e., through the repertoire of culturally intelligible images. Unfortunately, all such images are ideologically marked in some way; at the very least, they are carriers of sexual and racial difference, but they also project values of class, age, and nationality onto those who are seen through them. (*MSM* 353)

Freud's connection of the body ego to the psychic ego, as Silverman sees it, finds confirmation in how Tommy regards himself. Silverman writes "the ego is for Freud 'first and foremost a bodily ego' – or, as [James] Strachey explains in an authorized gloss, 'derived from bodily sensations, chiefly from those springing from the surface of the body'" (*MSM* 188). In *Seize the Day*, Tommy's bodily ego, his sense of his body and its relation to his identity, opposes his rational awareness of his potential. He sees his body through a psyche of masochistic self-hatred. After Rubin tells him, "Well, y'lookin' pretty sharp today." Tommy greedily grabs at the compliment: "And Wilhelm said gladly, "Am I? Do you really think so?" (*SD* 6)

However, Wilhelm cannot acquiesce to such a favorable view of himself. Looking at "his reflection in the glass cupboard full of cigar boxes, among the grand seals and paper damask and the gold-embossed portraits of famous men," he really sees himself as another object on display like the brand name cigars. "You had to allow for the darkness and deformations of the glass, but he thought he didn't look too good" (*SD* 6). Of course, he really sees the accumulated images of how he has seen himself in the past, usually as a groteseque animal-type figure such as a hippopotamus or as a "big clunk" (*SD* 6, 15, 29):

> He began to be half amused at the shadow of his own marveling, troubled, desirous eyes, and his nostrils and his lips. Fair-haired hippopotamus! – that was how he looked to himself. He saw a big round face, a wide, flourishing red mouth, stump teeth. And the hat, too; and the cigar, too. I should have done hard labor all my life, he reflected. Hard honest labor that tires you out and makes you sleep. I'd have worked off my energy and felt better. Instead, I had to distinguish myself – yet. (*SD* 6–7)

Reflecting in his mind on the reflection in the glass, he condemns himself to hard labor for how he looks and what he has done with his appearance. Interestingly, he contextualizes this inner vision of himself in terms of Hollywood images, thereby conflating, as Silverman suggests, both the external social image and interior psychic images.

> And if as a young man he had got off to a bad start, it was due to this very same face. Early in the nineteen-thirties, because of his striking looks, he had been very briefly considered star material, and he had gone to Hollywood. There for seven years, stubbornly, he had tried to become a screen artist. (*MSM* 7)

We soon learn, of course, that this Hollywood opportunity really grew out of a scam, and that even during this episode he was condemned as a failure who loses the girl to real stars. "Why, he thought, he cast me even then for a loser" (*SD* 21).

In the beginning of the novel, Wilky anticipates meeting his father, a successful and wealthy retired doctor, in the dining room of the New York City hotel where they both live in separate quarters. Dreading the encounter but punishing himself further through procrastination, he mentally reenacts his miserable situation. Realizing with masochistic relish that "His father was ashamed of him," Wilky also notes of him, "how we love looking fine in the eyes of the world – how beautiful are the old when they are doing a snow job!" (*SD* 13) Wilky's delayed entrance into the dining room to see his father gives spatial and temporal structure to the emotional chaos of the psychological distance between father and son.

> No wonder Wilhelm delayed the moment when he would have to go into the dining room. He had moved to the end of Rubin's counter. He had opened the *Tribune*; the fresh pages dropped from his hands; the cigar was smoked out and the hat did not defend him. He was wrong to suppose that he was more capable than the next fellow when it came to concealing his troubles. They were clearly written out upon his face. He wasn't even aware of it." (*SD* 14)

As the novel dramatizes the struggle in Wilky's mind, Bellow tightly entwines the relationship between his psychic anxiety and his presentation of himself to the world through his name. Significantly, for Wilky naming relates to his acting. Changing his name as an actor involves rebellion against his father whose punishing authority has been internalized within him as a relentless super-ego. Disowning the name of the father breaks the boundaries of the family and proposes maturity and independence. "In California he became Tommy Wilhelm. Dr. Adler would not accept the change. Today he still called his son Wilky, as he had done for more than forty years" (*SD* 24). Changing his name as part of an acting career literally presumes a new identity within a new environment. Wilky considers acting, name changing, and leaving home precisely this way as an act of manhood. "I was too mature for college. I was a big boy, you see. Well, I thought, when do you start to become a man?" (*SD* 15)

From a psychoanalytical point of view, the name change challenges the whole patriarchal order. The father's name involves the law-of-the-father, a linguistic fulfillment of the threat of castration. The law-of-the-father in the form of the father's name imposes the verbal sign of incorporation in the father's domain of authority. This authority provides the foundation for the meaning of all symbols of identity and authority. As Silverman notes, "Lacan also equates culture with the Name-of-the-Father." Quoting from Lacan's "The Function and Field of Speech and Language in Psychoanalysis" in *Ecrits*, Silverman writes: "It is in the *name of the father* that we must recognize the support of the symbolic function which, from the dawn of history, has identified his person with the figure of the law" (*MSM* 37). Silverman adds: "The Name-of-the-Father is also lived by the boy as the paternal legacy which will be his if he renounces the mother, and identifies with the father" (*MSM* 40).

Through this Oedipal process, the individual participates in the symbolic order of patriarchal ideology and power. Thus, by challenging the traditional order of the name-of-the-father, as Silverman suggests, one also subverts what she terms the "dominant fiction" of male and patriarchal authority in a way that questions the structure of society and inevitably also the nature of gender and sexuality (*MSM* 30, 34, 40, 41).

> Our dominant fiction calls upon the male subject to see himself, and the female subject to recognize and desire him, only through the mediation of images of an unimpaired masculinity. It urges both the male and the female subject, that is, to deny all knowledge of male castration by believing in the commensurability of penis and phallus, actual and symbolic father. (*MSM* 42)

Silverman further warns:

> [T]he dominant fiction not only offers the representational system by means of which the subject typically assumes a sexual identity, and takes on the desires commensurate with that identity, but forms the stable core around which a nation's and a period's "reality" coheres. (*MSM* 41)

In changing his name, Wilky begins a battle he cannot win, a war his own masochism foredooms to defeat. Changing his name merely reenforces his alienation from his father rather than asserting his own identity. Accordingly, Wilky finally goes to find his father in the dining room only after he has completed his own full course of psychic self-abuse by attacking himself, going down the entire menu of failures, guilts, and self-punishments until "he was nearly at the end of his rope." He spots "his father's small head in the sunny bay at the farther end, and heard his precise voice." Wilky then must walk a gauntlet of stares that elicits a visible awareness of his precarious situation. "It was with an odd sort of perilous expression that Wilhelm crossed the dining room" (SD 30).

Silverman's work suggests one possible insight into Wilky's "odd sort of perilous expression." The "perilous expression" transfers Tommy's psychic dismemberment to the look on his face, enacting an important principle in Silverman's Lacanian conception of castration. Using Lacan's shift in the definition of castration, Silverman emphasizes castration as a visual phenomenon. As Silverman says, Lacan's theory "repeatedly locates lack at the level of the eye, defining castration as the alterity of the gaze" (MSM 155). Tommy's expression as he crosses the dining room to his father makes a spectacle of his complicity in his impairment. It is in part a self-inflicted wound performed through the visualization of dismemberment. The expression reenforces the significance of symbolic castration in the novel. Thus, Tommy's wife's denial of his request to keep his beloved dog "Scissors" (SD 110), and the warnings of his surrogate father, Dr. Tamkin, about enjoying guilt all relate to Tommy's castration complex. Talking of Tommy's wife, Tamkin, a wonderful mixture of the comic and venal, says:

> "Why do you let her make you suffer so? It defeats the original object in leaving her. Don't play her game. Now, Wilhelm, I'm trying to do you some good. I want to tell you, don't marry suffering. Some people do. They get married to it, and sleep and eat together, just as husband and wife. If they go with joy they think it's adultery." (SD 98)

Tommy's walk through the dining room fulfills the association from the beginning of the novel of castration and external appearance, the connection between acting and the presentation to the world of a visible sign of the absence of manhood. Significantly, while Tommy saw acting as an attempt to achieve manhood, the novel repeatedly indicates that others' perception of him and perhaps even his own unconscious self-image really proffer homosexuality as his form of masculinity. Thus, we recall the peculiar reference by Tommy to his "Fagman" shirt. This epithet as a kind of badge of identity achieves greater significance in light of a later exchange between father and son. The father insinuates that perhaps Tommy was forced to leave a job because of a possible homosexual incident. Noting his son's obsession with his failures and perhaps intuiting an unconscious tension, the father says: "Since you have to talk and can't let it alone, tell the truth. Was there a scandal – a woman?" To which Wilhelm defends himself: "No, Dad, there wasn't any woman. I told you how it was." The father "wickedly" replies: "Maybe it was a man, then" (*SD* 51). The vigor of Tommy's immediate protest reveals an element of overcompensation:

> Shocked, Wilhelm stared at him with burning pallor and dry lips. His skin looked a little yellow. "I don't think you know what you're talking about," he answered after a moment. "You shouldn't let your imagination run so free. Since you've been living here on Broadway you must think you understand life, up to date. You ought to know your own son a little better. Let's drop that, now." (*SD* 51–52)

Moreover, homosexuality associates Tommy with a particular form of homosexuality of great interest to Silverman. Her study of marginalized male subjectivity relates homosexuality to moral masochism, the feminine, and the visualization of castration. Silverman argues that although Freud distinguishes between three forms of masochism – erotogenic or pleasure in pain, feminine, and moral – such distinctions immediately collapse. "However, no sooner are these distinctions enumerated than they begin to erode" (*MSM* 188). She argues that moral masochism and the feminine evolve into "homosexuality-as-feminine-corporeality" (*MSM* 348). Masochism and the feminine structure homosexuality as an alternative form of male subjectivity. "Implicit, then, in the notion of masochism, whether feminine or moral, would seem to be the experience of corporeal pleasure, or – to be more precise – corporeal pleasure-in-pain" (*MSM* 188).

Tommy exemplifies the character type Silverman describes. Even to some in the novel, he exists at some level of his psyche as a woman in the body of a man who wishes to be loved by the father rather than to identify with him. Indeed, Tommy's perennial groveling before his father for love and sympathy – "He was well aware that he didn't stand a chance of getting sympathy from his father, who said he kept his for real ailments" (*SD* 43) – relates to his unconscious conflicted identification with his mother and guilt over mixed and ambiguous feelings about her death. Thus, Tommy reminds his father about his mother's death with a sense of guilt he would like to share with him.

> "Wasn't it the year Mother died? What year was that?" He asked the question with an innocent frown on his Golden Grimes, dark blond face. *What year was it*! As though he didn't know the year, the month, the day, the very hour of his mother's death. (SD 27)

Put another way, Tommy's mental state compares to what Silverman terms as "this convergence of desire for the father and identification with his penetration of the mother" (*MSM* 173), a relationship analogous to Freud's classic case study of the Wolf Man whose neurosis derived from his "unconscious sexuality" (*MSM* 165) regarding his father. In trying to establish and then reinvent his identity as an actor, Tommy appears caught, as Silverman says, in "the possibility of assuming a subject-position at the intersection of the positive and the negative Oedipus complexes" (*MSM* 173). Trapped in the Oedipal dilemma between a positive relationship to his father that prohibits and represses the desire for the mother and a negative relationship that makes the father the object of desire so as to avoid the Oedipal attraction to the mother, Tommy founders in a regressive and nearly-infantile state that manifests itself in unclean and neurotic gestures. Thus, the doctor feels revulsion over what he sees as Wilky's "filth." "What a Wilky he had given to the world! Why, he didn't even wash his hands in the morning. . . . Wilhelm lived in worse filth than a savage" (SD 36–37). Wilky's incessant gestures are equally intolerable.

> But Dr. Adler was thinking, Why the devil can't he stand still when we're talking? He's either hoisting his pants up and down by the pockets or jittering with his feet. A regular mountain of tics, he's getting to be. (SD 28–29)

Also, the chaos of Tommy's sexual orientation and identification finds further confirmation in the way the book radically changes point-of-view and alters the subjective position and voice of the main characters. The book continually moves between Tommy's and his father's perspectives so that at the end of the novel, Tommy desperately strives to assert his subjective identity: "*I labor, I spend, I strive, I design, I love, I cling, I uphold, I give way, I envy, I long, I scorn, I die, I hide, I want*" (SD 115).

Bellow brilliantly brings together all of these highly complex and diverse elements of psychology, sexuality, and vision in a marvelously concrete and deceptively simple encounter between father and son that becomes the emotional and thematic climax of the novel. Tommy once again seeks out his father after he has lost all of his money in commodity market dealings engineered by the enigmatic Dr. Tamkin. Significantly, Tommy finds him in the massage room, a place of naked male bodies that emphasizes the key issue of sexuality, gender, and vision. "On the tables naked men were lying." The scene focuses on a man Tommy sees, "an athlete, strikingly muscled, powerful and young, with a strong white curve to his genital and a half-angry smile on his mouth" (*SD* 107–108). The "half-angry smile" and "genital" illustrate Silverman's fusion of the feminine and the masochist in the homosexual. Comparing in this "sexual territorialization of the body" (*MSM* 358), "the male mouth with the female genitals" (*SD* 10), Silverman argues that in this model "the homosexual subject does not so much flee from the mother as relocate her within himself" (*MSM* 372), a phrase that aptly describes Tommy and his latent attraction to the naked man.

Wilky's appearance before his father in the massage room dramatizes his sexually ambiguous relationship to him. At the level of spectacle, Tommy appears unnatural and abnormal to his father. "Dr. Adler opened his eyes into Wilhelm's face" (*SD* 108). The thrust of the sentence accentuates hostility and fear. "At once he saw the trouble in it, and by an instantaneous reflex he removed himself from the danger of contagion, and he said serenely, 'Well, have you taken my advice, Wilky?'" referring to his recommendation "To take a swim and get a massage." When Wilky appeals once again for help, the father reacts with horror. He says to his father "But one word from you, just a word, would go a long way. I've never asked you for very much. But you are not a kind man. You don't give the little bit I beg you for" (*SD* 109–110). The doctor responds viciously. In contrast to his son's masochism, he will not allow another person, not even his son, to become his cross. "You want to make yourself into my cross. But I am not going to pick up a cross. I'll see you dead, Wilky, by Christ, before I let you do that to me" (*SD* 110).

The father's next response to Wilky's whine summarizes the emotional and psychological center of the novel: "Go away from me now. It's torture for me to look at you, you slob!" (*SD* 110) The torture of the doctor's look upon his son matches his own fear of castration and women with his son's embodiment, in both their eyes, of deficiency and inadequacy. The combination of horror and guilt in the doctor's look relates directly to his ambivalence regarding the mother as part of his general disavowal of difference and weakness. In addition, Wilky's obsession over being normal reenforces the perception of his father and others about Wilky's sexuality (*SD* 51, 53, 73). He tells the doctor, "More than half of my life is over. More than half. And now you tell me I'm not even normal" (*SD* 54).

Wilky's condition of emasculation and his personification of the system of visual castration and masochism in combination with the feminine and the homosexual recalls Silverman's insistence that the "dominant fiction" of masculinity by definition denies and disavows castration and weakness. As already noted, she argues that the patriarchal order maintains a fiction of "unimpaired masculinity." She maintains that "traditional masculinity is predicated" upon the denial of "lack, specularity, and alterity" and that women are expected to reenforce this disavowal (*SD* 50–51). In radical contrast with this organization of power, she hopes "to show that male mastery rests upon an abyss" that must be recognized so that "every subject's encounter with the death drive might become in time more of an everyday occurrence – that the typical male subject, like his female counterpart, might learn to live with lack" (*SD* 65). Calling for a new "libidinal politics" that exposes "the murderous logic of traditional male subjectivity," Silverman aligns "marginal male subjectivities" with "the feminine" to subvert "the line of paternal succession" (*MSM* 389). The male subject that Silverman envisions will accede "to his castration, his specularity, and the profound 'otherness' of his 'self,'" thereby "embracing desires and identifications which are in excess of the positive Oedipus complex" (*MSM* 388). Say "'no' to power" (*MSM* 389) she says, as though offering a campaign slogan for gender reconstruction.

To some extent, Bellow's position on masculinity coincides with Silverman's program of reconstructing gender to counter the power of unitary masculinity. In *Dangling Man*, Bellow exhibits impatience with an attitude of unrestrained masculine power and aggression. In this novel, Bellow also anticipates the concern in *Seize the Day* for the relationship of external signs of behavior to inner being and character.

> For this is an era of hardboiled-dom. Today, the code of the athlete, of the tough boy – an American inheritance, I believe, from the English gentleman – that curious mixture of striving, asceticism, and rigor, the origins of which some trace back to Alexander the Great – is stronger than ever. Do you have feelings? There are correct and incorrect ways of indicating them. Do you have an inner life? It is nobody's business but your own. Do you have emotions? Strangle them. To a degree, everyone obeys this code.[6]

This view of masculinity mocks the dominance during this historical period of the Great Depression and the Second World War of a
Hemingway version of masculinity that pervaded not only Hollywood
but our entire culture as well. In the twelve years that separated
Dangling Man from *Seize the Day*, much changed in regard to the
values and ideals of masculinity. Wilky clearly embodies the opposite extreme of "hardboiled-dom." His desperate search for love and
punishment through the continual exposure of his inner feelings clearly
anticipates the way the internal has been unleashed with a vengeance in
contemporary culture. No longer strangled, internal feelings demand
instant expression and gratification in today's culture. Bellow's portrayal of Wilky demonstrates the need for some inhibition of this drive
toward public exposure of inner selves and inchoate needs. He seems to
be castigating what has become a character type in our times and what
he himself termed in another novel, "the victim." Ironically, Bellow's
presentation of Wilky's manhood may set him at odds with Silverman's
program of male subjectivity, while enlisting Tommy Wilhelm in her
cause.

Discussing a wide range of directors and authors from Frank Capra
and Rainer Werner Fassbinder to T. E. Lawrence, Henry James, and
Marcel Proust, Silverman articulates a program of alternative masculinities and gender relationships that challenges the power of unitary masculinity. In contrast to this program, Wilky, of course, never
directly confronts his symbolic castration, deals with his impulse toward death or recognizes the feminine in himself; he only represents
the consequences of these forces at the unconscious level. Nevertheless, in his passionate embrace of masochistic punishment, denial, and
emasculation, Tommy typifies in some ways Silverman's position of
proffering alternatives to traditional masculine power.

In *Seize the Day*, Bellow brilliantly conveys Tommy's emasculation
through a complex dynamic of interior monologue, fluid point of view,
unconventional use of narrative and time. While Tommy's rejection
of power and his accommodation to lack seem to exemplify some of
Silverman's proposals for forming new paradigms of male subjectivity,
his total immersion in weakness leaves him thoroughly isolated and
without any conceivable prospects for change. Because all of his experiences become internalized in the form of masochistic self-abuse,
he lives without the alliances that would enable him to construct a
promising future. His attempts to "seize the day" devour experience

and incorporate others within his psyche in a way that separates him from reality.

Tommy's position of absolute isolation creates a serious problem for the film version of the novel as to how visually to construct his place in society when the world of his mind encompasses his real living environment. The difficulty in a film of visually mapping out a social world without clear boundaries between inner and outer space requires a solution that an audience can visually recognize. Thus, in trying to put a face on Wilky's masochism, Robin Williams makes him merely a victim undergoing a nervous breakdown, a good guy forever down on his luck. As interpreted by Williams, Tommy's incapacity to respond effectively to his condition stems directly from the powerful forces arrayed against him – his father, his passive mother, an unsympathetic wife, an unfair boss, a devoted but inadequate lover, disloyal friends who won't help, including one played by Tony Roberts in a particularly pathetic business lunch scene in which Wilky picks up the tab out of false pride. Throughout the film, he refuses to defend himself against his wife's spiteful attacks, resisting his girlfriend's admonishments to be more aggressive, and he continues generous child support because of his affection for his children.

Williams's portrayal of Tommy as a total victim draws attention to the difficulties involved in visually articulating moral masochism and making marginalized male subjectivity an effective instrument for change. Instead of developing Tommy into a hero of absence and lack, Williams makes him an object of pity to win over the audience's support. By widening Tommy's internal war to include all that surrounds him, Williams's whining probably invites a sadistic response from some in his audience to equal Tommy's masochism.

Nevertheless, the intensity, depth, and range of Silverman's seminal theory demonstrate the potential for studying the complexity of male characters in films and literature. In fact, several recent studies consider representations of diverse masculinities in a broad range of important actors, including Silverman's own original analysis of Jimmy Stewart in Capra's *It's a Wonderful Life* (1946) and Fredric March and Dana Andrews in William Wyler's *The Best Years of Our Lives* (1946). Other significant works include Dennis Bingham's study of "masculinities in the films" of Stewart, Jack Nicholson, and Clint Eastwood in *Acting Male* and Graham McCann's portrayals of Montgomery Clift, Marlon Brando, and James Dean in *Rebel Males*. Also, James Naremore's work, *Acting in the Cinema*, includes indispensable interpretations of Stewart, Brando, Robert De Niro, Cary (among others.[7] All of these works expatiate upon the varieties o subjectivities presented by these actors. They attest to the pervasi in their performances of themes of importance to marginalized male subjectivity: castration, difference, specularity, otherness, the fragility of patriarchal positions, bisexuality. In innumerable films, these actors have complicated the representation of masculinity. From Clift in *From Here to Eternity* (1953) and *A Place in the Sun* (1951), Brando in *On the Waterfront* (1954), and Stewart in *It's a Wonderful Life* to more contemporary actors such as Al Pacino, Dustin Hoffman, Robert Redford, and most recently and remarkably, Clint Eastwood, all modify classic unitary masculinism to convey complexity, ambivalence, and a degree of bisexuality through speech patterns, physical positioning, and body language.

To some, Robin Williams belongs in this pantheon of actors of intelligence and sensitivity who dare to experiment with performances of alternative male identifications and subjectivities. For example, Lizzie Francke in a recent article, "Being Robin" in *Sight and Sound*, the journal of the British Film Institute, argues that since the inception of his career, Williams's acting persona "could be considered a symptom of the changes of the 70s, as feminism began to question notions of masculinity and femininity and the old models of maleness were revealed to be far from satisfactory."[8] Accordingly, Williams seems like a logical choice to play Tommy Wilhelm.

Unfortunately, the strategy of the film and Williams's performance rely excessively upon turning the inward spiral of Tommy's interior chaos into all kinds of maddening horizontal movement: driving insanely in his car to escape unseen forces; walking and running hysterically through the streets of New York to discover new ways of losing his money or himself; wandering abstractly through his New York hotel in search of the elusive father-figure locked tightly in some secret corner of his mind. Given the complex relationship of Tommy's masochism to gender, the feminine, and the homosexual, the challenge of the movie involves visualizing his psychic condition of castration. It must visually articulate this condition through performance and the other elements of film, including editing and mise-en-scene, without deteriorating into Williams's aggressive histrionics. It needs to place castration within the scopic regime itself to allow the film to exploit cinema's inherent specular text of the look and gaze that locates, again in Silverman's phrase, "lack at the level of the eye, defining castration as the alterity of the gaze" (*MSM* 155). As Silverman develops the relationship of the look and gaze to film, the "look" like language itself works to distinguish being from social definition and determination. Silverman says, "One of the crucial features of Lacan's redefinition of castration has been to shift it away from this obligatory anatomical referent to the void installed by language" (*MSM* 154–155). Like language, the look by organizing vision contests the existential unknown of human identity and emphasizes the intrinsic division of the human psyche. As Silverman writes:

> The implicit starting point for virtually every formulation this book will propose is the assumption that lack of being is the irreducible condition of subjectivity. In acceding to language, the subject forfeits all existential reality, and foregoes any future possibility of "wholeness." (*MSM* 4)

The look as a kind of abyss upon which the individual constructs subjectivity and dramatizes "lack at the level of the eye" can be found in many classic Hollywood films: on Montgomery Clift's face as he stands alone at a party at the Eastman mansion in *A Place in the Sun* or as he watches Donna Reed walk off with another soldier in *From Here to Eternity*; in Brando's scene with Rod Steiger in *On the Waterfront* when he admits to being a "bum" rather than a "contender"; in the stolid expression on Gary Cooper's face as he walks out of a saloon in *High Noon* (1952) and into the realization on the abandoned street that he stands absolutely alone in the town he has repeatedly saved from crime and desolation. The great moments in classic films often position the male characters alone in a confrontation with themselves and with their loss and inadequacy.

In contrast to such moments, Robin Williams in *Seize the Day* fills every scene with something substantial and palpable that essentializes his state of mind and his identity. Existential tension shrivels to self-pity. From the opening scene of Wilky's frantic driving, honking, and addictive smoking to the finale of hysterical weeping at a stranger's funeral, the screen spills over with the tears of his victimization. Thus, in the film's beginning, he greets road construction that delays his drive to nowhere with a whine, "Now what?" Similarly, the early flashbacks revisit his history of mistreatment by others.

The film's inability to engage the novel's linkage of masochism, castration, the body, and the feminization of homosexuality reveals itself in one early flashback that introduces Olive, his Catholic girlfriend.

Before presenting Olive, the film mechanically shows Wilky's hysterical tirade against his boss who has given Wilky's "territory" to a son-in-law. "What does he got that I don't have," Wilky screams before smashing his fist and arm through a glass window. The bandaged wound appears as a potential sign of both physical and psychological dismemberment in the next cut with Olive as Tommy describes the incident to her, wildly bragging about the impression his display made upon the other workers. His exaggerated expressiveness marks a form of verbal and physical overcompensation for his failure. As he talks, they both undress, intimating the sexual as well as the psychological dimensions of the self-inflicted wound. His frustrated and uncoordinated movements force him to struggle to remove his shirt. The shyness and fragility of Olive make the scene interesting, promising the potential exposure of weakness and ambivalence. Her drawn face and her thin body suggest a kind of spiritual anemia. She moves from the bed where she has lowered her stockings to a screen behind which she peers at Wilky as she undresses while he continues his tirade. The protection of the screen implies sexual difference and inhibition. However, the visual display of uncertainty becomes overwhelmed by his verbal bombast and wild gestures, her pleas for resolution to their situation, and the heavy-handed intention of Williams and director Fielder Cook to invest as much pathos in the scene as possible. Words smother the visual articulation of difference. Similarly, in a brilliant structural analysis of how "place, space, pace" change in moving from the novel to the film, Michael Shiels says the scene places Tommy "in what can only be viewed as an uneasily visualized relationship to his background."[9]

Moreover, rather than embracing the body in all of its ambiguity, vulnerability, and difference, the film of *Seize the Day* turns the body into the enemy. The film, thereby, epitomizes what an array of film theorists and directors, according to James Naremore, considers to be an inherent element in the aesthetic form of all film, namely its visible demonstration of death and biology. Naremore claims that Jean-Luc Godard summarizes the views of many other notables of film, including Jean Cocteau and Andre Bazin: "The person one films is growing older and will die. We film, therefore, a moment when death is working."[10] This symbiosis of death and cinema becomes an obsession with *Seize the Day* to the point of making the fear of death a crucial force in the film. The film of *Seize the Day* hates Dr. Adler not because he is a self-obsessed, self-centered, and selfish old man who psychologically violates his son as an unforgiving, uncompromising, and unrelenting moralistic super-ego, but because he is old and his friends are old and they all look old. From the moment the film enters the doctor's world at the Hotel Gloriana, we are in an uptown New York Auschwitz of the aging and the abandoned. Here the elderly, even when bound for glory, are by definition grotesque and horrific. Castration, sexual difference, and ambivalence have been personified and cast as elderly New York Jews who typify the cultural hatred of the body and biology. The aging body becomes a Jewish body, merging fears of death with fears of difference and otherness. Distorted lighting and restricted physical movements transmogrify the Gloriana residents into creeping aliens and revolting freaks with grotesque physical features, gestures, and expressions. The worst have physical deformities or own miserable, uncontrollable pets without adequate housetraining, perhaps emulating the difficulties of their aging owners. Even the relatively younger residents, who are retired such as Dr. Tamkin (Jerry Stiller) and his cardplayer cronies, are depicted as weird New York oddities.

As played with painful precision by the brilliant character actor Joseph Wiseman, Dr. Adler comes off as death incarnate, especially in the massage room scene. After a high angle shot reveals the fragility of Dr. Adler's thin body on the massage table, the camera shoots him in straight-on medium close-ups, keeping his head and body horizontal to the table, the embodiment of a ghostly death-in-life. Thus, without confronting any of the confusing complexity of castration, sexual ambivalence, parental authority, maturation, and identification, Wilky in the film finally has an enemy to share with everyone, his father as the personification of the grim reaper. In facing death in the figure of his father, Wilky represents the victimization of all people facing death. The whining, crying, pleading, frowning, cringing portrayal of manhood by Robin Williams institutionalizes victimization. The film's avoidance of symbolic castration and loss at the level of the look, meaning as an inexorable aspect of all human experience and all gender construction, male or female, trivializes the crisis of manhood and male subjectivity articulated by Bellow and Silverman. It, therefore, also avoids Silverman's challenge to live on the "abyss" with lack and loss, but it confirms Bellow's view of Wilky's manhood. The fierce intensity of Tommy's failed manhood resonates as a schism and uncertainty that extends beyond him into the suggestion of a general crisis of authority and stability. Tommy's distraught persona and frazzled demeanor are emblems of the transmogrification of the American hero into the American victim and the replacement of ideals of integrity and independence with an acceptance of dependence and death. Tommy becomes a victim for all seasons, unfortunately several decades too early to make it on afternoon talk shows as a perfect character type for our times. Poor Tommy, always the unhappy loser.

PART FOUR

DOCUMENTARY AND FICTION

CHAPTER SEVEN

DOCUMENTING THE BODY
IN *MODERN TIMES*

Love, Play, and Repression in Chaplin's Silent Classic

Performance makes the connection between fiction and documentary in film especially interesting for understanding and interpreting all aspects of film. The paradoxes that define the relationship between fiction and documentary in film grow sharper when considering acting. Discussing this aspect of his theory of documentary and fiction in film, Gilberto Perez quotes Jean-Luc Godard, the French auteur of *Breathless* (1959) and a leader of the New Wave. Godard says, "Every film is a documentary of its actors." Perez pursues and develops Godard's insight.

> A fiction movie constructs the fiction of characters from the documentary of actors. It is the documentary of a fiction enacted before the camera; and it is the fiction of a documentary of characters merged in our minds with their incarnation in the actors.[1]

This relationship in film between acting and documentary should be understood as a situation that differs essentially from the conditions of stage acting. Perez writes:

> Theater is founded on representation by performance, film on representation by documentary. The first signifying act of theater is to mark out a stage, set an area apart from the surrounding world for the purpose and the duration of a performance. The first signifying act of film is to train a camera on a subject, a piece of appearances to be documented.[2]

To focus upon film acting gives the tension that plays out between fiction and documentary in film a new significance. Performance grows out of this tension. An actor's performance in a film relates inescapably to the method, style, and technique of the documentation of that performance. To an extent, this argument about the importance of documentary and film performance – one related to James Naremore's theory of film acting – reenforces Lev Kuleshov's classic case that the juxtaposition of shots and editing organization determine meaning in film performance.[3] However, as Perez maintains, the relationship of documentary to acting helps to explain inherent differences between acting in film and other forms of performance. Since the nature of the presentation of a character on a screen derives at least in part from its documentation, film acting informs and enlightens any analysis of the relationship between fiction and documentary.

While the stature of actors discussed so far in these essays seems clear, in film history probably one figure achieves a truly special place as a founding and lasting force in expressing the full potential of film performance – Charlie Chaplin. Chaplin's career spanned film history from its beginning to its maturity; his character of The Tramp gained unprecedented universal recognition; and his diverse and multiple talents and genius have become benchmarks for film performance and filmmaking. The extraordinary significance of his career and work was given rather unusual recognition in a special multipage tribute to him by the Sunday *New York Times* that anticipated by a week the hundredth anniversary of his birthday. The headline for the series of articles and commentary speaks volumes about the influence of Chaplin on film: CHAPLIN, INVENTING MODERN TIMES.[4] The headline addresses the centrality of Chaplin as the embodiment of modern film representation and consciousness. However, it also puns on the special importance of his last silent classic, *Modern Times* (1936). A seminal work in modernism, and a crucial emblem of Chaplin's talent and genius, *Modern Times* has received considerable critical attention.

However, in the extensive Chaplin canon, *Modern Times* invites further commentary, partly because Chaplin, as director, star, and writer, uses his own and other's visual and physical performances in the film in ways that demonstrate and elucidate the Godard–Perez–Naremore arguments about film acting and documentary. Moreover, the development of film performance in *Modern Times* gains special importance because it not only shows acting as a signifying system, it also dramatizes the meaning of the film's title so well, the transformation of life and American values and ideals of renewal in modern times.

Ironically, in achieving such amazing influence, the performance by Chaplin that gets documented concerns a mediated representation, The Tramp. To paraphrase Godard, the performance by Chaplin entails a documentary of a disguised and costumed figure, The Tramp, that in turn becomes a documentary of the costumed actor himself, Chaplin.

The interaction between these various elements of The Tramp, Chaplin, and the documentary of the performance expresses the extraordinary intensity beneath the Chaplin persona of inner drives that motivate and propel him.

Rather than being a simple clown, the complex construction that entails The Tramp demonstrates Chaplin's insight into the way film performance through its relationship to the camera and documentary can become a signifying system of great creativity and complexity. Bill Irwin in the centennial tribute to Chaplin in the Sunday *New York Times* indicates the genius of Chaplin's understanding of how film acting works so that he could approach achieving film's expressive potential. Irwin writes:

> Chaplin is said to have told his actors, "Don't sell it; remember they're peeking at you." He seemed to be among the first to catch on to the difference between live witness and the camera eye.[5]

Appreciating this difference between live theatrical performance and acting for the camera, Chaplin in *Modern Times* converts his body into a complexly dynamic exhibition and enactment of contending forces that encompass the interior world of his own inner psyche and extend to external cultural, historic, and social forces that were in the process of transforming the relationship of the individual to history in modern times. In this silent film, Chaplin's performing and documented body becomes a carnival of multiple signifiers that expresses inner needs and desires as well as external forces of intimidation, stimulation, and repression. Chaplin the Old Man, Chaplin the Clown, Chaplin the Tramp, Chaplin the Loser–Schlemiel–Victim, and Chaplin the Triumphant Trickster all interact in an inner psychic arena that transforms itself through acting and film to express the very social forces of control, discipline, and reward that the Chaplin figures in all of their manifestations must engage.

Many have sought in Charlie Chaplin's biography, and in the inner recesses of his complex psyche, for the source of his creative genius and influence. His life, tortured relationships, notorious complexes, and unprecedented achievements engender such investigation and analysis. Chaplin was a man of extraordinary guilt, despair, and depression. Given to obsessive and compulsive behavior that originated, as several biographers and critics maintain, in the miseries of his youth, Chaplin justified performance, especially his comedy, as a kind of therapy and strategy for living. For Chaplin, humorous performance both protects and structures the individual psyche in the face of the pain of the human condition. As Constance Brown Kuriyama argues, "survival" helps explain the purpose of Chaplin's "art" of "impure comedy," meaning an artistically "mature" and "double-edged" comedy that acknowledges "the destructive power of the very forces it promises to contain."[6]

By the 1930s, however, Chaplin came to expand the range and depth of his concerns to ponder, not just how comedy could help the individual to survive in a sick world, but to ask if the exigencies and demands of current life had exceeded even comedy's ability to make any form of prolonged or meaningful happiness possible for most people. Critics and historians of film generally seem to agree that until *Modern Times*, Chaplin's classic silent comedy primarily dramatized the individual Tramp's struggle to overcome overwhelming difficulties. However, *Modern Times* expands its concerns to ask if society itself extracts so much from the individual as to doom everyone to permanent misery, and society to its own inevitable destruction. Society, the film suggests, rests upon a permanent foundation of sickness, what could be termed the unresolved tensions that Freud delineated between love and guilt, individual aggression and law and order.

Accordingly, *Modern Times* should not be dismissed as only a silent comedy of man's repression under modern industrialism and technology. As Charles Silver says, "The subject of man's increasing subservience to the machine was not new to film."[7] The famous visual metaphor in the opening shot that associates sheep with the mindless conformity and control of modern industrial man belies the film's greater visual, psychological, and ideological complexities. The representation in the film of the conflict between freedom and order actually supersedes in importance the film's more obvious romantic message of the control over modern man by the machine and its social system. The film's comedy intensifies the opposition of forces of love and repression within the individual and society. Of course, the comedy, which Chaplin saw as a source of relief of pain, invariably returns to and focuses upon the very difficulties and conflicts that constitute the source of pain.

Besides expounding upon some important themes about man and society, Chaplin's contribution in *Modern Times* involves his development of film performance as a complex system to communicate and dramatize ideas. Building on a lifetime of experience, Chaplin gives abstruse notions – individual freedom and society or sexuality and social order – concrete particularity by personifying and embodying them in two figures perfect for such representation at this moment in history. There is the nubile Paulette Goddard as a young waif, or Gamine, and, of course, Chaplin himself as the Tramp, the young girl's decidedly middle-aged companion. The performances and appearance of these two figures constitute an important development in the complexity of film performance and cinematic form. Their images run at once on several stratified layers of meaning.

Ironically, even as *Modern Times* seems primitive in its absence of dialogue, the film contributes to the hybrid nature or heterogeneity of cinematic form through the multilayered presentation of these characters. The Tramp–Gamine relationship develops in part through complex representations of their bodies in a kind of physical dialogue of differences of gender, age, and action. This representation of their bodies establishes an archeology of moving visual images. The contrast and clash of age and gender differences between the orphaned runaway girl and the older vagrant conflict with the surface presentation of the innocence of their relationship. By offering alternative perspectives of their possible relationship, the conflicting images disrupt the apparent simplicity of *Modern Times*'s narrative, complicating and deepening the film's themes of liberation and order.

Meanwhile, the real-life relationship and activities of the celebrity actor/director and his most recent ingenue suggest another layer of meanings. The offscreen Chaplin–Goddard connection contributes powerfully to the sexual overtones of the film, thereby exemplifying modern sexual liberation while at the same time manifesting the felt need for some form of opposition to such freedom.

While *Modern Times* marks an important break for Chaplin from the past, it also comes directly out of his classic film comedy. In fact, his continued resistance to sound in film and his insistence upon making *Modern Times* as primarily a silent film suggest not just a hesitancy to depart from a proven formula but also a fear of change. As David Robinson says, "Even at this stage Chaplin remained undecided about sound." Robinson reports a Chaplin interview in which he emphasized, "Dialogue may or may not have a place in comedy.... What I merely said was that dialogue does not have a place in the sort of comedies I make.... For myself I know that I cannot use dialogue."[8] Accordingly, *Modern Times* maintains all of the classic elements that comprise the Chaplin formula for past successes: The Tramp figure, sentimentality, gross and bawdy humor, physical slapstick, a simple narrative, a populistic ideological foundation for the plot, and the organization of visual images and music to elicit the most basic sympathy for and identification with the underdog.

At the same time, *Modern Times* dramatizes the emergence of a new Chaplin as both a public figure and artist with deep concerns about social and philosophical issues. As Robinson says:

> It was in the 1930s that Chaplin's critics – often the best-disposed of them – began to complain that he was getting above his station. The clown was setting himself up as a philosopher and statesman. He had mingled so much with world leaders (they said) that he had begun to think of himself as one. They regretted the lost, innocent purity of the old slapstick and shook their heads at the arrogance, conceit and self-importance of the man. If this had been true, it would have been less surprising than that Chaplin had remained as human and as conscious of reality as he did. No one before or since had ever had such a burden of idolatry thrust upon him. It was not he or his critics, but the crowds that mobbed him everywhere on his world tour that cast him in the role of symbol of all the little men of the world.[9]

Robinson regards Chaplin's political activities and social conscience sympathetically, seeing him as "a reasoning, reading, pensive man." He considers Chaplin as a man propelled into leadership by an anxious public whose fears and doubts about economic and political conditions stirred him to action. Such sympathies for Chaplin tend to make Robinson sound generally unconcerned about some of the inconsistencies between Chaplin's position and lifestyle. For example, Robinson unblushingly notes how Chaplin worked on the script and scenario for *Modern Times* in the Pacific waters off of California on his new boat called *Panacea*.[10] Robinson writes:

> That spring of 1933 Chaplin acquired a new toy, which was for years to provide him with therapeutic recreation. Disregarding financial stringencies, he ordered from Chris-Craft a 1932 model 38-foot commuting cruiser, with an 8-cylinder, 250 h.p. motor and a speed of 26 knots. It slept four, would ride twenty people, and had a one-man crew – Andy Anderson, a one-time Keystone Kop. It had luxurious cabin, galley and dining quarters and, provided with bedding, linen, stove, refrigerator and cooking utensils cost $13,950 at the Michigan factory.[11]

Although Robinson claims a kind of originality for Chaplin for the "burden of idolatry thrust upon him" by the masses for celebrity leadership, Chaplin in fact follows a reformist tradition by artistic and intellectual elites in America who identified with the "people" and advocated their causes but lived and associated with a rather select group of leaders. In this regard, as in so many other areas, Chaplin compares to the public life and private inner psychological world of Mark Twain. As Glauco Cambon, Hamlin Hill, and Walter Blair, among others, have noted, both Twain and Chaplin were part of a modern trend of finding heroes in popular culture among leading artists and thinkers.[12] Twain in his time was the most famous and popular of such figures, including William Dean Howells, the eminent writer, critic, and editor, and William James, the philosopher and psychologist. As has been noted, Twain's conflicted relationship with the masses was reflected in his ambivalence between his radical individualism and his sympathy for the situation of the underprivileged and oppressed that required some form of collective action.[13] Thus, in a telling phrase which proffers considerable insight into both men, Howells once described Twain and himself as "theoretical socialists and practical aristocrats."[14]

Similarly, Chaplin really lacked a coherent and systematic philosophical and political ideology but rather, like Twain, put his emotions into highly moralistic terms and obviously simplified political categories. His politics, as Robinson says, "probably represents capitalist utopianism rather than the socialism with which he was so regularly charged." Robinson further notes that "*Modern Times* is an emotional response, based always in comedy to the circumstances of the times."[15] In their mutual responses to the pressures put upon them by their own times and cultures, both Twain and Chaplin probably could be deemed anarchists in their fierce resistance to any form of domination or control.

Emotionally and psychologically Twain and Chaplin have much in common. In many ways, Chaplin resembled Twain in the depth and intensity of his sense of guilt as a pervasive manifestation of chronic depression. In his biography of Twain, Justin Kaplan calls him "a lifelong guilt seeker" and reports that "even so casual an acquaintance as Mrs. James T. Fields noted that 'his whole life was one long apology.'"[16] Both Kaplan and Henry Nash Smith emphasize Twain's misplaced feelings of guilt and responsibility over the accidental death of his son Langdon after the boy became exposed to bad weather during a carriage ride with his father.[17]

Similarly, Kuriyama describes Chaplin's guilt over events concerning loved ones that were beyond his control:

Chaplin blamed himself not only for his mother's illness but for all his family's disasters. Irrational guilt played a part in his painful breathing and suicidal wishes after his father's death and was even more evident in an incident that occurred at Hanwell School when he was only seven. During his first lengthy separation from his mother, Chaplin was falsely accused of setting a fire. Instead of denying the charge and trying to escape caning, a punishment he found "terrifying" to watch, he impulsively confessed.[18]

In addition, Twain and Chaplin were extremely self-centered egoists who often needed to distance themselves emotionally from those closest to them while at the same time intensely and sincerely loving humanity in the most general and abstract ways. Twain's own stories of family conflicts and outbursts are part of his legend, and Chaplin often seemed totally unable to put the feelings and needs of even loved ones ahead of his own ego. Chaplin reacted with ultimate conceit to the news of the impending death of his brother Sydney's wife, Minnie, by writing in a telegram only about his work. Robinson reports, "The telegram of sympathy which Chaplin sent to his brother during Minnie's last illness vividly illustrates how even genuine fraternal concern could not supersede his preoccupation with work." Chaplin relayed his sympathy with this account of his progress on *Modern Times*:

> I HAVE BEEN WORKING HARD ON THE PICTURE WHICH WILL BE READY FOR FALL RELEASE AND FROM ALL INDICATIONS WE SHALL HAVE A SENSATIONAL SUCCESS STOP IN TREATMENT IT WILL BE SIMILAR TO CITY LIGHTS WITH SOUND EFFECTS AND AUDIBLE TITLES SPOKEN BY ONE PERSON HOWEVER WE ARE GOING TO EXPERIMENT WITH THIS IDEA STOP.[19]

Twain and Chaplin brought much emotional and intellectual baggage to the issues of industrialism and technology in *A Connecticut Yankee in King Arthur's Court* (1889) and *Modern Times*. It has become commonplace to understand and interpret *A Connecticut Yankee* as a reflection of Twain's latent ambivalence to the progress of civilization as seen in the advances of modern industrialism. Although *Connecticut Yankee*'s wonderful vernacular hero, Hank Morgan, proudly celebrates all the advantages of bringing modern nineteenth-century industrialism and allegedly progressive Protestant thought to medieval Camelot, important events and symbolism subvert and countermand the surface optimism of the novel and suggest a profoundly pessimistic attitude toward technology and civilization. For example, critics, most notably and successfully Henry Nash Smith, have emphasized the significance of Twain's symbolism for a factory as a "serene volcano, standing innocent with its smokeless summit in the blue sky and giving no sign of the rising hell in its bowels."[20] Smith

indicates how such potent negative symbolism suggests Twain's ambiguity toward, not only technology, but progress, democracy, and human nature, as well.

Most significant, the novel ends with the use of modern technology
and armaments for the catastrophic slaughter of tens of thousands of
warring knights with the ensuing result of the destruction of civilization. Smith notes that this devasting ending invites "a psychological
explanation."[21] As an aspect of this psychological reading, he perceives an element of the "erotic" in Hank Morgan's "yearning for his
lost world." Smith continues:

> Since the Lost World is also identified with memories of childhood, one might
> conjecture that Mark Twain's latent hostility to industrialism is related to the
> psychological conflict between Eros and civilization that Herbert Marcuse
> has explored.[22]

In pursuing precisely such a theme in *A Connecticut Yankee*, I have
argued elsewhere how closely the novel anticipates Freud's theory of
the conflict within civilization between eros as opposed to guilt and the
death instinct. For Freud, such devastation originates in the failure of
eros to achieve maturity, stability, and permanence in society.[23]

For Smith, the "erotic" elements in *A Connecticut Yankee* in the form
of "prelogical fantasies...are buried too deeply to be more than
glimpsed."[24] However, if erotic impulses are indeed so latent in
Connecticut Yankee as to be barely perceptible to some, they are glaring in *Modern Times*. Thus, for some insights into *Modern Times*, we
can turn to the book mentioned by Smith in his discussion of Twain,
Marcuse's *Eros and Civilization*. In his program to radicalize Freudian
assumptions of eros and guilt by proffering the potential to eroticize
society through the liberation of repressive sublimation, Marcuse also
concentrates on dealing with and testing "the most 'disorderly' of all
instincts – sexuality." He asks "if the sex instincts can, by virtue of their
own dynamic and under changed existential and societal conditions,
generate lasting erotic relations among mature individuals." Marcuse
continues:

> We have to ask whether the sex instincts, after the elimination of all surplus-
> repression, can develop a "libidinal rationality" which is not only com-
> patible with but even promotes progress toward higher forms of civilized
> freedom.[25]

Chaplin's *Modern Times* presents an excellent engagement in
Marcuse's terms of sexuality with civilized freedom in the form of

Chaplin's classic Tramp figure and the young waif or Gamine played by Paulette Goddard. On the surface their relationship seems generally desexualized. Referring back to an earlier Chaplin film, *The Kid* (1921), with Jackie Coogan, Silver says of the Tramp and Gamine that "their companionship more closely resembles that of *The Kid* than any of the more overtly romantic or potentially sexual liaisons in intervening films." Silver emphasizes Chaplin's own word at one time for their relationship in the film as "playmates" and notes that "Like Charlie, the Gamine is a victim of contemporaneity, orphaned by industrial violence and a fugitive from the state's stewardship."[26]

However, at the very beginning of Silver's paragraph, almost in the same breath as his description of the basic innocence of the couple's relationship, Silver says: "Goddard's is an extraordinarily vibrant presence, far distant from the passive and pedestaled heroines of earlier Chaplin movies."[27] Thus, his written critique conveys the same tensions as the visual images.

As a film, *Modern Times* inescapably constitutes a documentary of the powerful and unmistakable sexuality of Goddard's performance. Many close-ups convey her youthful beauty, intensity, and sensuality, while medium shots and long shots of her body blatantly exhibit her seductiveness and flirtatiousness. When Goddard the Gamine waits barefoot in a tattered dress for Charlie to be taken into the department store where he fortuitously has found work as a night watchman, she appears brazenly erotic and could be mistaken even for a girl of the streets rather than simply homeless. The anxious, near desperate look on her face as she provocatively raises and bares her right leg and restlessly rubs the naked foot on the wall of the building against which she leans all add dramatically to the sensuouness of the moment. The purse she holds in front of her body suggests sexuality and business rather than an anticipated purchase of her own and emphasizes her impoverished abandonment.

Also, when she again waits for Charlie outside of prison for his release, she appears still barefoot and full figured, clearly attractive and sexual. Here she teases and plays and cavorts with him in a way that certainly could be seen as suggestive of an intimate relationship, a thought made manifest by her announcement that she has found them a home. They go off together arm in arm to establish a temporary "domestic" relationship. Similarly suggestive, the famous department store sequence exhibits their youthful play, including Chaplin wrapping her in a gorgeous fur coat and putting her to bed in the store's furniture

Figure 10. Charlie Chaplin loves and cherishes the orphan and waif Paulette Goddard in *Modern Times*. (Museum of Modern Art/Film Still Archives)

section. Many other aspects of the story also are sexually suggestive: her street dancing; her eventual employment in a saloon as a dancer where she finds Charlie a job; and, perhaps most significantly, the song Charlie sings in this saloon at the end of the film about, as Robinson says, "a tale of a seducer and a coyly yielding maiden."[28] The song obviously suggests one potential meaning of their relationship.

Accordingly, the visual images create a mise-en-scene of desire and eroticism that contradicts the initial impressions of a relationship of playful innocence between Charlie and the Gamine. Instead of a single movement of visual images and emotional tones conveying a comfortable companionship between a funny, kind but inept tramp and a victimized and helpless orphan, we get a dramatically different pattern of images with a potential meaning of abuse, exploitation, and illicit intimacies.

The documentary of Goddard's performance that reveals provocative sexuality also works as documentary, as James Naremore would suggest, of Goddard and Chaplin, the real public personalities. The documentary of performance doubles as documentary of real people and careers. The documentary images of the actors as real people comprise part of the film's visual text, complicating the fictional narrative. The film narrative incorporates the documentary images of its performers into the signifying chain of cinematic images. In *Modern Times*, widely-known stories of the celebrities Chaplin and Goddard insinuate themselves into the overall stratification and interaction of the film's images and meanings. The real and public Goddard and Chaplin, the charming and roguish Tramp and the vivacious but vulnerable Gamine, all contribute to the complicated and contradictory impulses of the film, increasing the tension between the patterns of innocent companionship and vigorous sexual activity.

Accordingly, the public and screen images of Chaplin and Goddard make a sexual reading of *Modern Times* not only possible but almost inevitable. They both brought their biographies and personal stories to the screen.

Goddard's story was fresher but no less compelling than Chaplin's ever-growing public legend. Basic sources and texts contradict each other regarding Goddard's first name, although they agree her family name was Levy. Ephraim Katz's *Film Encyclopedia* says Marion, while Robinson insists "her real name was Pauline."[29] Born on June 3, 1911, she came from a broken home on Great Neck, L.I. and was forced to help support her mother and family, becoming a Ziegfeld Girl known as "Peaches" at the age of fourteen, marrying a wealthy lumber industrialist, and then leaving and divorcing him in Reno to pursue a movie career in Hollywood. She began in Hollywood as a Goldwyn Girl in *The Kid from Spain* (1932), then signed a contract with Hal Roach's stock company when she met Chaplin. At least twenty years younger than Chaplin, she married him on a secret trip to Asia after making *Modern Times*, although here too there seems to be some controversy over whether they had actually secretly married three years earlier. In any case, Chaplin was in his forties at the time of the marriage and the age difference between them had to remind audiences that Chaplin's first wife, Mildred Harris, was sixteen or seventeen when they married in 1918, while his second wife, Lillita McMurray, later known as Lita Grey, was also a teenager when he married her at the age of thirty-five. The bitter and long divorce case with Lita involved their two sons and resulted in headlines around the world until the million dollar settlement. Many in the audience, therefore, knew exactly what they were seeing on the screen, and some could probably even correctly anticipate glamorous and controversial relationships for both Chaplin and Goddard in future years.

Interestingly and significantly, both on screen and offscreen, the Chaplin–Goddard relationship involved more than just liberated attitudes toward sexuality. They were also unconventional and anti-bourgeois people, living and behaving in ways that must have seemed threatening to audiences of ordinary people in the 1930s. Their life-styles challenged dominant mores and values, confirming the drastic contrast between Hollywood and the rest of America. Chaplin went on to face a paternity suit brought against him by Joan Barry, another young actress, and to be charged with violating the Mann Act for al-legedly transporting a minor across state lines for immoral purposes. Although not convicted on the morals charge, he was ruled the father of the child. He finally married Oona O'Neill in 1943 when she was eighteen and he was fifty-four against the strongest objections of her father, the great playwright, Eugene O'Neill. The marriage seems to have been his one really successful relationship with a woman.

Goddard, after divorcing Chaplin, married the actor Burgess Meredith, had a relationship with the revolutionary Mexican artist Diego Rivera, and then married the German novelist and author of *All Quiet on the Western Front*, Erich Maria Remarque. After Remarque's death in 1970, she continued to live as a famous, celebrated, and re-spected figure in social and cultural circles in both Europe and America.

The offscreen behavior and attitudes of Goddard and Chaplin reen-force some of the most interesting and challenging elements of their on screen relationship in *Modern Times*. Their individualistic, what some would call "bohemian," lives parallel the latent meanings of the sexu-ality in the film. This involves more than a certain fluidity of liberated libido but the organization and structure of eros in society.

Modern Times anticipates the melding in modern media, film, and culture of the public and private domains that generally destabilizes rigid narrative structures and ideological systems. Such crossings of the public and private proffer new perspectives and revisualizations of the cinematic text. Indeed, the collapse of the walls separating the public and private helps to form an ideology of the new that has characterized modernity since the end of the last century, including the emergence of the department store as a site for the commodification of personal desire, a social phenomenon dramatized by the reaction of the Gamine and the Tramp to such a store's pleasures. Moreover, the merger of the public and private incorporated within the film of the off-camera public lives of screen figures depends in part on the audience's awareness of the activities of the stars and the participation by the audience, therefore, in the process of the integration of the public and private.

Thus, offscreen sexual freedom in *Modern Times* compounds the sexual suggestiveness of the film itself to create an ideology of openness to countermand the offical institutional and cultural ideology of sexual repression. This disruptive force seems especially important in a film so dedicated to debunking and deflating all forms of institutional authority, ranging from the visit in *Modern Times* by the minister and his wife to Charlie's prison, to the public authorities who effectively prevent the Gamine from staying with her brother and sister after the death of their father in a labor demonstration. At the same time, in direct contrast to this impulse toward disruption, the film's sexual liberalism and its ridicule of middle-class values cause enough discomfort and fear to threaten society, frequently with the same audience entertained by the film's iconoclasm.

Accordingly, as dramatized by the complex heterogeneous and hybrid nature of film, *Modern Times* propounds the dilemma and paradox of modern sexuality. It advertises modern sexual freedom, while suggesting in some of its images the need for its control. It illustrates the suffocation by public-custodial forces of the independence of inner impulses for passion and love and yet raises fears of sexual anarchy.

The film's symbolism of machinery suggests the contradiction in modernism between external strength and movement as opposed to internal, emotional numbness, alienation, and isolation. Machinery means opportunity and enterprise but also inner death through the suffocation of creativity and personal freedom. Machinery as a metaphor for "modern times" articulates the crisis of the inner psyche and the organization of eros as well as the domination of the individual by technology and industrialism. From the opening images of sheep and workers, already mentioned, to the sequence when Charlie goes "crazy" on an assembly line, machinery represents man alienated from his labor by a brutal, dehumanized society that mimics the ideas of industrial management set forth by Frederick Taylor during the early decades of the century. Other scenes sustain this theme of alienated labor including, of course, the labor strife throughout the film and Charlie's arrest as a Communist after he is mistakenly identified as a leader because he picks up a fallen red flag. Caught between contending forces of marchers and the police, the Tramp finds himself swept up in forces beyond his control, the perennial alien from and victim of both sides.

However, in the various machinery sequences, once again images operate on multiple levels and require an archeological interpretive process. Machines and the human body become interchangeable. In the food feeding scene, the machine enters Charlie's mouth and body just as in the bathroom scene the image of the boss on the enormous screen in the bathroom invades Charlie's privacy and insists on the authority to intrude upon and control even his bodily functions. The time of the industrial process becomes internalized inside the biological and psychological body of the working individual.

Similarly, in many comic scenes from the beginning of *Modern Times*, Charlie enters the body of the machine as does his supervisor. These various entrances and exits of human bodies and machines have a definite sexual connotation. The interventions and intrusions into and between bodies and machines represent sexual aggression and signify not just the transformation of the human into a machine but also the collapse of love and tenderness in personal and human relations. This machinery dramatizes the turning of sex and eros into inner death. The machinery embodies extreme repression and excessive sublimation. The vulgarity of lower body functions that Chaplin found so useful in his humor loses its effectiveness in the surrender of the individual to the state and economic machine. Gas and gurgling are mechanical activities to machines that operate without taste, embarrassment, or etiquette. As Marcuse suggests, a society of machinery turns the body into an instrument in which pleasure becomes alien. "In a repressive order, which enforces the equation between normal, socially useful, and good, the manifestations of pleasure for its own sake must appear as *fleurs du mal*."[30]

At the same time, Charlie as The Tramp represents and embodies the most dangerous enemy to such a repressive state, not mere sexual licentiousness and abandonment that can be controlled by the law and the state and manipulated and directed by the media and entertainment industry but the idea of pleasure for its own sake. Unable to beat the system of the machine on its own terms, Charlie intuitively changes the rules through pleasure. Using Freud's terminology from *Three Essays on the Theory of Sexuality*, Marcuse labels such pleasure as "perversions."

Against a society which employs sexuality as means for a useful end, the perversions uphold sexuality as an end in itself; they thus place themselves outside the dominion of the performance principle and challenge its very foundation. They establish libidinal relationships which society must ostracize because they threaten to reverse the process of civilization which turned the organism into an instrument of work.[31]

The Tramp's inability to satisfy the performance principle's demands to sustain work and to make his body an instrument of efficiency for production challenges the social order.

However, the Tramp's capacity for pleasure, his penchant for infusing play into the social order and the work environment entails a revolutionary potential for society. Here Chaplin's Tramp comes closest to proffering an actual plan for change, a program that in fact anticipates the radicalization of Freud in the Counter Culture days of the 1960s and 1970s. This program of pleasure builds on the complex relationship between the erotic and repression that comprises *Modern Times*'s central psychological and philosophical conflict for contemporary culture. Marcuse delineates this program for change, succinctly summarizing how the program contrasts with the normal system of surplus-repressive sublimation:

> With the emergence of a non-repressive reality principle, with the abolition of the surplus-repression necessitated by the performance principle, this process would be reversed. In the societal relations, reification would be reduced as the division of labor became reoriented on the gratification of freely developing individual needs; whereas, in the libidinal relations, the taboo on the reification of the body would be lessened. No longer used as a full-time instrument of labor, the body would be resexualized. The regression involved in this spread of the libido would first manifest itself in a reactivation of all erotogenic zones and, consequently, in a resurgence of pre-genital polymorphous sexuality and in a decline of genital supremacy. The body in its entirety would become an object of cathexis, a thing to be enjoyed – an instrument of pleasure. This change in the value and scope of libidinal relations would lead to a disintegration of the institutions in which the private interpersonal relations have been organized, particularly the monogamic and patriarchal family.[32]

Marcuse articulates in this paragraph many of the ideas that made his writing so popular during the heady days of counterculture activism: sexuality and the body as ends in themselves for pleasure, a rebirth of sexuality in the body to overcome death in life. He asserts:

> However, the process just outlined involves not simply a release but a *transformation* of the libido; from sexuality constrained under genital supremacy to eroticization of the entire personality. It is a spread rather than explosion of libido – a spread over private and societal relations which bridges the gap maintained between them by a repressive reality principle.[33]

Assuming the sexual dimension of Charlie the Tramp's relation to the Gamine in *Modern Times*, he could be seen to embody the kind of

Figure 11. Charlie Chaplin tries to overcome Paulette Goddard's fears about the future in *Modern Times*. (Museum of Modern Art/Film Still Archives)

return of polymorphous sexuality that Marcuse advocates. The Tramp clearly presents his body as a force for pleasure, a self-contained carnival of gestures played for laughs, although ironically such performances indicate the exact opposite of abandoned pleasure in that Chaplin literally became neurotically obsessed with the repetition of innumerable scenes and takes in the compulsive pursuit of perfection. Significantly, he drove himself even harder in dangerous and life-threatening scenes, apparently responding to some inner compulsion that links death with work and achievement. As Kuriyama says of his work on an earlier film, *The Circus* (1928):

> He insisted on over 700 takes on the tightrope, some with monkeys crawling all over him, and more than 200 takes in cages with lions, one of which was so aggressive and unpredictable that Chaplin later claimed the terror on his face in one shot included in the film was completely genuine.[34]

For Charlie the Tramp as opposed to Chaplin the sick perfectionist, work and play become the same so that the only job manageable for him requires singing and dancing to a mindless song about lascivious sexuality. As a kind of prelinguistic gibberish, the song also suggests the infantilism of his sexuality. While Chaplin probably intended the song as an example of the superiority of mime and dance to spoken, verbal language and dialogue in film, the form of the song suggests deeper meanings for language and the arts that carry over to serious political matters and cultural concerns. Charlie's challenge to traditional linguistic forms undermines the inevitability of inherited structures of patriarchal authority so hated by the New Left of Marcuse's day. This attack on conventional power continues throughout *Modern Times* in which Charlie taunts the police, bosses, and bullies, although nothing in the film quite equals the opening scene of *City Lights* (1931) for deflating cultural authority. In that opening scene, the city's most prominent people formally assemble for the unveiling of a stone monument of three figures symbolizing "Peace and Prosperity." The size and design of the monument exemplify self-congratulatory public authority and rhetoric. As the cover of the monument slowly rises, the Tramp appears sound asleep in the lap of the woman figure. To escape, The Tramp sits on the face of another figure, steps on its crotch, and suffers the statue's sword through the seat of his pants. The scene ends brilliantly with The Tramp's nose on the thumb of the open hand of one statue, thereby making a mocking nose-thumbing gesture. Thus, Chaplin's body and antics insult the self-important gathering, while also besmirching their sacred standards and beliefs.

The Tramp's love interest in *City Lights* also anticipates the Goddard Gamine in *Modern Times*. However, crucial differences concerning these women also obtain. In *City Lights*, almost to the very end, the young love object remains blind and totally innocent of seeing Charlie as the Tramp and of allowing herself to be truly interested in him sexually. The sexuality operates throughout in a sublimated and sentimentalized form. The camera in *City Lights* never endows the blind flower girl (Virginia Cherrill) with the provocative sensuality and sexuality it gives Goddard. It never violates her quality of detached unawareness and innocence.

In contrast, the sexual power of *Modern Times* actually helps to energize and motivate the call for social and cultural change, thereby inviting the powerful countermovement for greater repression and the clash of extremes that Marcuse anticipates could lead to the loss of all meaningful society: "These prospects seem to confirm the expectation that instinctual liberation can lead only to a society of sex maniacs – that is, to no society."[35]

Modern Times ends in just that way with "no society" to speak of as the Tramp and the Gamine walk on a desolate road by themselves in a continuing flight from reality. In contrast to the themes of individual and cultural renewal and the reembodiment of America that occur in other films in this study, *Modern Times* concentrates on survival, nonconformity, and covert resistance. The body not only fails to revivify the American idea, it both internalizes and exhibits dreadful forces of destruction.

In addition, Charlie and the Gamine fulfill the greatest fears raised by the movie. They enact every parent's worst nightmare, the vision of a lost daughter on a road to nowhere in California with a bum.

Today another consideration of *Modern Times* resonates as suggestively as it did sixty years ago: Charlie belongs in jail. Generations ago, Charlie's crime was the refusal to work and conform to a society desperately needing to escape the Depression but unwilling to adopt radical reform. In our own day, concerns about sexual molestation and harassment and pronounced fears of child abuse align the police and social services agencies with the official hegemony in calling for sexual control and administration. The crimes and ideologies have changed, but the criminal remains the same. Thus, Chaplin can rest easily. The Tramp remains as potent and dangerous as ever, still walking on the borders of society, a deviant outcast and alien with only the love of a beautiful child for comfort.

CHAPTER EIGHT

SPIKE LEE, DENZEL WASHINGTON, AND THE REBIRTH OF MALCOLM X

Cinetext for a Black American Dream

In countries throughout Europe during the early decades of the last century, brilliant filmmakers pioneered in making documentary into a significant art form and a social and cultural institution. Innovators of documentary discussed or mentioned at the beginning of this study include Dziga Vertov in Russia, Walter Ruttmann and Leni Riefenstahl in Germany, Luis Buñuel in Spain and France, and John Grierson of the British documentary movement. Their work dramatizes many of the inexorable paradoxes and tensions in film between documentary and fiction of interest to contemporary critics such as Gilberto Perez and James Naremore. In America, the films of Robert J. Flaherty (*Nanook of the North*, 1922) and Pare Lorentz (*The Plow that Broke the Plains*, 1936; *The River*, 1937) made similar strides in developing the documentary form and articulating the inherent dichotomy in film between photographic documentary and fiction.

However, it could be argued with some irony that in America during these decades of documentary innovation, the most powerful articulation of the dilemma of synthesizing fictional narrative and documentary presentation occurs in the work of a man without a camera, John Dos Passos. Deemed by Alfred Kazin as "one of the great achievements of the modern novel," Dos Passos's trilogy, *U.S.A.* (1938) can be read and studied as an attempt to fuse fiction and documentary in the written word.[1] The novels in the trilogy are: *The 42nd Parallel* (1930), *1919* (1932), and *The Big Money* (1936). For innumerable scholars and students, the overall genius and achievement of *U.S.A.* involve Dos Passos's use of a thoroughly original four-level narrative structure to dramatize an enormous panorama of American life during the first decades of the century. Fictional and historic characters and events merge under the power of the continuity and coherence of Dos

Passos's rhythmically pulsating narrative prose. For many, the narrative structure enables Dos Passos to fulfill his ambition of writing a novel to proffer the vast complexity of American life. As Kazin says, "But the framework holds the book together and encloses it; the narrative makes it."[2] The four narrative techniques and levels are: the "Newsreel," a running commentary of media moments and events that reflects the news, music, social and cultural behavior of the nation; biographies of different lengths that compactly but dramatically present the lives of a wide range of American leaders in diverse fields from presidents such as Woodrow Wilson, to inventors and thinkers such as Thomas Alva Edison, Luther Burbank, and Thorstein Veblen, to leaders of industry and finance such as J. P. Morgan and Andrew Carnegie, and mavericks and rebels such as Eugene V. Debs and "Big Bill" Haywood; the technique of "The Camera-Eye," an on-going direct expression of the author's incessant stream of consciousness that follows a developmental pattern throughout the three novels of maturing from infantile incoherence to an organized involvement of inner experience with external events; a fictional narrative of many individual characters and cultural types who interact with and affect each other.

At least two of Dos Passos's narrative modes relate immediately to documentary, mostly obviously the Newsreels of events, images, and personalities, and the Camera-Eye, suggestive of a psychological version of Vertov's kino-pravda, which directly and mechanically reports the flow of individual inner thoughts and feelings, just as the Newsreels report public events and life. The Biographies also have a documentary aspect to them as stories of leaders, historic figures, and celebrities. The merger of these techniques with a complex fictional narrative insinuates documentary reality and context into fiction and establishes the relevance of fictional organization and structure to coherent documentary styles and techniques.

The documentary consciousness of *U.S.A.* derives directly from the authenticity of Dos Passos's intense commitment as a writer and intellectual to merging fiction and history. Dos Passos biographer and scholar, Townsend Ludington, summarizes how Dos Passos's ideas and theory of the novel and history help explain the form and meaning of *U.S.A.*

> Dos Passos understood that the kind of blend of history and fiction he was writing would confuse readers, and in 1928 he wrote a "Statement of Belief" that effectively summarized his concept of fiction. "The only excuse for a novelist," he wrote, "aside from the entertainment and vicarious living his

books give the people who read them, is as a sort of second-class historian of the age he lives in." Dos Passos may have denigrated the value of fiction – fiction often treats matters of more lasting import than does narrative history – yet his intent to bridge the gap between history and the writer's imaginative re-creation of his own experiences was apparent. "The best kind of narrative," he asserted, would combine fiction and history, which was precisely what he had set out to do.[3]

In *U.S.A.* the visual and cinematic techniques of Newsreels, Camera-Eyes, and imagistic and sensational Biographies transform Dos Passos's historic self-awareness into documentary consciousness. Moreover, this documentary consciousness coheres and comes alive through the continuing, unfolding dramatic interaction of concrete moments of deeply-felt personal and individual experiences. Dos Passos particularizes and individualizes experience on all the levels of his narration for his fictional and historical characters.

Thus, for Dos Passos, documentary and fiction come together in language. Throughout *U.S.A.*, Dos Passos proclaims and institutes an artistic and political faith in the power of the word to achieve the kind of marriage of documentary and fiction that occurs for many in film. Obviously, his literary commitment contrasts with the view of critics and scholars of film that we have discussed. These film scholars emphasize how the photographic image of film infuses fiction with documentary, while the art of the documentary form compromises the absolute purity of documentary reality with aspects of fiction. In contrast, the structure, form, and social and political content of *U.S.A.* assert Dos Passos's commitment to language to represent reality, articulate meaning, and suggest visual images through the word's intersection of fiction and documentary. Dos Passos's credo of the word and faith in the documentary power of spoken and written language assume the potential union of individual and social consciousness. In an introductory literary vignette written to set the mood and tone for the published collection of the trilogy, Dos Passos writes, "words call out on mountain pastures, drift slow down rivers widening to the sea and the hushed beaches. . . . it was the speech that clung to the ears, the link that tingled in the blood; U.S.A." Compiling a Whitmanesque series of catalogues and concatenations, he concludes: "But mostly U.S.A. is the speech of the people."[4]

Dos Passos's recognized genius in attempting to create in literature a documentary consciousness of America in transition during the early decades of the last century dramatizes the universality of the paradoxes involving fiction and documentary. *U.S.A.* thrives on the inexorable tension and connection between fiction and documentary. Dos Passos's literary experiment of negotiating between the two realms of fiction and documentary makes his work a crucial part of the modernist imagination. In these novels, fiction and documentary punctuate, subvert, and sustain each other in compelling ways. As a result of this exchange between fiction and documentary, the novels provide one of modern literature's most vivid representations of the transformations of modern life by forces of overwhelming change: urbanization, industrialization, alienation, ideological and political conflict, family disruption, sexual confusion, moral and emotional chaos.

Arguably however, as documentary, the multiple literary techniques invented and employed by Dos Passos ultimately call for a form of electricity that must come from a source other than the author's imagination, energy, and vitality. In terms of structure and form, the attempt at documentary through Newsreels, Camera-Eyes, and Biographies simply accentuates the importance of visual images and sound. Inevitably, as part of a documentary impulse, the absence of a cinematic semiotics of moving visual images and frames and a sound track coordinated with the image track places an excruciating burden on the power of the word in *U.S.A.* So brilliant in rendering a modernist documentary consciousness and so prescient in anticipating the nature, form, and structure of documentary, the inner drama of the novels involves Dos Passos's effort to make words and language match his moral, political, and aesthetic imagination.

The heart of Dos Passos's efforts and the motivation that propels and directs Dos Passos's energies center on his moral and political consciousness. *U.S.A.* manifests Dos Passos's felt and articulated mandate to put literature in the service of the democraticization of American society, to make the word a fierce combatant against economic, social, and cultural forces of repression, a mission redolent of the dedication and vitality of American literary realism as advocated and practiced in an earlier time by many writers and thinkers such as William Dean Howells. Like these earlier writers, Dos Passos strives to describe the conditions of modern existence and to delineate the causes behind social situations that require action and change. He wishes to impregnate his own work with a moral and political consciousness to inspire such change. As manifested in his documentary sensibility, Dos Passos hopes his extravagant literary ambitions and intentions will sustain his social and political idealism.

However, just as Dos Passos's style of literary documentary can be compared to cinematic documentary, so too should his political program and social sensibility be considered in the light of historic change. Ironically, in terms of political and social content, as well as changing values and attitudes, the absence of people of color and of a strong feminist awareness of gender issues dates Dos Passos's trilogy. It would be hard to imagine such omissions in contemporary cinematic documentary.

Nevertheless, Dos Passos's documentary imagination in literature provides a grounding for considering the issues of documentary and fiction that have become so important in modern film. His manner of isolating, detailing, and integrating different techniques and modes of documentary informs and enlightens discussion about the significance and complexity of documentary. His insight into the complexities and ambiguities of the relationship between fiction and documentary helps in developing clearer and closer analysis of such tensions in contemporary works that also attempt a fresh synthesis of the so-called visually real and historically accurate with the imaginary of artistic construction. The documentary imagination and consciousness as conceived and implemented by Dos Passos in his greatest novels achieve renewal in the proliferation of contemporary documentary film.[5] Contemporary documentary films also revivify today the controversy that Dos Passos engaged with his effort to merge fiction and documentary.

From Dos Passos's time to our own, the documentary techniques and sensibilities in *U.S.A.* remain available to documentary filmmakers. Newsreels, Camera-Eye techniques, Biographies, and narrative constructions constitute conventional rhetorical and cinematic strategies for documentary film. However, even when charged and enlivened with electricity, so to speak, for moving visual images and sound, such documentary techniques still must deal with the dilemmas and paradoxes of fiction and documentary that we have been discussing throughout this study. In both the public mind and the academic and critical community, the position for the current filmmaker most often associated with negotiating such issues about documentary and fiction probably belongs to Oliver Stone. Stone has received enormous critical attention because of the notoriety and controversy of such films as *JFK* (1991) and *Nixon* (1995).[6]

However, another contemporary filmmaker – Spike Lee – has dedicated his life and creative and intellectual energies to work that deals directly with the question of fiction and documentary as it relates to issues of profound historic and cultural urgency. In the work of Spike Lee, especially his landmark film, *Malcolm X* (1992), I think Dos Passos's narrative techniques and his vision of a democratic aesthetic achieve a form of current fulfillment. The techniques of the Newsreel, the Camera-Eye, Biography, and fictionalized narrative all cohere in Lee's film to espouse freedom and equality in our time. Moreover, the history, structure, ideology, and social and artistic significance of *Malcolm X* make it an important work not only in the unfinished fight for equality, freedom, and unity in America but also in the continuing discussion of documentary and fiction.

Issues that have recurred throughout this study surface again with relevance and significance in Lee's work, especially *Malcolm X*. As in films discussed earlier such as *Mississippi Masala* (1992), *Lone Star* (1996), and *When We Were Kings* (1996), Lee approaches and dramatizes the issue of race from a thoroughly modernistic perspective of cultural and historic change. The body of Lee's work illustrates the changing racial and ethnic character of America. By dramatizing racial conflict and vehemently expressing the need for new values and attitudes, Lee's films fulfill the historic function of conventional film documentary to present and describe social conditions. At the same time, his work presents a modernist consciousness through the priority he places upon his art and the independence he exudes as a filmmaker. As a modernist, his work exhibits a self-reflexivity and self-consciousness about film as an art form and medium, as in his frequent experimentation in various films with colors, camera angles, time, and story construction. Such Lee films reflect modernistic values and sensibility of ambiguity, violence, uncertainty, psychic and cultural division, social and cultural insecurity.

Moreover, the modernism of Lee's work manifests itself in the way he develops the relationship in his films between fiction and documentary. The inherent documentary nature of film contributes to its potential for modernistic self-reflexivity. Especially in *Malcolm X*, Lee also employs the documentary nature of the visual film image to authenticate the social and cultural contexts for his fiction. This cultivation by Lee of the tensions and ambiguities in the interaction between documentary and fiction in *Malcolm X* dramatically compounds the complexity of the film and demonstrates the modernistic impulse behind Lee's thought and work.

Lee's exploitation of the documentary nature of film occurs with particular artistic profit and cultural significance in his collaboration with Denzel Washington in *Malcolm X*. Together, Washington and Lee fully capitalize upon the intrinsic connection of documentary to film performance, turning Washington's portrayal of Malcolm into a total, coherent system of performance semiotics. As directed by Lee, Washington becomes what James Naremore describes in his seminal work on film performance as "a field of signs" that creates through acting a "systematic ostentatious depiction" of a national ideology in turmoil, a culture in chaos, and an individual psychology of transforming energy and authority.[7]

In terms of this study of film, modernism, and America, Washington's performance in *Malcolm X* sustains, propels, and completes – without concluding – a process of proffering a new racial representation of America on the screen. Washington maintains a trajectory of film performance throughout his career that embodies and dramatizes cultural transformation. The documentary of his acting career converges with his enactment of his idea of Malcolm and with Lee's recreation, through a fusion of documentary and artistic sensibilities, of the historical and autobiographical figure of Malcolm. For Washington, personal biography, career, and image all merge with his representation and performance of Malcolm on the screen and with Lee's reconstruction of America from a racial perspective.

Recalling Washington's work in *Malcolm X* and anticipating, mistakenly as it turns out, Washington's winning the Academy Award for best actor in 2000 for *The Hurricane* (1999), Elvis Mitchell recently observed:

> This year, the odds seem to be in Denzel Washington's favor for *Hurricane*, though if he wins it could be seen as a consolation award for his Malcolm, one of the best performances of the 1990s. As Malcolm, he embodied, to use a phrase Kenneth Tynan once affixed to a Laurence Olivier performance, "a panther among doves." Specifically, he portrayed the anguish of passing from the hell of unfocused anger, through the purgatory of alienation and prison into the heaven of self-awareness.[8]

It should be emphasized that Washington enacts the innumerable changes of Malcolm's character with depth and intensity, never becoming a visual and performative cliché or stereotype and always conveying both a sense of inner struggle and outer social and cultural significance. Literally, in his scenes throughout the film, Washington finds a way

Figure 12. Denzel Washington in *Malcolm X* reinvents the life of the historic black leader and addresses supporters outside the Apollo Theater in Harlem while also advancing his own career as a creative and charismatic leading actor and major film star. (Museum of Modern Art/Film Still Archives)

to create through facial expression, physical gesture, movement, and speech something unique about the character of Malcolm. Each phase of Malcolm's tortured life finds expression through Washington's interpretative acting. Washington's ability to move so convincingly through so many different character changes from thief and hustler to convict and convert and yet retain solid coherence and consistency constitutes a true acting triumph in American film. Washington turns Malcolm's journey into an authentic pilgrim's progress of genuine growth and learning. Indubitably, Lee's direction helps create the dynamic, condition, and environment for Washington's stellar performance.

In *Malcolm X*, inseparable performance and documentary make Washington's work a fulfillment of Spike Lee's artistic, cultural, and historic imagination that in turn derives from Lee's own personal biography as a black man as well as his basic regard for and attitude toward Malcolm X. For Lee, no doubt, in attempting and making *Malcolm X*, the personal and the political came together. The film culminated a calculated effort over years by Lee to propound his total commitment as an artist to filmmaking and to promote his self-image of being on a special mission as a black filmmaker. An early form of such validation of Lee, the unique black filmmaker, occurred in a collection of essays about him in 1991, a year before the release of *Malcolm X* but amazingly only a few years after his first feature film, *She's Gotta Have It* (1986), which was followed relatively soon by *School Daze* (1988), *Do the Right Thing* (1989), *Mo' Better Blues* (1990), and *Jungle Fever* (1991). Following an introductory essay by Lee, who seems to have helped bring them together, the contributors included influential scholar Henry Louis Gates, Jr., author Charles Johnson, filmmaker Melvin Van Peebles, writer Toni Cade Bambara, journalist Nelson George, and author Terry McMillan, each writing about a different film by Lee.[9] Earlier, as another sign of his seriousness, Lee also published and edited a book about the production of *Do the Right Thing* that included the working script.[10]

Even after such success, *Malcolm X* seemed to many to signify a new dimension of filmmaking for Lee, one that suggested a new beginning and direction of great importance. In a brilliant article and thorough review of measured and careful critical analysis, Lisa Kennedy considers the film such a landmark, dubbing it "a turning point." She wrote:

> There is an overwhelming sense that *Malcolm X*, the movie, will be looked back on as a turning point, not just for the nation, but for the film's director. If Oliver Stone's *JFK* could lead to the opening of sealed congressional reports, what might *X* bring about?[11]

Lee insists that he always venerated Malcolm X as a leader, advocate, and activist to advance the situation of blacks in America and the world. Although he famously ended *Do the Right Thing* (1989) with long quotations from Dr. Martin Luther King, Jr. and Malcolm X that ostensibly give the viewer a choice between opposing views toward violence, Lee's personal attraction to Malcolm stands out both in the film's violently riotous conclusion and in Lee's own stated opinions. Explaining how he conceived of the film's conclusion, he wrote:

> I had to find a way to tie these two great men into the finale. King and Malcolm. Both men died for the love of their people, but had different strategies for realizing freedom. Why not end the film with an appropriate quote from each? In the end, justice will prevail one way or another. There are two paths to that. The way of King, or the way of Malcolm.[12]

Declaring that "the days of twenty-five million Blacks being silent while our fellow brothers and sisters are exploited, oppressed, and murdered have to come to an end," Lee makes his own preference for Malcolm X obvious. "Yep, we have a choice, Malcolm or King. I know who I'm down with."[13]

The two famous quotations from King and Malcolm propose profoundly different attitudes toward violence as a means for achieving justice and racial equality. The King quotation states: "Violence as a way of achieving racial justice is both impractical and immoral.... Violence ends by defeating itself. It creates bitterness in the survivors and brutality in the destroyers."[14] In contrast, the Malcolm X statement proclaims that because "bad" white people "are the ones who seem to have all the power," then,

> you and I have to preserve the right to do what is necesary to bring an end to that situation, and it doesn't mean that I advocate violence, but at the same time I am not against using violence in self-defense. I don't even call it violence when it's self-defense, I call it intelligence. (*Means* 4)

In his book about making the film of Malcolm, Lee declares that "Malcolm has always been my man" (*Means* 2). In statements and comments at the time of the film's production and release, Lee elaborated on the influence of Malcolm X upon him. For example, in an interview for *Sight & Sound*, when James Verniere asked Lee how long he had been thinking of making *Malcolm X*, he responded:

> Since I made *Do the Right Thing*. I read *The Autobiography of Malcolm X* – the most important book I'll ever read – when I was in junior high school. I began to look at the world with a new set of eyes. It showed me how we are portrayed in the media, how African-American stars in sport and show business smile and say all the right things, but never speak out, and how it all ties in.[15]

Apparently Malcolm's idea of using any necessary means, including violence, for reaching the objectives of black equality and freedom profoundly impresses Lee as political strategy and rhetoric, as well as a sign of commitment and dedication. Malcolm uses such terminology about necessity on several occasions and contexts. Recalling speeches he made about his "new position regarding white people" since leaving the Black Muslims, Malcolm says: "I firmly believe that Negroes have the right to fight against these racists, by any means necessary."[16] Also, in a typical statement in an interview in 1964, he said repeatedly "that our people should start doing what is necessary to protect ourselves" and "that we should get whatever is necessary to protect ourselves" and "that it's only fair to expect elements to do whatever is necessary to protect themselves."[17]

Lee identifies with and incorporates this language so completely as his own way of thinking that he repeats Malcolm's slogan, "By Any Means Necessary," in his discussion of King versus Malcolm in his book, *Do the Right Thing*.[18] Lee, in fact, goes on to adopt this very phrase for the title of his book about making *Malcolm X* as the most appropriate, accurate, and succinct language for describing the challenge involved in making the film. The book's title, *By Any Means Necessary: The Trials and Tribulations of the Making of Malcolm X*, reflects the cumulative challenges the project presented Lee as well as his great effort to overcome such obstacles and complete the film. The title also suggests the depth and intensity of his desire to fulfill his ambition of bringing Malcolm X's story and message to the screen.

At the same time, an irony also suggests itself in the use of the word "means." The title indicates perhaps a subtle alteration and reversal of the ends and means. The original ends of dramatizing and explaining the importance of Malcolm to a mass audience of blacks and whites gets somewhat displaced by making the making of the film an end in itself. For Lee, the making of the film becomes so dominant that the film perhaps shares and even competes for importance with its subject, Malcolm X.

In a manner consistent with modernist sensibility and consciousness, the alteration in means and ends not only elevates Washington and Lee to special prominence, such a sharing of focus also places special emphasis upon process. This shared focus on Washington and Lee with Malcolm X shifts the weight of the film from the subject and theme of Malcolm X, the signified, toward the process and form of the film, the signifier, thereby deepening its modernist sensibility. Lee asserts plainly: "My means is filmmaking . . ." (*Means* 15).

Lee's appropriation of Malcolm's words to describe his own view of his efforts to make a film about Malcolm X at first may seem merely narcissistic and self-centered. However, to be fair to Lee, it should be noted how the controversial history of Lee's involvement with the project helped inflame his obsession to make it. Skepticism about Lee's assumed commercialism and opportunism as a filmmaker caused many who honored Malcolm X's memory to feel that Lee would not do justice to Malcolm.[19] Evelyn Nieves in the *New York Times* summarized the intensity of the controversy and the depth of the opposition to Lee. The article suggested that an anti-Lee rally in Harlem with about two-hundred protestors signaled an organized effort to stop his work on the film. She writes:

> But as the martyred black nationalist leader's popularity grows 26 years after his assassination, an intense debate is stirring over what exactly Malcolm X's legacy is or should be.
>
> So hot is the debate that even before Spike Lee has started filming his treatment of Malcolm X, a movement is afoot to stop him. None of the two dozen or so protest organizers, led by the poet Amiri Baraka, has seen the film's script. But they say that based on their scrutiny of Mr. Lee's past films, they are sure he will exploit the Black Muslim's life, corrupt his history and forever taint the legacy of one of the country's most revered leaders of the black liberation movement.[20]

The article noted that at the Harlem rally, Baraka, known earlier in his career as the playwright and activist LeRoi Jones, explained that he wanted "to bring the issue of Mr. Lee's exploitation film to the masses." Baraka said: "We will not let Malcolm X's life be trashed to make middle-class Negroes sleep easier." Attacking each of Lee's films for misrepresenting and exploiting the situation and lives of black people, Baraka said, "Spike Lee is part of a retrograde movement in this country." Summarizing the concerns of Lee's opponents, Nieves writes:

> The protestors' main worry is over which part of Malcolm X's life Mr. Lee's film will focus on. Some said they feared too much attention would be given to Malcolm X's days as a pimp called Detroit Red.
>
> Or worse, they fret that the film will make him seem in the end like Martin Luther King, Jr. – a revisionist portrait, some said, that is being pushed by the middle class to take the edge off some of Malcolm X's most militant writings.[21]

Perhaps even more personally painful, as well as embarrasing, to Lee, Betty Shabazz, Malcolm X's widow, also appeared in the article expressing some of her own concerns, although she herself was a consultant to the film. She said:

> "I think what is happening is that people who really knew Malcolm and who understood the thrust and importance of his leadership have a right to question anyone who is doing anything on Malcolm. Just because Spike Lee is doing a film, don't mean he owns Malcolm."[22]

In his book about the making of *Malcolm X*, Lee argues that in themselves such matters raised by Baraka and Shabazz should be viewed primarily as personal attacks. More important to him than any potential substantive validity to their questions and objections was his feeling of being personally challenged and tested, as though by a force greater than himself that placed him in a position to make the film. He insists that such obstacles only increased the significance of his efforts. He writes:

> Problems. Big problems. I will admit it is hard, with the problems we had early in the shoot. Big problems. I think we're being tested. I know I am. Hurdles are being thrown in our path – personal and otherwise – and we have to overcome them. And we will. I know it. I know 'cause I have to know it. (*Means* 94)

He lists "the so-called controversy with the writer Amiri Baraka" as the first problem. Baraka, Lee writes, "didn't want me directing this film, said I was too middle class" (*Means* 94). Lee essentially dismisses Baraka's criticism as a personal complaint. He writes:

> I know Baraka. I used to go out with one of his two daughters, Lisa Jones . . . and she collaborated on three books with me. But out of nowhere, even before we began principal photography, here comes Baraka on a blitzkrieg, attacking me, saying that the masses of Black people didn't want Spike Lee directing this film, that I was a petit bourgeois Negro who had no claim to the legacy of Malcolm – some serious blathering. (*Means* 99)

Lee further responds to such so-called "blathering" with his own counter assaults on Baraka, including a complaint that Baraka never raised any objections to the idea of the film being directed by Norman Jewison, the successful Canadian-born white director of many major films, who was an early consideration for directing the film and went on recently to direct Washington in *The Hurricane*.

Lee also attributed Betty Shabazz's concerns about the film to her personal situation as opposed to any weakness of the script or film. Saying "I wish we had gotten a lot more input from Betty, but at the same time I realize that it must be painful for her still," Lee writes:

> Betty Shabazz has been asking and asking for a script, and finally I let her see it. And my instincts were right. She hated the script – hated it. She said it was the worst piece of shit she'd ever read in her life. She came and told me she and Malcolm never fought. Now what married couple in the history of the world has never had an argument? (*Means* 98)

As Lee relates Shabazz's reaction to the film, her idealization of her marriage to the assassinated black leader epitomizes a key source behind the opposition of so many to Lee's work. As already suggested, for many, Malcolm X had become the stuff of myth and legend, so that any effort to present him on the screen inevitably would seem to fail for those who saw him as greater than life. In their extensive coverage of the difficulties and the controversy surrounding the film, the *New York Times* quickly appreciated this aspect of the story involving the mystique and myth of Malcolm. Thus, Caryn James wrote "The Search Continues for the Real Malcolm X," while Sheila Rule discussed, "Malcolm X: The Facts, the Fictions, the Film."[23] Also, in a photo caption with pictures of Malcolm X and Denzel Washington that accompany additional commentaries, the newspaper asserts that "27 years after his assassination, his complicated life has been refracted through the prisms of history and myth."[24]

Even the actual review of the film by Vincent Canby tends to treat Malcolm X as a mythical figure who arouses mystery and awe. Under the headline, 'MALCOLM X,' AS COMPLEX AS ITS SUBJECT, Canby says that "Malcolm was already something of a myth when he was assassinated at the Audubon Ballroom in New York on Feb. 21, 1965, just three months short of his 40th birthday." Canby writes:

> Malcolm X lived a dozen different lives, each in its way a defining aspect of the black American experience from nightmare to dream. There was never any in-between for the man who was initially called Malcolm Little, the son of a Nebraska preacher, and who, when he died, was known by his Muslim name, El-Hajj Malik El-Shabazz. Malcolm traveled far, through many incarnations to become as much admired as he was feared as the black liberation movement's most militant spokesman and unrelenting conscience.[25]

No doubt the mythic, almost superhuman mystique of Malcolm X as much as Lee's own charisma and dedication inspired many black celebrities and leaders to contribute their own money to help Lee overcome yet another extraordinary obstacle in the form of the great financial problems that threatened to kill the film.[26] Ironically, while the veneration of Malcolm placed great demands upon Lee to make a film to match the expectations of his audience, the same regard for Malcolm in the final analysis helped Lee find the financial support and encouragement to finish and release *Malcolm X.*

The importance of the mythology of Malcolm X to understanding the significance of Lee's film also interests many scholars and critics. In "'Myth' and the Making of 'Malcolm X,'" Gerald Horne writes: "What is called the civil rights movement or the post–World War II trajectory of African-American history has developed a certain mythology that Spike Lee's estimable and worthy epic, *Malcolm X,* seeks to replace with an alternative mythology." Horne adds that, "With his usual audacity, Spike Lee has dared to create a competing myth akin to what Oliver Stone has attempted in his alternative myth of Camelot, *JFK*."[27] In a somewhat similar vein, Nell Irvin Painter argues that the film and the Malcolm X autobiography reinvent history and biography to establish their own truths about Malcolm X. She writes, "Both *The Autobiography of Malcolm X* and the film *Malcolm X* simulate history by purveying autobiographical rather than biographical truths, for the source of each representation is Malcolm's own recomposition of his life from the vantage point of 1964." She maintains that while Alex Haley helped to shape Malcolm X's autobiography as it was told to him and as he understood it, so also the film's screenplay as it was developed by the celebrated writer James Baldwin, Arnold Perl, and Lee himself "recasts the published autobiography for the 1992 film."[28] Painter dramatically emphasizes: "While each of these retellings invents a new narrative, neither the book nor the film is congruent with the life that Malcolm Little/Malcolm X lived, day by day, between 1925 and 1965."[29] Similarly, Michael Eric Dyson says, "Lee's Malcolm is inevitably a creation of Lee's own oversized ambitions." At the same time, Dyson's understanding of Malcolm places such exaggeration by Lee within a broader cultural and historic context. He writes: "The cultural rebirth of Malcolm X, then, is the remarkable result of complex forces converging to lift him from his violent death in 1965."[30]

Simply by virtue of making *Malcolm X*, Lee insinuates himself into the debate concerning history and myth and fact and fiction that surrounds the historical and biographical Malcolm X. Apparently, Lee happily enters this discussion. Like Oliver Stone, whom he regards as a "good" friend, Lee relishes his public involvement in controversial issues that instigate intense debate among experts as well as the general public (*Means* 124). Thus, he strongly approves of Stone's *JFK*, saying of it, "Great film; a result of great filmmaking" (*Means* 125). Moreover, the polemical and didactic thrust of *Malcolm X* as manifested in its rhetoric and its documentary style indicates Lee's self-conscious awareness of involving himself in a debate of the utmost importance to the black community and to America as a whole. However, crucial differences also stand between Stone and Lee and their major work. Stone's argument in *JFK* of a right-wing, reactionary conspiracy of a vast and intricate network of leaders to kill President John F. Kennedy remains intrinsic to the film.

In contrast, the singular search for the putative truth about an allegedly real and accurate Malcolm X stands as a secondary concern to Lee. His primary interest rests on presenting his personal vision of Malcolm X the man and black leader instead of pursuing one dominant theme about the man. The reversal of means and ends that made completion of the film so important to him, obtains in his arrogating to himself the right to proffer his own idea of Malcolm X as opposed to providing a record of historical interpretation and insight. Lee places precedence upon his vision as an artist as opposed to being a trained historian, journalist, or pure documentary filmmaker. Thus, he concludes *Malcolm X* with a tiny-print disclaimer after the endless credits that some of Malcolm's language and some characters have been changed for purposes of dramatization.

Lee also asserts the priority of his artistic vision at the outset of his book on Malcolm X, as though to inoculate himself against any potential charge of historical or biographical inaccuracy. Along with such inoculation, this prefatory statement also expresses his values as a filmmaker and artist. Articulating a romantic notion of the artist, Lee says, "Artists have been blessed with God-given talents that must be allowed to flourish. It's their life, that's why they were put here on the planet, they have no other choice" (*Means* xiii–xiv). Proclaiming his place within this group of artists, he relates this artistic creed to his project regarding Malcolm X. Lee says:

> I'm an artist. I live, breathe, and will die for my art, for CINEMA. *Malcolm X* is my artistic vision. The film is my interpretation of the man. It's nobody else's. I do not want to sound egotistical either. I stand behind it all the way and everyone involved has contributed to a great piece of cinema. As Malcolm often said, "All credit is due to Allah, the lord of all the worlds and only the mistakes have been mine." (*Means* xiv)

Lee's argument for his artistic independence and integrity as a filmmaker reaffirms his self-image as a modern consciousness and sensibility. Rather than proffering a textbook study of Malcolm, his background, life, and influence, Lee strives to create a modernist work that shifts attention from the boundaries of the streets to the borders of the screen, that manipulates the focus between recording social history and art. Rather than presenting a photographically, sociologically, and politically correct Malcolm, the film synthesizes fiction and documentary to make its own statement about black leadership and the situation and condition of blacks in America today.

However, Lee does not always achieve such artistic excellence and cultural and social brilliance in *Malcolm X*. For a considerable part of the film, Lee's aesthetic impulse and intelligence operate in a fairly conventional way to construct and convey the story of Malcolm along standard lines of cinematic storytelling. For a good part of the three hours of *Malcolm X*, Lee applies sophisticated filmmaking techniques to create an illusion of a real Malcolm, even while reinventing Malcolm just as Malcolm rewrote himself in the autobiography and Haley interpreted what he learned from Malcolm. To affect and project his idea of Malcolm, through most of the film Lee contrives a documentary style in which Washington immerses himself. As Painter says, "This movie is not a documentary, but it wraps itself in manufactured images of documentary truth."[31] One example of artificial documentary stylistics occurs in the last thirty minutes of the film when Washington/Malcolm faces reporters at a JFK airport press conference upon returning from his momentous trip to Mecca. Using almost a jump cut technique, Lee shoots the scene of the airport press conference by switching back and forth between black and white and color. He changes angles and positions and varies the sound. He moves the camera around, erratically changing its concentration upon Malcolm, his family, his entourage, the reporters, and the crowd. All of this activity creates an illusion of viewing the conference both as an event in color and as a black-and-white documentary of Malcolm confronting the press. This excessive artifice confuses fiction, reality, and historical accuracy to generate an emotional reaction from the audience without contributing much to our understanding.

Lee uses this technique of documentary stylistics in other scenes when Malcolm meets the press, including a disastrous conference after the assassination of President Kennedy and a conference with less radical shifts in sound and camera movement when Malcolm announces his break with the Black Muslims. Also, on the trip to Mecca, color footage changes to black and white shooting that suggests official documentary filming by the C.I.A. or other American operatives following Malcolm X to Africa.

Barry Alexander Brown, the editor for the film, discusses the film's documentary technique as an attempt to demonstrate different levels of reality in the film. Describing the press conference scene when Malcolm leaves Temple No. 7 to find himself surrounded by the waiting white press, Brown indicates the degree of improvisation involved in this technique and suggests the meaning of the method came to him and

Lee as an act of self-discovery, a process of learning the meaning of their own work through experiencing it. Brown says of this particular scene:

> Most of it is an improvisation, if not all of it, and one of the angles was shot 16 millimeter, as if it were actual news footage of that time. You can actually see the 16 camera in the shot at times. Good. I want it there. I knew what I was going to do with that, back and forth between the 35 and the 16. Looking at reality and in reality. But then there is also the matter of what are we trying to say here? What is the theme of the scene? How is it helping the story? Is it just that it is an impromptu press conference? Well, that's not enough. Everything has to build. (*Means* 142)

According to Brown, they found the content and point behind their efforts by working with and developing this technique. He says:

> And then it hit us. The press was trying to put words in his mouth. They know they need to get a hot story to go anywhere in New York, and they were trying to get him to say it, to give them that story. What they were trying to get him to say was that he was anti-white and pro-violence. (*Means* 143)

This scene like the others just described remains an artificial construction, a mixture of documentary style and fiction to create an illusion of reality and evoke a false emotional response from the viewer.

Moreover, through much of the film, Washington's brilliant performance enables Lee to sustain such documentary stylistics. Washington's thoroughly convincing portrayal and his careful emulation of public images of Malcolm lend credibility to the docudrama aspects of Lee's direction. Especially in the portion of the film that occurs after Malcolm's conversion, Washington becomes Malcolm. More accurately, through studious detail and intense control and discipline, Washington creates a lasting image and symbol of himself as the public figure and leader, Malcolm X. Giving Washington less credit than he deserves for a performance of extraordinary range and depth, Painter observes:

> For a 1993 audience, Denzel Washington is a good-enough Malcolm X: he looks and talks like Malcolm did in the 1960s; and, from this vantage point, it only matters slightly that Washington is significantly darker-skinned than Little/X and much older than Malcolm during much of the action.[32]

However, Lee dramatically and significantly transcends such imitation and illusion to take the film to another dimension of artistry and level of meaning when he establishes a dialogue between fiction and documentary. *Malcolm X* achieves the brilliance and originality many wish for it when the film imaginatively deals with the tension at its core between fiction and documentary. Lee invents interactions between fiction and documentary that compel reconsiderations of social, political, and moral reality. These engagements push Lee's creative imagination to its limit and make his and Washington's views of Malcolm into provocative perspectives of the black experience in America.

Lee initiates the process of such engagement between fiction and documentary early in the film, in part by using his greatest asset, Denzel Washington. Through Washington, Lee strikes at a basic tension between fiction and documentary in film in the form of the inevitable breach between the documentary image of the actor and the character the actor plays.

Thus, Lee establishes the grounding for the excellence and originality of Washington's performance by instigating a radical disjuncture between the actor and his character, Malcolm. He begins *Malcolm X* by breaking the very thing that for so many seems to make the film and define Washington's success, the apparent merger on the screen of Washington and Malcolm. This break between actor and character actually builds upon the relationship between documentary and fiction in acting that such directors as Jean-Luc Godard cultivate. By developing this aspect of separation or alienation in film acting, Lee replicates the creative and intellectual insight of earlier models of modernism in film as proffered by Godard and others.

Yet again, Gilberto Perez's study of fiction and documentary proves helpful in explaining and articulating Lee's success in *Malcolm X*. Perez focuses on the "marked separation between the actor and the character" that both Bertolt Brecht and Godard set up. As noted earlier in this study, Perez repeats Godard's idea that "Every film is a documentary of its actors," and emphasizes: "To separate actor and character... is in each medium a different undertaking...."[33] This crucial distinction between actor and character allows for a concentration upon the distinction between the signifier and the signified in film. Perez notes, "Both Brecht and Godard induce a break between signified and signifier – between the means of representation and expression and the things being represented and expressed...."[34]

Lee opens *Malcolm X* with precisely such parallel distinctions between actor and character, documentary and fiction, and signifier and signified. The modernist impulse behind these differences suggests an intentional self-consciousness and seriousness about the film's subject matter – Malcolm and blacks in America – and its artistic form and style. Certainly it should be noted that some critics, such as Jonathan Rosenbaum, strongly dispute the credibility and power of this opening scene.[35] However, it seems to me, that in spite of some possible pretentiousness, the opening works in that it sets the stage for the rest of the film by immediately indicating that complex, interconnected levels of meaning will obtain for the film, including, of course, Washington's performance. As in Perez's reading of Godard's *Breathless*, the confrontation between documentary and fiction in *Malcolm X* concentrates considerable attention on the artistic process and the operations of the signifier.

The opening immediately pits fiction against documentary and indicates the high stakes for the film by emphasizing its message about the meaning of Malcolm X for race in America. The opening also insists upon directing attention to its own artistic values and intellectual credibility. The initial visual images and sounds embattle each other in an engagement of conflicting ideas and forms – signifieds and signifers – until they eventually cohere in a kind of cinematic poetry of prophetic meanings for America. Opening images and symbols, words and sounds suggest a multilevel and multidimensional understanding of the history of race in America. Also, the opening indicates a self-conscious history of film that invariably involves African Americans in complex ways. Moreover, Lee's combative style remains consistent in *Malcolm X* with Sharon Willis's notion of how the visual contends in Lee's work with other cinematic means of communication, what Christian Metz, Godard, and others consider the various semiotic tracks of the heterogeneous cinematic text. Referring primarily to *Jungle Fever*, Willis writes:

> That is, what the visual offers is never fully erased or withdrawn by subsequent narrative accountings. What the visual does do, however, is interfere with, interrupt, throw into question, and even overturn what a film asserts at the discursive level. This is part of what Lee's films play on, the work of contradiction that goes on between the visible and the arguable or discursive, work that seems particularly important in a film intent on displaying the contradictions embedded in racial visibility.[36]

A basic division between signifiers and signifieds separates actor Denzel Washington from Malcolm X when the film opens with a resonating voiceover from Washington reciting Malcolm's explosive words of indictment against the viciousness and prejudice of white people toward people of color. Because the words resound without a face on the screen – neither Denzel's nor Malcolm's – to match the voice, the voice remains disembodied. Washington's voiceover, therefore, helps to create division and to separate the actor from himself and from his character.

This separation of actor and character induces a quality of alienation in the film's beginning that renders even greater power to the extraordinary opening visual image that consumes the screen – a full screen image of the American flag. Given the division between Washington and Malcolm, the flag image becomes overwhelmingly dominant, especially since it also resonates immediately, as Lisa Kennedy notes, as a "*Patton*-like" image, carrying all of the ideological weight and power of *Patton* (1970), the multi – Academy Award winning film starring George C. Scott.[37] The cheers of an unseen crowd precede Denzel's voice, suggesting the support of a community and the power of his message. As Washington's voice and Malcolm's words reverberate in rage, they stand in opposition to the flag but also to Hollywood's representation of the flag. At first, the voice and words also must resist what sounds like the militaristic music of a drum roll and cymbal. However, the horns and drums quickly assume a funereal quality that adds poignancy to the spoken words of anger and sorrow. Denzel's voice declares: "Brothers and sisters, I am here to tell you that I charge the white man, I charge the white man with being the greatest murderer on earth. I charge the white man with being the greatest kidnapper on earth. There is no place in this world that that man can go and say he created peace and harmony."[38] As Washington speaks, the shouts and cries of the unseen audience call out in agreement.

Especially interesting in the context of this mixture of sound, music, and speech, as Washington proclaims his anger at the white man, the visual image on the screen suddenly changes from the symbolism of the flag to a documentary image of the secretly videotaped scene of Los Angeles police beating Rodney King on the evening of March 3, 1991. For the rest of the film's approximate two-minute opening portion, Washington's voiceover, a steadily increasing musical crescendo of intensity and anger from Terence Blanchard's score, and the shouts and cries of an impassioned audience all play to cuts between the beating of King and the slow burning of the American flag.

At the same time, adding to the visual and audio complexity of the opening, the lower left corner of the flag burns, while a fresh choral sound enters the pulsating music, a hymnal theme filled with religious tones and moods that seem to echo the music and sound track of another film, *Glory* (1989), about the 54th Massachusetts Regiment of black volunteers during the Civil War, which was directed by Edward Zwick. For his work in *Glory*, Washington received the Academy Award for best supporting actor. Awards also were given to the film for best sound and cinematography. What reasonably can be heard in some of the opening music of *Malcolm X* as a similarity to certain themes and moods in *Glory* compares to Lee's use of the full-screen American flag. The music constitutes a commentary on the treatment of blacks in film history as well as in American history in general. Of course, Lee's film contrasts ironically with the highly evocative, patriotic, and idealistic *Glory* that assimilates not only Washington but also Morgan Freeman and other powerful black actors in the Union cause. Thus, through the multiple semiotic effect of cinema, Lee opens his film with intertwined levels of meaning that cohere in their reference to and development of national and cultural history, film history, Malcolm X's view of American racial history, and current events.

As a filmmaker with strong modernistic proclivities, Lee has always been attracted to blending documentary and fictional styles. For example, in *Do the Right Thing*, the use of an Italian cultural milieu and the controversial conclusion with conflicting quotations from Malcolm X and Martin Luther King, Jr. indicate Lee's documentary interests. Similarly, *Jungle Fever*, as Willis notes, contains a considerable documentary sensibility.[39] In *Jungle Fever*, a creative geographical introduction to New York using street signs in the opening sequence and the development of street and neighborhood scenes culminating in the horrible visit to the so-called "Taj Mahal," the local drug den, demonstrate such efforts at documentary realism. Since making *Malcolm X*, this documentary interest has been pursued somewhat in Lee's work in *Get on the Bus* (1996), about the Million Man March on Washington, D.C., but even more so in *Four Little Girls* (1997), about the bombing on September 15, 1963 of the 16th Street Baptist Church in Birmingham, Alabama, which received an Academy Award nomination, and to a minor extent in *Summer of Sam* (1999), about the culture and life of New York during the summer of 1977 when David Berkowitz terrorized the city.

For Lee himself, in *Malcolm X* apparently the combination of the burning flag and the beating of Rodney King by Los Angeles police provides a way in the film's opening to make a powerful editorial statement about the absence of meaningful change in America involving race. He told James Verniere of *Sight and Sound*:

> I think the inclusion of the Rodney King video footage in the opening of our film, along with the image of the burning American flag and the words of Malcolm X, say that things haven't changed much. Things have opened up to some individuals, but not to the masses. There are more black people in the underclass than ever before: under Reagan and Bush, the country seemed to be moving backwards.[40]

In his book about making *Malcolm X*, Lee reports that one of his "favorite touches in *Malcolm X*" involves "the opening, a full-frame of the American flag, which then burns down to an American red-white-and blue X" (*Means* 159). The second occurs at the end as Malcolm drives from the New York Hilton to the Audubon Ballroom on February 21, 1965. The music in the background is Sam Cooke singing, "A Change is Gonna Come" (*Means* 159–160). To Lee, both scenes "are so evocative of what it truly means to be an African-American in this country today." Amazingly, he then emotionally equates the significance of these scenes to his own personal crisis as the director. He writes, "There's our reality, and then there's the hope inside that reality. The reality was that it was now May 4, and I was screening X for the second time to the suits at Warner Brothers in Hollywood."

Relating his personal tensions and difficulties to the King incident, but apparently misremembering the dates, Lee then recounts: "This was on a Thursday, the day after the infamous Rodney King verdict came down from Ventura County, California, north of the L.A. basin" (*Means* 160).[41] Somewhat melodramatically, he emphasizes: "It was a bad day to be an American, and maybe the perfect day to think of and reflect on the man they'd called 'Brother Minister'" (*Means* 160). To Lee, "the jury's verdict of not guilty" in the King case against the police "meant they actually believed the police were beating an animal" on March 3, 1991 (*Means* 160). He continues:

> The American system was one of injustice, not justice. And everywhere you went, if you watched any sort of electronic media, the images were there. You saw the last five seconds of Rodney King being handcuffed, after the serious, sadistic beating was over, and then you saw a white truck driver named Reginald Denny, who was being beaten up after being pulled out of [a] truck on the corner of Florence and Normandie. No way are these two images of an equal weight to me. (*Means* 161)

Leaving aside the validity of Lee's interpretation of the meaning of the Rodney King – LA police – Reginald Denny incident for the issue of race in America, it remains significant that in these comments, Lee's frustrations, anxieties, and anger over his problems with making and completing the film help to frame and shape his view of the issue in its broadest dimension. The importance he gives to his "reality" of confronting studio executives compares his situation to the outrageous injustices levelled against King. Once again, ends and means get blurred for Lee over this film.

Nevertheless, Lee's frustration and rage inspire the successful marriage in the opening sequence of moral imagination and artistic sensibility to create a rare coherence in film of art and ideology. The explosive mixture of symbols, images, and ideas in the opening establishes a symbolic and intellectual foundation for the film. The scene becomes a living cinematic jeremiad about the meaning of America as contending promises and failures involving destruction and redemption, damnation and salvation, slavery and freedom, nightmare and the dream of paradise. Contradictions and ambiguities persist, providing ideas and symbols for the rest of the film. The tension between documentary and fiction in the opening also sustains the intellectual conflict. Especially when viewed retrospectively in the light of the entire film, even while the flag burns and King suffers, all of the elements of the scene call for change and redemption as opposed to total destruction and rejection.

Contrary to an initial impression of the opening as an absolute rejection of America, the scene exists and builds upon an adherence to American values and terms. The moral outrage of Malcolm's words proclaims the continued existence of a moral dimension based on the expressed meaning of America, in spite of a history of violations of its promises. In fact, the implied meaning of the flag defines the horror and outrage over the beating in the footage of King. The heat of the tension between the ideal of the American Creed as symbolized by the flag and the harsh reality of racism erupts into the flames that consume the flag.

Malcolm's insistence in the opening speech on the failure of democracy for blacks constitutes a demand for a real democracy. The hope for inclusion in America ultimately structures the outrage, as indicated when Malcolm becomes a martyr to a new idea for him of accepting and tolerating whites. Whatever the presumably real Malcolm felt or believed, especially during his last days after his break with the Black Muslims, the film itself never gives up on the flag. The flag burns in

sorrow and anger, but echoing Lee's own words about the King incident and the trial of the police, the film looks toward better days to be
an American. Malcolm's jeremiad in the beginning of the film entails
an attack on American hypocrisy and can be read and heard today as a
profound and provocative rhetorical gesture and political strategy for
renewing the American Creed by insisting upon inclusion, justice, and
freedom for all Americans. Malcolm in that opening declares:

> Being born here does not make you an American. I am not an American. You
> are not an American. You are one of the 22 million black people who are the
> victims of America. You and I, we've never seen any democracy. We ain't seen
> no democracy in the cotton fields of Georgia. There wasn't no democracy
> down there. We didn't see any democracy in the streets of Harlem, and the
> streets of Brooklyn and the streets of Detroit, and Chicago. There ain't no
> democracy down there. No we've never seen democracy. All we've seen is
> hypocrisy. We don't see any American dream. We've experienced only the
> American nightmare.

Malcolm X's explosive use of words and concepts that become charged
in this speech – American, democracy, American Dream – hold out the
possibility for their true potential relevance to all black Americans in
a just society. Especially in the film's terms of Malcolm X's evolving
acceptance of whites in the final stages of his life, Malcolm's rhetorical
and political strategy in this speech relates to the classic American
jeremiad of Thoreau, Whitman, and others of attacking and criticizing
America for failing to exemplify and advance the principles and values
of what came to be called the American Creed.[42] Of course, the degree
of Malcolm's commitment to any coherent idea of America as a creed
or ideology should not be exaggerated and cannot compare to Martin
Luther King's model of American rhetoric in the "I Have A Dream"
oration. Still, Malcolm X's strategy of protest thrives by revivifying the
American ideology that it attacks.

Just as the relationship in film between fiction and documentary
cultivates film performance, so it also structures and articulates the
tension between the ideal of America and the reality of racism, as
expressed in Malcolm X's opening speech. Crucial scenes that sustain
the thrust of artistic renewal and achievement and overcome the film's
enervating mode of artificial documentary also serve to perpetuate the
rhetorical tension between the American ideal and reality. Together
Washington and Lee perpetuate these creative tensions of form and
ideology within the film that originate in the uniqueness of the opening
flag burning and documentary sequence.

In one key sustaining sequence of this inner movement of regeneration in the film between documentary and fiction, Lee uses a vigorous montage of scenes that interconnect a major address by Malcolm with his return to his home. At home, Malcolm/Washington sits on a bed and watches actual documentary footage on the television screen that includes images of Martin Luther King, Jr., racial riots and demonstrations, and police brutality. In this particular scene, Washington seems to step out of himself and his role, to be providing yet another perspective on the worlds inside and outside of the film. The real documentary footage alienates the fictional documentary. This moment of tension between fiction and documentary takes the film out of the realm of illusion and docudrama to a form in which documentary and fiction question, challenge, and elevate each other. In this modernist moment, the film becomes a self-reflexive interaction of documentary and fiction that examines its own premises as a work of art while also surveying and studying the world it wishes to dramatize and explain. This scene anticipates the film's treatment in its concluding portion of Malcolm's assassination. Again documentary footage, this time of the real Malcolm and his world, alters the fictional and documentary boundaries of the film. As Painter says, "When the images are real – as in the footage of Martin Luther King's remarks after the assassination of Malcolm X, the effect can be chilling."[43]

Washington himself understood the need to recognize the gap between himself and Malcolm. He appreciated the importance to his best possible performance of capitalizing on the film's inherent tensions. He says:

> I remember when we were shooting in Rahway Prison, I spoke to what you might call the graduating class, and I told them I could feel some of the brothers out there, I could see how they were looking at me – so I told them straight out I wasn't Malcolm X and could never be Malcolm X. But I did also tell them that if for a second I tried to make myself bigger than that same spirit that made him, then all would be lost. (Means 115)

This insight into the danger to his acting and the film of trying to achieve the impossible by truly becoming one with his role helped Washington to realize the potential of his unique function and mission as an actor. He writes: "I got very calm once I realized I couldn't be Malcolm X. There was something more important than Malcolm X here, much more important than any of us, and that is the betterment of all of us" (Means 115).

Washington's appreciation for his specific function as an actor and for the broader purposes of the film indicates his collaboration with Lee in making a film that strives to be both art and a catalyst for change. Indeed, the prescience of Washington's comments suggests his awareness of a kind of double construction and parallelism in *Malcolm X* that makes the film at least two films. The first obviously concerns the story of Malcolm X, what Perez calls the fiction of a documentary, the fictional construction that attempts to portray Lee's personal vision of a heroic figure of almost indescribable importance to this particular director. The second film constitutes the documentary of the fiction as enacted by Denzel Washington, the documentary of an acting performance of a lifetime. The film of Malcolm X's story dramatizes a world of social, political, and cultural significance that still remains the focus of excruciating investigation and study by scholars, students, and critics after decades of controversial examination. This subject of study involves the question of Malcolm's place and meaning as a man and as a symbol in American and African American history and culture. How blacks and whites regard Malcolm X today, of course, says much about the current condition of race relations and issues in America.

The documentary of Denzel Washington also requires serious study and investigation. It concerns the changing significance of the black actor in America and needs to be considered in the context of the evolving relationship of black culture and history to America and American film. In this broader context, the documentary of Washington's work in *Malcolm X* relates immediately to Lee's direction and imagination. Lee's vision of this film, his passion for his work as an independent artist, his absolute commitment to the subject of the film and the culture and people it represents and attempts to speak for, his obsession with the film as an end in itself that justified any means necessary for its completion, demonstrate his awareness of an idea that in its modern form in America goes at least as far back as Dos Passos's hopes for a democratic literature to help renew democracy in America. Recently, Lee has spoken vituperatively about what he perceives as a trend among some in African American cinema and television to gain popularity with mass white audiences by returning to classic stereotypes of blacks as passive enablers and supporters of white domination. He clearly sees himself and Washington as resisting this trend through their commitments to both artistic authenticity and the struggle for equality and justice for blacks in America, values that to Lee should parallel and sustain each other.[44] In spite of Lee's chronic anger and pessimism, bitterness and skepticism, the making and finishing of *Malcolm X* and the performances and collaborative work that comprise it constitute an historic sign of change, a potentially crucial transition for the future of American culture and what America and Americans will look like. As in all major filmmaking in American history, now Washington and Lee work together in the remaking of America as they make films.

NOTES

Introduction: Film and Modernism in America

1. See Gertrude Stein, *Wars I Have Seen* (New York: Random House, 1945), pp. 257–258. Jay Martin, *Harvest of Change: American Literature, 1865–1914* (Englewood Cliffs, N.J.: Prentice-Hall, 1967), p. 15, puts this comment in a valuable context of intellectual, social, and literary history.
2. Gilberto Perez, *The Material Ghost: Films and Their Medium* (Baltimore & London: Johns Hopkins University Press, 1998), p. 280, says:

    > If, in the older arts, it is not quite clear what the avant-garde, what modernism is, in the art of film it is even less clear. If the avant-garde characteristically strives to "make it new," if that defines the art of modernism, then it may be concluded either that the art of film, because new, is automatically modern, or that it is automatically not modern because, being new to begin with, it cannot be part of the striving to make it new. For some devotees of the avant-garde, film is an inherently modern art betrayed by Hollywood into the way of traditionalism, whereas for others, devotees of the Hollywood movie, film has been exempted from the imperatives of the modern and enabled to flourish as the last traditional art.

3. Ibid., p. 262.
4. Dudley Andrew, "The 'Three Ages' of Cinema Studies and the Age to Come," *PMLA* 115 (May 2000): 342, states: "For modernity enters over the threshold of cinema, as even those who distrust the medium agree."
5. Miriam Bratu Hansen, "America, Paris, the Alps: Kracauer (and Benjamin) on Cinema and Modernity" in *Cinema and the Invention of Modern Life*, eds., Leo Charney and Vanessa R. Schwartz (Berkeley: University of California Press, 1995), pp. 365–366.
6. Ibid., p. 364.
7. Ibid. She adds, p. 390n.6:

    > If we take modernism, in the widest sense, to refer to the articulated intellectual, artistic, political responses to modernity and to processes of modernization, then the distinction between the terms can only be a sliding one: Baudelaire, for example, did not simply record the phenomenon he perceived as saliently new and different in "modern" life but also wrote them into significance – and, as a new type of literary intellectual, was also part of them. Nonetheless, it seems important not to collapse the two terms if we wish to maintain the heuristic

claim that modernity comprises the material conditions of living (regardless of what intellectuals thought about them) as well as the general social horizon of experience, that is, the organization of public life as the matrix in which a wide variety of constituencies related to these living conditions and to each other and did or did not have access to representation and power.

8. Ibid., p. 365. Similarly, Christine Stansell, *American Moderns: Bohemian New York and the Creation of a New Century* (New York: Metropolitan, 2000), p. 7 asserts:

    Modernity, we are taught, is about machines, speed, electricity, explosions, abstractions, the autonomy of language, the autonomy of paint, the death of God, and the divided self. All true, and yet this first full-blown generation of American moderns experienced the imperatives of the age as plainer, if no less complex: the pressures of democracy and the claims of women.

9. See Girgus, *The Law of the Heart: Individualism and the Modern Self in American Literature* (Austin: University of Texas Press, 1979), p. 3. See Ellmann and Feidelson, *The Modern Tradition: Backgrounds of Modern Literature* (New York: Oxford University Press, 1965), p. v.
10. See Irving Howe, "Introduction: The Idea of the Modern" in *Literary Modernism* (New York: Fawcett, 1967), pp. 11–23.
11. Ibid., pp. 23–40.
12. James Naremore and Patrick Brantlinger, "Introduction: Six Artistic Cultures" in *Modernity and Mass Culture*, eds. Naremore and Brantlinger (Bloomington: Indiana University Press, 1991), p. 8.
13. Peter Nicholls, *Modernisms: A Literary Guide* (Berkeley: University of California Press, 1995), p. 46.
14. Stansell, *American Moderns*, p. 4.
15. See Thomas Crow, *Modern Art in the Common Culture* (New Haven: Yale University Press, 1996), pp. 3–48.
16. Nicholls, *Modernisms*, p. 25.
17. Hansen, "America, Paris, the Alps," p. 364.
18. Perez, *The Material Ghost*, p. 43. See also, Andre Bazin, *What Is Cinema?* trans. Hugh Gray (Berkeley: University of California Press, 1967).
19. Kevin Macdonald and Mark Cousins, "The Kingdom of Shadows" in *Imagining Reality: The Faber Book of Documentary*, eds. Macdonald and Cousins (London: Faber and Faber, 1998), pp. 4–6.
20. Seth Feldman, "'Peace Between Man and Machine': Dziga Vertov's *The Machine with a Movie Camera*" in *Documenting the Documentary: Close Readings of Documentary Film and Video*, eds. Barry Keith Grant and Jeannette Sloniowski (Detroit: Wayne State University Press, 1998), p. 40.
21. From Vertov, *The Council of Three* in *Imagining Reality: The Faber Book of Documentary*, eds. Macdonald and Cousins, p. 55.
22. See *Imagining Reality*, p. 54.
23. Bill Nichols, *Representing Reality: Issues and Concepts in Documentary* (Bloomington: Indiana University Press, 1991), pp. 29–30.
24. Ibid., pp. 107, 108.
25. Ibid., p. 108.
26. Ibid., p. 109.

27. Noel Carroll, "Nonfiction Film and Postmodernist Skepticism" in *Post-Theory: Reconstructing Film Studies*, eds. David Bordwell and Noel Carroll (Madison: University of Wisconsin Press, 1996), pp. 292, 296.
28. Nichols, *Representing Reality*, p. 43.
29. Quoted in Perez, *The Material Ghost*, p. 345.
30. Ibid., pp. 302–303.
31. Ibid., pp. 300–301.
32. See James Naremore, *More Than Night: Film Noir In Its Contexts* (Berkeley: University of California Press, 1998).
33. Norman Mailer, *The Fight* (1975; rpt. New York: Vintage, 1997), p. 43.
34. For my discussion of the relationship of several of these films to American ideology and culture, see, Girgus, *Hollywood Renaissance: The Cinema of Democracy in the Era of Ford, Capra, and Kazan* (New York: Cambridge University Press, 1998).

Chapter 1: *Mississippi Masala*

1. See "America's Immigrant Challenge," *Time*, Special Issue, Fall 1993, p. 3. See also Susan Gubar, *Racechanges: White Skin, Black Face in American Culture* (New York: Oxford University Press, 1997), p. xvi.
2. "America's Immigrant Challenge," *Time*, Special Issue, Fall 1993, p. 3.
3. See Eric Schmitt, "New Census Shows Hispanics Are Even With Blacks in U.S.," the *New York Times*, March 8, 2001, p. A1 and Schmitt, "For 7 Million People in Census, One Race Category Isn't Enough," the *New York Times*, March 13, 2001, A1, A14; Susan Sachs, "Redefining Minority," Week in Review, the *New York Times*, March 11, 2001, p. 1. See also, Steven A. Holmes, "The Politics of Race and the Census," the *New York Times*, Week in Review, March 19, 2000, p. 3, on census politics and ethnicity and race. Also, Deborah Sontag and Celia W. Dugger, "The New Immigrant Tide: A Shuttle Between Worlds," the *New York Times*, July 19, 1998, pp. 1, 12–13 on globalization and immigration.
4. Sanford J. Ungar, "Film View: Immigrants' Tales, in Subtle Shades of Gray," the *New York Times*, June 23, 1996, Arts & Leisure, pp. 15, 28.
5. Herman Melville, *Redburn* (Harmondsworth: Penguin Classics, 1986), p. 238.
6. See Judith M. Redding and Victoria A. Brownworth, "Mira Nair: Exiles, Expatriates and Life on the Margins" in *Film Fatales: Independent Women Directors* (Seattle: Seal Press, 1997), p. 161.
7. Samuel G. Freedman, "One People in Two Worlds," Film, Arts & Leisure, the *New York Times*, February 2, 1992, p. 14.
8. Ibid.
9. Ibid.
10. Janice C. Simpson, "Cinema: Focusing on the Margins," *Time*, March 2, 1992, p. 67. Concerning her love for and relationship with her husband and son, Redding and Brownworth, *Film Fatales*, p. 168, more recently report: "Despite the hard work, Nair loves filmmaking in all its aspects, except being separated from her husband and young son, Zohran. 'I love

it, I really do. Even though I have to be separated from him [Zohran] for periods of time, which is the hardest thing, it is just so exciting, never boring, always fresh.'"

11. Freedman, "One People in Two Worlds," p. 14.
12. *Film Fatales*, pp. 158, 161.
13. Ibid., p. 161.
14. *Film Fatales*, p. 170.
15. Freedman, "One People in Two Worlds," p. 13.
16. Ibid., p. 14.
17. Walt Whitman, *Complete Poetry and Selected Prose*, ed. James E. Miller, Jr. (Boston: Riverside/Houghton Mifflin, 1959), p. 28.
18. *Film Fatales*, p. 170.
19. See Freedman, "One People, Two Worlds," p. 14.
20. Ibid., p. 13.
21. Ericka Surat Andersen, "Review of *Mississippi Masala*," *Film Quarterly* 46 (Summer 1993): 24.
22. Ibid., p. 25.
23. Of course, Capra's classic film carries the great weight of an extraordinary burden of cultural and critical commentary. For my own view of the cultural and ideological significance of the film as well as a survey of previous commentary about it, see Girgus, *Hollywood Renaissance: The Cinema of Democracy in the Era of Ford, Capra, and Kazan* (New York: Cambridge University Press, 1998), pp. 86–107.
24. In contrast to the way the scene appears, Choudhury describes how uncomfortable she felt during the shoot. She says, "My first time nude was with a woman director, so I thought it would be easy, but it wasn't. I got my period just before." See Mim Udovitch, "The Pressure to Take It Off," the *New York Times Magazine*, June 25, 2000, p. 42.
25. Laura U. Marks, *The Skin of the Film: Intercultural Cinema, Embodiment, and the Senses* (Durham: Duke University Press, 2000), p. 5, says: "The rise of Mira Nair to panderer of cultural exoticism for white audiences... is but one example of how the commercialization of multiculturalism tends to evacuate its critical effects." See also E. Ann Kaplan, *Looking for the Other: Feminism, Film, and the Imperial Gaze* (New York & London: Routledge, 1997), pp. 173–179.
26. From Bharati Mukherjee in *The World of Ideas* With Bill Moyers, Public Broadcasting System, June 24, 1990, quoted in Girgus, "The New Ethnic Novel and the American Idea," *College Literature* 20 (October 1993): 68.

Chapter 2: *Lone Star*

1. Quoted in Peter Gay, *Freud: A Life for Our Time* (New York: Norton, 1988), pp. 170–171 from *The Wolf-Man by the Wolf-Man*, ed. Muriel Gardiner (1971): 139.
2. See Gay, p. 171.
3. Ibid., pp. 171, 172.

4. Quoted in Gay, p. 321 from *Standard Edition of the Complete Psychological Works of Sigmund Freud*, trans. James Strachey, IX: 40.
5. Ibid., p. 171.
6. Dennis West and Joan M. West, "Borders and Boundaries: An Interview with John Sayles," *Cineaste* 22(3) (1996): 15.
7. Ibid., p. 14.
8. Ibid.
9. John Sayles, *Men With Guns and Lone Star* (London: Faber & Faber, 1998), p. 108. All subsequent references to this screenplay and to the introduction to the screenplay will be to this edition and will be included parenthetically in the text as *LS*.
10. *Sayles on Sayles*, eds. John Sayles and Gavin Smith (Boston: Faber & Faber, 1998), p. 217.
11. Ibid., p. 218.
12. Ibid.
13. Ibid., p. xiv.
14. Ibid., 219.
15. "Borders and Boundaries," *Cineaste*, p. 16.
16. *Sayles on Sayles*, p. 228.
17. Ibid., p. 219.
18. See Francois Truffaut, *Hitchcock*, rev. ed. (New York: Touchstone, 1985), p. 138.
19. "Borders and Boundaries," *Cineaste*, p. 15.
20. Arthur M. Eckstein, "Darkening Ethan: John Ford's *The Searchers* (1956) from Novel to Screenplay to Screen," *Cinema Journal* 38(1) (Fall 1998): 3–24. See also Girgus, *Hollywood Renaissance: The Cinema of Democracy in the Era of Ford, Capra, and Kazan* (New York: Cambridge University Press, 1998).
21. For a discussion of the complexity of the character Wayne plays see also, Girgus, *Hollywood Renaissance: The Cinema of Democracy in the Era of Ford, Capra, and Kazan*, pp. 19–55; and Gary Wills, *John Wayne's America: The Politics of Celebrity* (New York: Simon & Schuster, 1997).
22. "Borders and Boundaries," *Cineaste*, p. 16.
23. Ibid.
24. *Sayles on Sayles*, p. 232.
25. Ibid., p. 221.
26. Ibid., p. 223.
27. Ibid., p. 231.
28. Ibid., p. 228.
29. Ibid., p. 232.
30. Slavoj Žižek, *The Sublime Object of Ideology* (London: Verso, 1989), p. 140.

Chapter 3: *Raging Bull*

1. See David Bordwell and Kristin Thompson, *Film Art: An Introduction*, 5th ed. (New York: McGraw-Hill, 1997), pp. 426–427.

2. See Jake La Motta, *Raging Bull: My Story* with Joseph Carter and Peter Savage (rpt; 1970. New York: Da Capo, 1997), pp. 6–7, 170–171, 116.

3. See Nick Tosches, "Introduction," *Raging Bull: My Story* by Jake La Motta, pp. ix, xii.

4. La Motta, *Raging Bull*, p. 2.

5. Ibid., pp. 2–3.

6. Ibid., p. 4.

7. Ibid.

8. Ibid., p. 3.

9. For an accessible development of this concept of body ego and psychic ego, see Janine Chasseguet-Smirgel, *The Ego Ideal: A Psychoanalytic Essay on the Malady of the Ideal*, intro. Christopher Lasch, trans. Paul Burrows (New York: Norton, 1985), pp. 76, 4–5.

10. Leo Braudy, *The World in a Frame: What We See in Films* (1976; rpt. Chicago: University of Chicago Press, 1984), p. 101.

11. Lizzie Borden, "Blood and Redemption," *Sight and Sound*, 5 (February 1995): 61. Borden also states that De Niro gained "more than 100 lbs for his role," whereas others give the figure of more than 60 pounds.

12. See Robert Phillip Kolker, *A Cinema of Loneliness: Penn, Kubrick, Scorsese, Spielberg, Altman*, 2nd. ed. (New York: Oxford University Press, 1988), p. 179.

13. In contrast, Morris Dickstein, "Self-Tormentors," *Partisan Review* 61 (Fall 1994): 661, says, "Compared to most boxing movies, the fight scenes in *Raging Bull* aren't especially real or convincing. Sometimes Scorsese gives us only a few seconds of a round, really just a graphic shorthand for what the fighter goes through."

14. David Ehrenstein, *The Scorsese Picture: The Art and Life of Martin Scorsese* (New York: Birch Lane Press, 1992), p. 155.

15. As quoted in Ken Keyser, *Martin Scorsese* (New York: Twayne/Macmillan, 1992), pp. 120–121, Reed called the film "a relentlessly despairing look at a punchy, inarticulate, ignorant, sub-mental punching bag from an Italian neighborhood in the Bronx who lives a thoroughly loathsome life from the first frame to last." John Simon wrote: "*Raging Bull* does not even communicate what the rage of this bull is about...."

16. See Keyser, *Martin Scorsese*, p. 122 and Dickstein, "Self-Tormentors," p. 659, says, "Scorsese made *Raging Bull* at the end of a difficult and self-destructive period in his own life, after the failure of his most ambitious film, *New York, New York*, when drugs, illness, and a failed marriage nearly killed him."

17. Mary Pat Kelly, *Martin Scorsese: A Journey* (New York: Thunder's Mouth Press, 1991), p. 125.

18. See *The Cambridge Companion to Brecht*, eds. Peter Thomson and Glendyr Sacks (New York: Cambridge University Press, 1994), pp. 191, 193, 262.

19. Sumiko Higashi, "*Walker* and *Mississippi Burning*: Postmodernism versus Illusionistic Narrative," in *Revisioning History: Film and the Construction of a New Past*, ed. Robert A. Rosenstone (Princeton: Princeton University Press, 1995), pp. 188–190.

20. Ibid., pp. 190, 201.
21. Joyce Carol Oates, *On Boxing*, photographs by John Ranard (Garden City: Dolphin/Doubleday, 1987), p. 15.
22. *Existence: A New Dimension in Psychiatry and Psychology*, eds. Rollo May, Ernest Angel, Henri F. Ellenberger (New York: Clarion, 1958), pp. 71, 120.
23. D. N. Rodowick, *The Crisis of Political Modernism: Criticism and Ideology in Contemporary Film Theory*, 2nd. ed. (Berkeley: University of California Press, 1994), p. xiv. All references to this work will be to this edition and will be made parenthetically in the text.
24. Ibid., p. xx.
25. Ina Rae Hark, "Animals or Romans: Looking at Masculinity in *Spartacus*," in *Screening the Male: Exploring Masculinities in Hollywood Cinema*, eds. Steven Cohan and Ina Rae Hark (London: Routledge, 1993), p. 156.
26. Linda Williams, "A Provoking Agent: The Pornography and Performance Art of Annie Sprinkle," in *Dirty Looks: Women, Pornography, and Power*, eds. Pamela Church Gibson and Roma Gibson (London: British Film Institute Publishing, 1933), pp. 179, 180. See also, Williams, *Hard Core: Power, Pleasure, and the "Frenzy" of the Visible* (Berkeley: University of California Press, 1989).
27. See La Motta, *Raging Bull*, p. 87. See the next chapter for a more extensive discussion of this issue of La Motta's attitude toward black fighters.
28. Bordwell and Thompson, *Film Art: An Introduction*, p. 430.
29. Kaja Silverman, *Male Subjectivity at the Margins* (New York: Routledge, 1992), pp. 188, 348.
30. Ibid., pp. 358, 10.
31. Keyser, *Martin Scorsese*, p. 120.
32. Ibid.
33. Kelly, *Martin Scorsese*, p. 119.
34. Keyser, *Martin Scorsese*, p. 115 and Kelly, *Martin Scorsese*, p. 125.
35. Robyn Wiegman, "Feminism, 'The Boyz,' and Other Matters Regarding the Male," in *Screening the Male*, p. 179.
36. Interestingly, Borden, "Blood and Redemption," p. 61, sees "fat as a de-sexualized protection against [his] own violence." She also argues "Jake's pleasure in being punched is redemptive, but it's also a form of sexual masochism."
37. Susie Orbach, *Fat is a Feminist Issue: The Anti-Diet Guide to Permanent Weight Loss* (rpt; 1978. New York: Berkeley Books, 1986). See, Susan Bordo, *Unbearable Weight: Feminism, Western Culture, and the Body* (Berkeley: University of California Press, 1993).
38. Hark, "Animals or Romans: Looking at Masculinity in *Spartacus*," in *Screening the Male*, pp. 165, 164.

Chapter 4: The Black Gladiator and the Spartacus Syndrome

1. Jake La Motta, *Raging Bull: My Story* with Joseph Carter and Peter Savage (1970; rpt. New York: Da Capo, 1997), p. 185.
2. Ibid., pp. 185–186, 184.

3. Dave Anderson, Foreward, *Sugar Ray: The Sugar Ray Robinson Story* by Sugar Ray Robinson with Dave Anderson (1970; rpt. New York: Da Capo Press, 1994), pp. ix–x.
4. See Arnold Rampersad, *Jackie Robinson: A Biography* (New York: Knopf, 1997).
5. La Motta, *Raging Bull*, p. 87.
6. *Sugar Ray*, p. 5.
7. Ibid., p. 186.
8. Ibid.
9. See Stephen J. Whitfield, *The Culture of the Cold War* (Baltimore: Johns Hopkins University Press, 1991), p. 219. See also *The Cambridge Companion to Brecht*, eds. Peter Thomson and Glendyr Sacks (Cambridge: Cambridge University Press, 1994), pp. 26, 49.
10. See Kirk Douglas, *The Ragman's Son* (New York: Pocket Books, 1988), pp. 295–296. For Douglas's discussion of the film's history and production, see pp. 276–306.
11. Ibid., p. 305.
12. See Donald Bogle, *Dorothy Dandridge: A Biography* (New York: Amistad, 1997) and Bogle, *Toms, Coons, Mulattoes, Mammies, & Bucks: An Interpretive History of Blacks in American Families*, New Expanded Edition (New York: Continuum, 1989).
13. See Woody Strode, with Sam Young, *Goal Dust* (Lanham, MD.: Madison Books, 1990).
14. See Arthur M. Eckstein, "Darkening Ethan: John Ford's *The Searchers* (1956) from Novel to Screenplay to Screen," *Cinema Journal* 38 (1) (Fall 1998): 3–24; Sam B. Girgus, *Hollywood Renaissance: The Cinema of Democracy in the Era of Ford, Capra, and Kazan* (New York: Cambridge University Press, 1998), pp. 1–61.
15. Gary Wills, *John Wayne's America: The Politics of Celebrity* (New York: Simon & Schuster, 1997), p. 264.
16. Vincent LoBrutto, *Stanley Kubrick: A Biography* (New York: Da Capo, 1999), pp. 176–177. Strode, *Goal Dust*, p. 195, says: "Kubrick couldn't find anyone physical enough for my part in *Spartacus*. They needed a black actor who could scale a twelve-foot wall up to a balcony where Sir Laurence Olivier was sitting, watching the fighting in an arena down below."
17. Ibid., p. 182.
18. LoBrutto, *Stanley Kubrick*, pp. 46–47.
19. Ibid., p. 47.
20. Ibid., p. 64.
21. Ibid., p. 69.
22. See Douglas, *The Ragman's Son*, pp. 276–306.
23. See, for example, LoBrutto's extensive discussions of Kubrick and Strode and their work on the film in *Stanley Kubrick: A Biography*.
24. Michael Rogin, *Blackface, White Noise: Jewish Immigrants in the Hollywood Melting Pot* (Berkeley: University of California Press, 1996), p. 212.

25. Ibid., p. 215.

26. Ibid., p. 218.

27. Thomas Cripps, *Making Movies Black: The Hollywood Message Movie from World War II to the Civil Rights Era* (New York: Oxford University Press, 1993), p. 212.

28. Crowther quoted in Bogle, *Toms, Coons, Mulattoes, Mammies, & Bucks*, p. 140.

29. Rogin's question occurs in Rogin, *Blackface, White Noise*, p. 219.

30. Ibid., p. 216.

31. See Cripps, *Making Movies Black*, pp. 213–214.

32. See Nat Fleischer and Sam Andre, *A Pictorial History of Boxing* rev. ed. (New York: Citadel, 1993), pp. 151–158.

33. David Remnick, *King of the World: Muhammad Ali and the Rise of an American Hero* (New York: Random House, 1998), pp. 5, 8.

34. Norman Mailer, *On the Fight of the Century: "King of the Hill"* (New York: New American, 1971), pp. 38, 40.

35. Remnick, *King of the World*, p. 14.

36. Fleischer and Andre, *A Pictorial History of Boxing*, p. 159.

37. Ibid., p. 162.

38. Remnick, *King of the World*, p. 274.

39. Ibid., p. 276.

40. Ibid., p. 280.

41. Quoted in Remnick, *King of the World*, p. 23.

42. Ibid., pp. xiii, 291.

43. Ibid., pp. 291, 287.

44. Fleischer and Andre, *A Pictorial History of Boxing*, p. 174.

45. Remnick, *King of the World*, pp. 200, 280.

46. Ibid., p. 207.

47. Ibid. Jimmy Cannon was famous for his enthusiastic support for and coverage of heroes like Louis and Joe DiMaggio. He was the writer who famously called Louis "a credit to his race, the human race."

48. Norman Mailer, *The Fight* (1975; rpt. New York: Vintage, 1997), p. 43.

49. Ibid., p. 44.

50. See Bill Nichols, *Representing Reality: Issues and Concepts in Documentary* (Bloomington: Indiana University Press, 1991), pp. 107–109. For a discussion of Nichols's theory of documentary and its relationship to conflicting issues of fiction and narrative as well as its potential impact upon the concern for a democratic aesthetic in film and documentary, see the Introduction to this work.

51. Remnick, *King of the World*, p. 81.

52. Ibid., p. 83.

53. Mailer, *The Fight*, p. 47.

54. Jeffrey C. Stewart, "The Black Body: Paul Robeson as a Work of Art and Politics" in *Paul Robeson: Artist and Citizen* (New Brunswick: Rutgers University Press, 1998), p. 162.

55. Ibid.

56. From Chris Matthews, *Hardball*, CNBC, June 6, 1999.

57. See the *New York Times*, June 7, 1999, p. A13.
58. Richard Sandomir, "Book Portrays Ali as Something Less Than 'the Greatest'" the *New York Times*, May 21, 2001, D3.
59. Ibid. Sandomir quotes Remnick as saying of Ali in response to Kram's book, "He had a sense of the popular culture, comedy and politics.... And he was the best fighter of his time. Had he been without personality, would Norman Mailer have gone to Africa to see him fight?"

Chapter 5: "Fresh Starts"

1. On David Selznick and "the desire for textual fidelity" concerning these classic films, see James Naremore, "Introduction: Film and the Reign of Adaptation" in *Film Adaptation* (New Brunswick: Rutgers University Press, 2000), p. 11–12.
2. George Bluestone, *Novels into Films* (Berkeley: University of California Press, 1957), pp. 5, 61.
3. Naremore, "Introduction," *Film Adaptation*, p. 2. In this essay, Naremore challenges Bluestone's assumptions and practice regarding the translation of novels into film.
4. See Jeffrey Walker, "Deconstructing an American Myth: *The Last of the Mohicans*" in *Hollywood's Indian: The Portrayal of the Native American in Film*, eds. Peter C. Rollins and John E. O'Connor (Lexington: University of Kentucky Press, 1998), pp. 170–186. Twain famously teases about Cooper's literary excesses of style and language in his essay, "Fenimore Cooper's Literary Offenses" that originally appeared in the *North American Review* in July 1895. For example, Twain jokingly notes that "In one place in *Deerslayer*, and in the restricted space of two-thirds of a page, Cooper has scored 114 offenses against literary art out of a possible 115. It breaks the record." See Twain, "Fenimore Cooper's Literary Offenses" in *Selected Writings of Mark Twain*, ed. Walter Blair (Boston: Houghton Mifflin Riverside, 1962), pp. 227–238.
5. See Joel Engel, "A Fort, a War and the Last Thousand or So Mohicans," the *New York Times*, Arts & Leisure, September 20, 1992, pp. 9, 12. Janet Maslin, "Cooper's Hawkeye as Swashbuckler," the *New York Times*, September 25, 1992, B2. See also D. H. Lawrence, *Studies in Classic American Literature* (1923; rpt. Garden City: Doubleday Anchor, 1951); Henry Nash Smith, *Virgin Land: The American West as Symbol and Myth* (1950; rpt. Cambridge: Harvard University Press, 1973); Richard Slotkin, *Regeneration Through Violence: The Mythology of the American Frontier, 1600–1860* (Middletown: Wesleyan University Press, 1973).
6. Walker, "Deconstructing an American Myth: *The Last of the Mohicans*" in *Hollywood's Indian*, p. 178.
7. "If Gatsby Had Been a Goodfella," *Newsweek*, December 16, 1991: 75.
8. See for example, *Levinson on Levinson*, ed. David Thompson (London: Faber and Faber, 1992) and James Toback, *Bugsy: An Original Screenplay* (New York: Citadel, 1991). All subsequent references to *Bugsy* will be to this edition and will be included parenthetically in the text, while all

subsequent references to *Levinson on Levinson* will be to this edition and will be cited parenthetically in the text as Levinson.

9. "A Playboy Meets Miss Right," *Time*, December 9, 1991: 90.
10. See "A Question of Control," an interview with Gavin Smith in *Film Comment*, 28 (January 1992): 28–37; Michael Eaton, "Bugsy and Clyde," *Sight and Sound*, March 1992: 4; Jaci Stephen, "Las Vegas Nights," *New Statesman and Society*, March 20, 1992: 40–41; Brian D. Johnson, "A Hollywood Hoodlum: Bugsy Siegel had big visions – and big rages," *MacLean's*, 23 December 1991: 50; Michael Kinsley, "TRB: From Washington: Et tu, *Bugsy?*" *The New Republic*, February 3, 1992: 4; Stanley Kauffmann, "Gangster Love," *The New Republic*, December 23 & 30, 1991: 30.
11. See Peter Wollen, *Signs and Meaning in the Cinema*, 3rd ed. (Bloomington: Indiana University Press, 1972).
12. Edith Wharton, *The Age of Innocence* (1920: rpt. New York: Modern Library, 1948), p. 42.
13. F. Scott Fitzgerald, *The Great Gatsby* (1925; rpt. New York: Scribner's, 1953), p. 93. All subsequent references to this novel will be to this edition and will be included parenthetically in the text.
14. See Girgus, *Desire and the Political Unconscious in American Literature* (New York: St. Martin's Press, 1990), pp. 182–194.
15. See Christian Metz, *The Imaginary Signifier: Psychoanalysis and the Cinema*, trans. Celia Britton, Annwyl Williams, Ben Brewster an Alfred Guzzetti (Bloominton: Indiana Univeristy Press, 1982).
16. See Freud, "A Child is Being Beaten: A Contribution to the Origin of Sexual Perversions" (1919) in *Freud: Sexuality and the Psychology of Love*, ed. Philip Rieff, intro. Rieff (New York: Macmillan/Collier, 1963), pp. 107–132.

Chapter 6: Imaging Masochism and the Politics of Pain

1. See Gerhard P. Bach, "'Howling like a Wolf from the City Window': The Cinematic Realization of *Seize the Day*," *Saul Bellow Journal* 7 (1988): 71–83.
2. Daniel Weiss, "Caliban on Prospero: A Psychoanalytic Study of the Novel *Seize the Day*, by Saul Bellow" in *Psychoanalysis and American Fiction*, ed. Irving Malin (New York: Dutton, 1965), p. 287.
3. Ibid., pp. 291–292.
4. See Kaja Silverman, *Male Subjectivity at the Margins* (New York: Routledge, 1992), pp. 1–12. All subsequent references to this book will be to this edition and will be included parenthetically in the text.
5. Saul Bellow, *Seize the Day* (New York: Viking, 1956), p. 3. All subsequent references to this book will be to this edition and will be included parenthetically in the text.
6. Bellow, *Dangling Man* (New York: Avon, 1944), p. 7.
7. See Dennis Bingham, *Acting Male: Masculinities in the Films of James Stewart, Jack Nicholson, and Clint Eastwood* (New York: Rutgers

University Press, 1994); Graham McCann, *Rebel Males: Clift, Brando, and Dean* (New York: Rutgers University Press, 1993); James Naremore, *Acting in the Cinema* (Berkeley: University of California Press, 1988).

8. Lizzie Francke, "Being Robin," *Sight and Sound* 4 (April 1994): 28.
9. Michael Shiels, "Place, Space, and Pace: A Cinematic Reading of *Seize the Day*" in *Saul Bellow at Seventy-Five: A Collection of Critical Essays* (Tubingen: Gunter Narr Verlag, 1991), pp. 59, 55.
10. Naremore, *Acting in the Cinema*, p. 20.

Chapter 7: Documenting the Body in *Modern Times*

1. See Gilberto Perez, *The Material Ghost: Films and Their Medium* (Baltimore: Johns Hopkins University Press, 1998), p. 343.
2. Ibid., p. 344.
3. See James Naremore, *Acting in the Cinema* (Berkeley: University of California Press, 1988), pp. 15–17. See Naremore also on Kuleshov, p. 240 as well as his chapter on Chaplin.
4. See, "Chaplin, Inventing Modern Times," the *New York Times*, April 9, 1989, Arts & Leisure, pp. 1, 20–21.
5. Bill Irwin, "How a Classic Clown Keeps Inspiring Comedy," the *New York Times*, April 9, 1989, Arts & Leisure, p. 20.
6. Constance Brown Kuriyama, "Chaplin's Impure Comedy: The Art of Survival," *Film Quarterly* 45 (Spring 1992): 26, 29.
7. Charles Silver, *Charles Chaplin: An Appreciation* (New York: The Museum of Modern Art, 1989), p. 38.
8. David Robinson, *Chaplin: His Life and Art* (New York: DaCapo, 1994), p. 465.
9. Ibid., p. 455.
10. Ibid., pp. 456, 455.
11. Ibid., pp. 454–455.
12. See Glauco Cambon, "Mark Twain and Charlie Chaplin as Heroes of Popular Culture," *Huck Finn Among the Critics: A Centennial Selection: 1884–1984*, ed. Thomas Inge (Washington: Forum: USIA, 1984), 193–200; Hamlin Hill, *Mark Twain: God's Fool* (New York: Harper & Row, 1973); Walter Blair and Hamlin Hill, *America's Humor: From Poor Richard to Doonesbury* (New York: Oxford University Press, 1978).
13. See for example, Girgus, "Individual Conscience and Mass Culture in Mark Twain," *Journal of American Culture* 4 (Fall 1981): 156–163.
14. Mildred Howells, ed. *Life in Letters of William Dean Howells* 2 vols. (Garden City: Doubleday, Doran, 1928): I:417.
15. Robinson, *Chaplin: His Life and Art*, p. 458.
16. Justin Kaplan, *Mr. Clemens and Mark Twain* (New York: Pocket Books, 1968), p. 169.
17. See Henry Nash Smith, *Mark Twain: The Development of a Writer* (New York: Atheneum, 1967), pp. 132, 168.
18. Kuriyama, "Chaplin's Impure Comedy," p. 27.
19. Robinson, *Chaplin: His Life and Art*, pp. 473–474.

20. Mark Twain, *A Connecticut Yankee in King Arthur's Court* (New York: Harper & Brothers, 1960), p. 78–79.
21. Henry Nash Smith, *Mark Twain: The Development of a Writer*, p. 168.
22. Smith, *Mark Twain's Fable of Progress: Political and Economic Ideas in A Connecticut Yankee* (New Brunswick: Rutgers University Press, 1964), p. 106.
23. Girgus, *Desire and the Political Unconscious in American Literature* (New York: St. Martin's Press, 1990), pp. 167–177.
24. Smith, *Mark Twain's Fable of Progress*, p. 106.
25. Herbert Marcuse, *Eros and Civilization: A Philosophical Inquiry into Freud* (New York: Vintage, 1962), pp. 181, 182.
26. Silver, *Charles Chaplin: An Appreciation*, p. 40.
27. Ibid.
28. Robinson, *Chaplin: His Life and Art*, p. 468.
29. See Ephraim Katz, *The Film Encyclopedia* (New York: Harper & Row, 1979), p. 489 and Robinson, *Chaplin: His Life and Art*, p. 447.
30. Marcuse, *Eros and Civilization*, p. 46.
31. Ibid. See also, Freud, *Three Essays on the Theory of Sexuality* (New York: HarperCollins Basic Books, 1975).
32. Marcuse, *Eros and Civilization*, pp. 183–184.
33. Ibid., p. 184.
34. Kuriyama, "Chaplin's Impure Comedy," p. 35.
35. Marcuse, *Eros and Civilization*, p. 184.

Chapter 8: Spike Lee, Denzel Washington, and the Rebirth of Malcolm X

1. Alfred Kazin, *On Native Grounds: An Interpretation of Modern American Prose Literature* (1942; rpt. New York: Doubleday Anchor, 1956), p. 276.
2. Ibid., p. 277.
3. Townsend Ludington, *John Dos Passos: A Twentieth-Century Odyssey* (New York: Dutton, 1980), p. 257.
4. John Dos Passos, *U.S.A.* (1938; rpt. Boston: Houghton Mifflin Sentry Edition, 1960), pp. v–vi.
5. It is worthy of special note as an important sign of the recognition today of documentary as both an art form and cultural product, that in recent years newspapers such as the *New York Times* as well as magazines in the popular press regularly review on a daily and weekly basis new documentary films with the same attention and depth they give fiction films.
6. See for example, Paul Mitchinson, "Natural Born Historian," *Lingua Franca* (April 2000): 19–20.
7. James Naremore, *Acting in the Cinema* (Berkeley: University of California Press, 1988), pp. 96, 23.
8. Elvis Mitchell, "Black Actors Locked Down or Locked Out," the *New York Times*, Arts & Leisure, March 19, 2000, p. 13.
9. *Five for Five: The Films of Spike Lee*, photographs by David Lee, intro. Spike Lee (New York: Stewart, Tabori, & Chang, 1991).

10. See Spike Lee (with Lisa Jones), *Do the Right Thing* (New York: Simon & Schuster, 1989).
11. Lisa Kennedy, "Is *Malcolm X* the right thing?" *Sight & Sound* (February 1993): 6.
12. Lee, *Do the Right Thing*, p. 282.
13. Ibid.
14. Quoted in Spike Lee (with Ralph Wiley) *By Any Means Necessary: The Trials and Tribulations of the Making of Malcolm X* (London: Vintage, 1993), p. 4. All subsequent references to material in this book will be from this edition and will be included parenthetically in the text as *Means*.
15. James Verniere, "Doing the Job," Interview with Spike Lee, *Sight and Sound*, February 1993, p. 10.
16. Malcolm X, *The Autobiography of Malcolm X*, with the assistance of Alex Haley, intro. M.S. Handler, epilogue Alex Haley (New York: Grove Press, 1966), p. 367.
17. Malcolm X, "Whatever is necessary to protect ourselves," Les Crane interview, December 27, 1964, in *Malcolm X: The Last Speeches*, ed. Bruce Perry (New York: Pathfinder, 1989), p. 84.
18. Lee, *Do the Right Thing*, p. 282.
19. Phil Patton, "Marketeers Battle for the Right To Profit From Malcolm's X," the *New York Times*, November 9, 1992, B1, B4, describes some of the commercial atmosphere surrounding the film that raised concerns at the time of the film's production and release.
20. Evelyn Nieves, "Film on Malcolm X, Yet to Be Made, Creates Firestorm," the *New York Times*, August 9, 1991, B1.
21. Ibid., pp. B1, B5.
22. Ibid., p. B1.
23. See Caryn James, "The Search Continues for the Real Malcolm X," *The New York Times*, 3 December 1992, B1, B4; Sheila Rule, "Malcolm X: The Facts, the Fictions, the Film," the *New York Times*, November 15, 1992, Arts & Leisure, pp. 1, 23.
24. See, David Bradley and Thulani Davis, "Reflections on the Lessons of Malcolm," the *New York Times*, 15 November, 1992, Arts & Leisure, p. 22.
25. Vincent Canby, "Malcolm X, as Complex as Its Subject," the *New York Times*, November 18, 1992, B1, B6.
26. See Lena Williams, "Spike Lee Says Donors Saved His *Malcolm X*," the *New York Times*, May 20, 1992, B1. The article includes the following as donors: Bill Cosby, Oprah Winfrey, Michael Jordan, Earvin (Magic) Johnson, Janet Jackson, Prince, Peggy Cooper Cafritz. The article also details Lee's difficulties, which he also discusses in his book about the film, with the Completion Bond Company that had taken financial control over the movie. Lee noted that the final cost of the film would be around $40 million as opposed to the original costs of between $28 million to $33 million and that "he had used $2 million of his own $3 million salary on the project."
27. Gerald Horne, "*Myth* and the Making of *Malcolm X*," *American Historical Review* 98 (April 1993): 440, 441.

28. Nell Irvin Painter, "Malcolm X across the Genres," *American Historical Review* 98 (April 1993): 433.
29. Ibid.
30. Michael Eric Dyson, "Spike's Malcolm" and "Malcolm X and the Resurgence of Black Nationalism" in *Making Malcolm: The Myth and Meaning of Malcolm X* (New York: Oxford University Press, 1995), pp. 132, 82.
31. Painter, "Malcolm X across the Genres," p. 434.
32. Ibid.
33. Gilberton Perez, *The Material Ghost: Films and Their Medium* (Baltimore: Johns Hopkins University Press, 1998), pp. 341, 343, 345.
34. Ibid., p. 345.
35. Jonathan Rosenbaum, *Movies as Politics* (Berkeley: University of California Press, 1997), p. 147 writes:

    > When he begins his movie with a speech by Malcolm X *and* clips of the Rodney King video *and* shots of an American flag burning down to an X *and* a full serving of Terrence [sic] Blanchard's overloaded score, all delivered more or less at once and at full blast, I'm forced to conclude that he doesn't respect any of these ingredients enough to allow them to be heard or seen with close attention – which is another way of saying that he doesn't really respect his audience either.

36. Sharon Willis, *High Contrast: Race and Gender in Contemporary Hollywood Film* (Durham: Duke University Press, 1997), p. 170. On this idea of Lee and the contradiction between the visual and other forms of communication, see Ed Guerrero, "Spike Lee and the Fever in the Racial Jungle" in *Film Theory Goes to the Movies*, ed. Jim Collins, Ava Preacher Collins, and Hilary Radner (New York: Routledge, 1993), p. 178. On Metz, Godard and semiotic channels of communication, see Robert Stam, Robert Burgoyne, and Sandy Flitterman-Lewis, *New Vocabularies in Film Semiotics: Structuralism, post-structuralism and beyond* (London: Routledge, 1992), pp. 56–59.
37. Kennedy, "Is *Malcolm X* the right thing?" *Sight and Sound*, p. 9.
38. A source for the origins of this opening speech by Malcolm X can be found in "The Verdict is 'Guilty' – The Sentence is Death" in C. Eric Lincoln in *The Black Muslims in America* 3rd ed. (Grand Rapids, Mich: William B. Eerdmans Publishing, 1994), p. 1 and comes from the unpublished typescript of the television documentary "The Hate That Hate Produced," presented by Mike Wallace and Louis Lomax on New York's WNTA-TV, July 10, 1959. The rest of Malcolm's speech in the opening of the film follows:

    > Everywhere he's gone, he's created havoc. Everywhere he's gone, he's created destruction.
    > So I charge him, I charge him with being the greatest kidnapper on this earth, I charge him with being the greatest murderer on this earth, I charge him with being the greatest robber and enslavor on this earth. I charge the white man with being the greatest swine-eater on this earth, the greatest drunkard on this earth.
    > He can't deny the charges. You can't deny the charges. We're the living proof of those charges. You and I are the proof. You're not an American. You are the victim of America. You didn't have a choice coming over here. He didn't say, black man, black woman come on over and help me build America. He said nigger get down in the bottom of that boat, and I'm taking you over there.

Being born here does not make you an American. I am not an American. You are not an American. You are one of the 22 million black people who are the victims of America. You and I, we've never seen any democracy. We ain't seen no democracy in the cotton fields of Georgia. There wasn't no democracy down there. We didn't see any democracy in the streets of Harlem, and the streets of Brooklyn and the streets of Detroit, and Chicago. There ain't no democracy down there. No we've never seen democracy. All we've seen is hypocrisy. We don't see any American dream. We've experienced only the American nightmare.

39. Willis, *High Contrast*, pp. 180, 184.
40. "Doing the Job," *Sight and Sound*, p. 11.
41. Actually, the verdict occurred on April 29, 1992. See Ronald Takaki, *A Different Mirror: A History of Multicultural America* (Boston: Little, Brown, 1993), p. 4.
42. For a discussion and analysis of the jeremiad and of America as an ideology and creed see: Gunnar Myrdal, *An American Dilemma: The Negro Problem and American Democracy* (1942; rpt. New York: Harper & Row, 1962); Sacvan Bercovitch, *The American Jeremiad* (Madison: University Wisconsin Press, 1978). For a discussion of these concepts in classic American film see, Girgus, *Hollywood Renaissance: The Cinema of Democracy in the Era Ford, Capra, and Kazan* (New York: Cambridge University Press, 1998).
43. Painter, "Malcolm X across the Genres," p. 434.
44. Lee made such remarks in talks for the Student Speakers Committee at Vanderbilt University, April 24, 2001, Nashville, Tennessee.

INDEX